THE JPS RASHI I
TORAH COMMEN

The Jewish Publication Society expresses its gratitude for the generosity of the following sponsors of this book:

Alan and Gittel Hilibrand

In honor of **David and Gayle Smith**, whose tireless efforts and generosity help so many.

In loving memory of **Bernard Lieberman**, who was such a special paternal presence in the family.

And with love for the newest family addition, **Eva Smith**.

University of Nebraska Press
Lincoln

THE JPS RASHI DISCUSSION TORAH COMMENTARY

Steven and Sarah Levy

The Jewish Publication Society
Philadelphia

Library of Congress Cataloging-in-Publication Data
Names: Levy, Steven, 1966– author. | Levy, Sarah,
1972– author.
Title: The JPS Rashi discussion Torah commentary /
Steven and Sarah Levy.
Description: Lincoln: University of Nebraska Press;
Philadelphia: The Jewish Publication Society, [2017]
| Series: JPS Study Bible Series | Includes index.
Identifiers: LCCN 2017034936 (print) | LCCN
2017035115 (ebook) | ISBN 9780827612693 (pbk.: alk.
paper) | ISBN 9780827613478 (pdf)
Subjects: LCSH: Rashi, 1040–1105. Perush Rashi 'al
ha-torah. | Bible. Pentateuch—Commentaries.
Classification: LCC BS1225.S6 (ebook) | LCC BS1225.
S6 L48 2017 (print) | DDC 222/.107—dc23
LC record available at https://lccn.loc.gov/
2017034936

Set in Iowan Oldstyle by Scribe Inc. (scribenet.com).

CONTENTS

❖ Numbers

❖ Deuteronomy

PREFACE

Steven: In a 2013 (5774) Rosh Hashanah sermon, my rabbi asked his congregants to set a meaningful goal for the new year and share it with another person. As I contemplated the rabbi's words, I thought about committing to learn the weekly Torah portion with Rashi's commentary—something I had begun tentatively in the past, but never come close to completing. At lunch following services, I shared with our guests the rabbi's proposition and declared my intention to learn Rashi's commentary over the coming year.

As I began reading Rashi's commentary, certain insights resonated with me, and I thought it would be a shame to continue without at least noting these points so I could review them later. Some of the ideas I recorded seemed as if they would be of interest to others, particularly if they were supplemented with questions geared toward generating discussions around the Shabbat table. Given that my wife, Sarah, is a psychologist with keen insight into human nature, I asked her if she would like to join me in preparing these weekly essays. She agreed (once again) to be my partner, and thus began the project that resulted in this book.

Sarah: Although I was present at the Rosh Hashanah lunch when Steven announced that he would like to learn the weekly Torah portion with Rashi's commentary, I was surprised when he later asked, "How would you like to write a book with me?" That was the beginning of many weekly meetings reviewing ideas from the week's Torah portion and—before the Shabbat deadline—formulating questions that would engage the reader. We shared these essays, which we called "Thought for Food," with family and friends so they could use them at their Shabbat tables. Steven also handed them out on Friday night as people exited the synagogue. We were gratified to receive feedback that these essays were engaging readers in meaningful conversations.

Working on this project together proved to be a bonding experience for us as a couple. As we drew on our respective backgrounds, interests, and life experiences, we learned more about each other. I have always been intrigued by the intersection of Torah with science and psychology, and was delighted to be able to explore this further, in collaboration, through the prism of Rashi's comments. I would like to thank my beloved husband for inviting me to join him in this project. I am always inspired by his insatiable thirst for learning new things.

I also want to highlight an important link between this endeavor and the Judaica created by my great-great-grandfather Aryeh Steinberger, who was a scribe and *shochet* (ritual slaughterer) in Hungary. His Torah scroll, Scroll of Esther, and illuminated Haggadah are in the possession of family members and still used today, while his decorative sukkah liner and illuminated Scroll of Antiochus are displayed in New York's Museum of Jewish Heritage and serve to connect Jews to the broad tapestry of Jewish life. This legacy provides his descendants with a tangible link to him and his values. In a similar vein, we hope that this book contributes in a meaningful way to our five daughters' Jewish identities and their relationship to the Torah. Thank you Shira, Daniella, Ariella, Avigail, and Elana for your patience throughout this process, and for understanding why we invested ourselves in it.

I would like to acknowledge my dear parents, Bernard and Eva Lewis. From as early as I can remember, they would invite all those seated at their Shabbat table to share a teaching from the Torah. Making Torah a focal point of the meal had a powerful impact on me. This tradition provided me with a feeling of personal connection to the Torah's lessons—as an active participant rather than merely a passive listener. We hope that this book will enable others to have a similar experience.

Steven and Sarah: We would like to thank The Jewish Publication Society, its director, Rabbi Barry Schwartz, and editors Carol Hupping and Joy Weinberg for their dedication, professionalism, and invaluable assistance in transforming the manuscript they received into the volume before you. We also wish to thank rabbis Gerald Friedman and Neal Gold for reviewing an early manuscript and offering many constructive comments. We also acknowledge the University of Nebraska Press for generously committing its resources and expertise to the publication of this book.

At this project's inception, our synagogue was Atlanta's Congregation Beth Jacob, and we greatly appreciate the encouragement we received from Rabbi Ilan Feldman and members of the community.

Steven: I am forever indebted to Rabbi Emanuel Gettinger, *zichrono livracha* (may his memory be for a blessing), and his wife, Rochel (may she live and be well), whose kindness, scholarship, and piety left an indelible impression on me and provided, at a critical juncture, a model of refined Jewish living.

I am grateful to my parents, Norman and Roslyn Levy, who have always encouraged my growth and development, providing me with the support and allowing me the autonomy to pursue my dreams. Throughout the writing of this book their backing remained constant, as it had with my previous endeavors. I also want to acknowledge my brother David for his assistance in editing the manuscript, and my siblings Debi and Kenneth for their encouragement.

This book would never have been written without the constant input and unflinching support of my wife, who not only generously devoted her time and insights to its writing, but also assumed additional responsibilities to afford me time to work on this project. As we wrote the manuscript, I remarked to her more than once, "If we're going to disagree, it should at least be in matters of Torah." I also acknowledge our daughters for allowing us to spend time on this book and for providing helpful and candid ("say that in kids' language") feedback as we shared the essays at our Shabbat table.

Steven and Sarah: We would like to dedicate this book to our grandparents: Dr. Marvin and Ethel Levy; Dr. Sidney and Dorothy Friedlaender; Rabbi Dr. Daniel Lewin, a pulpit rabbi, prison chaplain, and scholar of Jewish history, and his wife, Inez; and Sadie Lewis (and her mother, Rachel Perkel), all of whom dedicated themselves selflessly to their families.

Steven and Sarah Levy
Yad Binyamin, Israel
Shevat 5777/February 2017

INTRODUCTION

Introducing Rashi

Shlomo Yitzchaki (1040–1105, known as Rashi [Rabbi **Sh**lomo **Yi**tzchaki]) was a medieval French rabbi who authored monumental commentaries on both the Hebrew Bible and the Babylonian Talmud.

Born in Troyes, France, Rashi was an only child. His primary Torah teacher during his youth was his father.

At age seventeen he married and went to learn in yeshiva in Worms, Germany, studying under a relative who was the chief rabbi of Worms. He then moved to Mainz, Germany, where he studied under another relative, who was the chief rabbi of Mainz.

Rashi returned to Troyes at the age of twenty-five. Joining the city's rabbinic court, he subsequently became its head. In addition, he founded and headed a yeshiva called Yeshivat Ga'on Yaakov (The Yeshiva for the Glory of Jacob). He is believed to have earned his living as a vintner.

In 1096, twelve thousand Jews were murdered during the People's Crusade, a military expedition to restore Christian access to the Holy Land that swept through the Lorraine region in which Rashi lived. This tragedy prompted Rashi to write a number of penitential prayers (*Selichot*), seven of which still exist.

Rashi died at age sixty-five. He was buried in the Jewish cemetery of Troyes.

His three daughters all married Torah scholars. His grandsons included Shmuel ben Meir (Rashbam) and Yaakov ben Meir (Rabbeinu Tam), prominent Tosefists (scholars) whose commentaries appear opposite Rashi's on the pages of the Babylonian Talmud.

The Written and Oral Law

To better appreciate what Rashi accomplished in writing his commentary on the Torah, it is helpful to understand the origins of the Torah.

According to Jewish tradition, when the Jews received the Torah at Mount Sinai more than thirty-three hundred years ago, they received both the Written Law (*Torah she-bi-khetav*) and the Oral Law (*Torah she-be-al peh*). This dual nature of the Torah is alluded to in the verse (Lev. 26:46): "These are the laws, rules, and instructions [literally "Torahs"] that the Lord established, through Moses on Mount Sinai, between Himself and the Israelite people," on which the Rabbis comment, "This teaches that Israel was given two Torahs, one written and one oral" (*Sifra, Be-ḥukkotai* 12, 8). The Written Law consists of the Five Books of Moses (often called the Torah, or *Humash*, from the Hebrew word *hamesh*, meaning "five"), plus the books of the Prophets (Nevi'im) and the Writings (Kethuvim). Together, these twenty-four books compose the Hebrew Bible (Tanakh). The Jews also received at Mount Sinai—through their prophet Moses—the Oral Law, an explanation of the Written Law.

The Oral Law was, as the name implies, transmitted orally from teacher to student. This practice of an exclusively oral transmission continued from the time of the Revelation at Mount Sinai until the second century of the Common Era—a period during which the Romans severely persecuted the Jewish community in Israel, eliciting concern that the Oral Law would be lost. As a result, Rabbi Judah the Prince, the leader of the Jewish community, organized the entire corpus of Jewish law into a codification known as the Mishnah.

In the ensuing centuries the oral explanations of the Mishnah were organized into a further codification known as the Gemara (consisting of both the Jerusalem Talmud and the Babylonian Talmud). The Mishnah and Gemara form the foundation of a vast commentary on the Torah known as the Oral Law.

It is clear from the Torah itself that it cannot be understood without an accompanying oral tradition. For example, the paragraph containing the *Shema* (a fundamental affirmation of Jewish faith) states, "Bind them ['these instructions with which I charge you this day'] as a sign on your hand and let them serve as a symbol on your forehead" (Deut. 6:8). This verse describes the mitzvah (commandment) of tefillin (phylacteries), the black-leather boxes worn on the arm and head during the weekday morning prayers. The Torah itself, however, does not provide any details concerning tefillin—their shape, color, contents, construction material, or how they are affixed to the body. All these details are provided in the Oral Law, which accompanied the Written Law.

With this background one can better appreciate what Rashi did in writing his monumental commentary on the Torah. Rashi drew from an encyclopedic knowledge of the vast corpus of the Oral Law. His commentary on the Torah (Five Books of Moses) is regarded as the most authoritative of all commentaries. For centuries it has been an indispensable aid in Torah study. In fact, the first printed Hebrew book was Rashi's commentary on the Torah, printed in Italy in 1475. Since then Rashi's commentary has been part of the standard format of the printed *Humash*.

About Rashi's Commentary

Rashi himself informs us of the purpose of his commentary: "I have come only to give the plain meaning [*peshat*] of Scripture and the rabbinic interpretations [*aggadah*] that serve to clarify the words of Scripture" (Rashi, Gen. 3:8). Still, generations of scholars have sought to reconcile his stated goal with certain of his comments that seem to depart from the text's plain meaning.

Many Rashi readers have puzzled over why Rashi commented on the text in certain instances and not in others. Here it is helpful to know that Rashi's commentary was originally printed as a stand-alone publication, unaccompanied by the Torah text. Because his treatise was essentially a compilation of his comments, each being prefaced by particular words on which he was commenting, it is helpful to focus on those introductory words (*dibur ha-matchil*) to understand what prompted Rashi's individual comments.

His comments tend to fall into one of a handful of categories:

1. Rashi defines a difficult or obscure word, essentially acting as a dictionary (see "An Observant Jew," Parashat Va-yeshev, where he defines the unusual Hebrew word *zoafim* [sad]).
2. Rashi comments when there is an inconsistency or seeming contradiction (see "National Unity," Parashat Yitro, where he comments on why, in the same verse, the word "encamped" is used both in the singular and the plural to describe the Jewish people).
3. Rashi fills in missing information that leads to a more complete understanding (see "Your Money or Your Life," Parashat Va-yera', where he explains why Lot was reluctant to flee the impending destruction of Sodom).
4. Rashi comments when the text is ambiguous and therefore presents more than one possible understanding (see "Not in Heaven," Parashat Nitsavim/Va-yelekh, where he provides the proper inference to be drawn from the fact that the Torah "is not in the heavens").
5. Rashi comments on what can be learned from seemingly superfluous words (see "The Immigrant Experience," Parashat Lekh Lekha, where he explains what is learned from the additional word *lekha* [to/for youself] in *Lekh lekha* [Go to/for yourself]).

6. Rashi highlights ethical principles that can be learned (see "Good Neighbors," Parashat Be-midbar, where he comments on the positive influence that can be exerted by good neighbors, citing as an example the influence of Moses and Aaron on the tribes that encamped adjacent to them).

How to Use This Book

The Torah not only describes the history of the Jewish nation, but, more importantly, provides the framework for the ongoing development of the Jewish people, on both an individual and a collective level. The issues the Torah addresses—the origins of humankind, the mission of the Jewish people, the way a person relates to others—are as relevant today as they were at any time in the past.

One of the most ancient and influential civilizations, the Jewish nation interacted with the Egyptians, Persians, Greeks, and Romans of antiquity. Whereas some of these latter civilizations exist today principally in museums and history books, the Jewish nation, which they all subjugated at one time or another, remains a vital actor on the world stage.

Today, as in antiquity, the Torah—its values, perspectives, and language—remains the central repository of what is unique about the Jewish nation. By studying it, we can better understand the history of the Jewish nation and its destiny in the modern era. This book is a modest attempt to relate the Torah's timeless messages to the experiences of our modern lives.

Since most Jews' exposure to the Torah comes through hearing the weekly parashah read in the synagogue, this book uses the parashah as the vehicle for delving into the Torah and draws on Rashi's comments to highlight relevant messages. For every parashah there are three essays, each quoting a Torah verse and a comment by Rashi, and then developing a related theme or idea. To generate lively discussions, each essay then concludes with three questions that draw on a variety of universal life experiences. For example, for Parashat Va-yishlaḥ, instead of a typical question, "How did Jacob prepare for his meeting with the more powerful Esau?" you'll discover, "What preparedness advice would you give a child who is being bullied?"

This book is written for all who wish to further their understanding of Torah through Rashi's insightful lens. You do not need any knowledge of Hebrew or familiarity with the Torah or Jewish practice to learn from it. All Torah verses and comments by Rashi are quoted in both Hebrew and English (the English translations of biblical verses are taken from the NJPS TANAKH), and enough relevant background is provided for less conversant readers to understand the quoted verses in their proper context. All Hebrew terms are defined, and Jewish concepts that may be unfamiliar are explained.

The book is also designed to be used for a variety of aims and in many settings, among them, Hebrew and Sunday school, day school, bar and bat mitzvah preparation, teen education, adult education, and family time. Given its focus on discussion, we encourage you to use it in the company of others. We've made it easy for you to discuss Rashi's insights at the Sabbath table: every parashah has three essays, one for each of the three meals traditionally eaten on Shabbat.

We hope that *The JPS Rashi Discussion Torah Commentary* provides you with an opportunity to engage in meaningful conversations about the timeless concepts in the Torah.

THE JPS RASHI DISCUSSION
TORAH COMMENTARY

Genesis

BERE'SHIT

❖ Contesting the Inheritance

There's a famous quote among newspaper editors: "If a dog bites a man, that's not news. But if a man bites a dog, that's news." It is the unusual or controversial nature of a story that makes it newsworthy. From this vantage point, one might ask why the State of Israel, whose size and population are roughly equivalent to those of New Jersey, has been the subject of so many newspaper headlines around the globe. It seems it is the Jewish claim to the Land of Israel, in particular, that arouses such controversy among the nations of the world. Their reaction might come as little surprise to the sages of the Talmud, whose opinion on this matter is recorded by Rashi on the opening verse of Parashat Bere'shit:

בְּרֵאשִׁית בָּרָא אֱלֹהִים אֵת הַשָּׁמַיִם וְאֵת הָאָרֶץ: (בראשית א, א)

When God began to create heaven and earth. (Gen. 1:1)

Rashi is bothered by why the Torah, which is ostensibly a book of laws, does not begin with the first commandment. He therefore presents the opinion of a talmudic sage to resolve this difficulty:

בראשית: אמר רבי יצחק לא היה צריך להתחיל [את] התורה אלא מ (שמות יב, ב) מהחודש הזה לכם, שהיא מצוה ראשונה שנצטוו [בה] ישראל, ומה טעם פתח בבראשית, משום (תהלים קיא, ו) כח מעשיו הגיד לעמו לתת להם נחלת גוים, שאם יאמרו אומות העולם לישראל לסטים אתם, שכבשתם ארצות שבעה גוים, הם אומרים

להם כל הארץ של הקב"ה היא, הוא בראה ונתנה לאשר ישר בעיניו, ברצונו נתנה להם וברצונו נטלה מהם ונתנה לנו: (רש"י,שם)

When [God] began: Said Rabbi Isaac: It was not necessary to begin the Torah except from "This month shall mark for you" (Exod. 12:2), which is the first commandment that the Israelites were commanded. Now for what reason did it begin with "When God began"? Because of [the verse] "He revealed to His people His powerful works, in giving them the heritage of nations" (Ps. 111:6). For if the nations of the world should say to Israel, "You are robbers, for you conquered by force the lands of the seven nations [of Canaan]," they will reply, "The entire earth belongs to the Holy One, blessed be He; He created it and gave it to whomever He deemed proper. When He wished, He gave it to them, and when He wished, He took it away from them and gave it to us." (Rashi, Gen. 1:1)

While one might be inclined to regard Rashi's comment as being of interest only to biblical scholars and believers, its relevance is much broader. Rashi penned these words almost a thousand years ago, and he quoted a talmudic sage who preceded him by another thousand years. Ignoring the theological implications of this talmudic statement, it frames the question of Jewish sovereignty over the Land of Israel against a historical backdrop extending back almost two millennia. A proper understanding of the issues concerning the State of Israel is premised on this recognition: the question of Jewish sovereignty in the Holy Land extends back to antiquity. Israel's detractors distort the Jewish connection to the Holy Land, claiming that it began in the nineteenth century, with the resettlement of Jews from elsewhere that culminated in the founding of the State of Israel in 1948. Such a blatant fabrication, however, cannot withstand even a cursory examination of the historical record. Just as the Acropolis in Athens attests to the history of the ancient Greeks, so too the Temple Mount in Jerusalem attests to a Jewish presence in the Holy Land that extends back millennia and predates the founding of both Christianity and Islam—an inconvenient truth for those who seek to deny the Jews their patrimony.

Questions for Discussion

1. Does the existence of the State of Israel make a difference in your life? In what ways?

2. Rashi's words are from almost a thousand years ago, and he quotes a talmudic sage who preceded him by another thousand years—thereby carrying on a chain of Jewish tradition and thought. What meaning does a chain of Jewish tradition hold for you?

3. Describe how the founding of your country may be controversial to those who regard themselves as native inhabitants of your country's territory. How do the territorial claims on which your country was founded compare to those underpinning the State of Israel?

❖ Rest: An Affirmative Creation

Since the Industrial Revolution, consumers have been enticed with repeated promises that each new invention—the sewing machine, automobile, telephone, and so forth—would simplify their lives and provide them with more leisure time. With "multitasking" now part of everyday parlance, people are understandably skeptical about the extent to which today's technological marvel—the smartphone—streamlines and thereby enhances the quality of their lives. Here, the concluding passage of this parashah's Creation narrative has a particularly relevant message:

וַיְכַל אֱלֹהִים בַּיּוֹם הַשְּׁבִיעִי מְלַאכְתּוֹ אֲשֶׁר עָשָׂה וַיִּשְׁבֹּת בַּיּוֹם הַשְּׁבִיעִי מִכָּל מְלַאכְתּוֹ אֲשֶׁר עָשָׂה: (בראשית ב, ב)

On the seventh day God finished the work that He had been doing, and He ceased on the seventh day from all the work that He had done. (Gen. 2:2)

Since we are told elsewhere that "in six days the Lord made heaven and earth" (Exod. 31:17), what remained to be "finished" on the seventh day? Rashi answers:

ויכל אלהים ביום השביעי: מה היה העולם חסר, מנוחה, באת שבת באת מנוחה, כלתה ונגמרה המלאכה: (רש"י, שם)

On the seventh day God finished: What was the world lacking? Rest. The Sabbath came and so came rest. The work was completed and finished. (Rashi, Gen. 2:2)

We are informed that rest is not merely the cessation from work, but rather is itself an affirmative creation: a fundamental creation in and of itself. Another way to think about it is to distinguish "rest" from "respite." Whereas "respite" is merely the pause between the activities that precede and follow it, "rest" requires creating a clearing that is free of all the surrounding clutter. While "respite" existed in the six days of Creation, "rest" only came into being with the entry of the Sabbath on the seventh day.

Questions for Discussion

1. Describe any activities or intrusions that prevent you from spending quality time with your family and friends. Does having a smartphone, engaging on social media, or using the Internet help or hinder those efforts?
2. What do you do—and what more might you do—to enhance the quality of the time you spend with people you care about?
3. How do you relate to the importance of "rest" as an affirmative creation in your life? Give an example of how you have carved out (or have contemplated carving out) time for yourself.

❖ What the First Man Could Have Learned from the Thirty-Third U.S. President

Harry Truman, the thirty-third president of the United States, had a sign on his desk in the Oval Office that read, "The Buck Stops Here," reflecting his belief that the president must make decisions and accept responsibility for them. Adam, the first man, would have been well served had he demonstrated similar accountability. The parashah relates how he responded to God's question as to whether he did the one thing God forbade him to do: eat from the Tree of Knowledge.

וַיֹּאמֶר הָאָדָם הָאִשָּׁה אֲשֶׁר נָתַתָּה עִמָּדִי הִוא נָתְנָה לִּי מִן הָעֵץ וָאֹכֵל: (בראשית ג, יב)

The man [Adam] said, "The woman You put at my side—she gave me of the tree, and I ate." (Gen. 3:12)

Not only did Adam fail in exercising self-restraint, but, as Rashi points out, he compounded his failure by blaming his wife:

אשר נתת עמדי: כאן כפר בטובה: (רש"י, שם)

You put at my side: Here he [Adam] showed his ingratitude. (Rashi, Gen. 3:12)

Adam lived in a veritable paradise where everything he required was provided for him. Furthermore, God even fulfilled Adam's one unmet need by creating a mate especially for him. Rather than show proper gratitude for this gesture, Adam blamed his actions on her.

Assuming responsibility is one of Judaism's fundamental values. A Jewish boy or girl becomes responsible for observing mitzvot (commandments) on becoming bar or bat mitzvah. Jews that own animals may not eat unless they first feed their animals (see *Bavli Berakhot* 40a). Moreover, a talmudic precept teaches that all Jews are responsible for one another (see *Bavli Shevuot* 39a).

Questions for Discussion

1. Describe a way in which you have taken "the buck stops here"-type of responsibility in your life. What did or does this mean to you?
2. Describe a time when you, someone you know, or a public figure used another person to deflect culpability for his or her actions. What was the immediate result, and what did you learn from the experience?
3. Do you believe that all Jews should be responsible for one another? What should our responsibilities be?

NOAH

❖ Nature versus Nurture

There is a long-running debate concerning the extent to which a person's personality is a function of genetic makeup (nature) or environmental (familial and societal) influences (nurture). While a consensus about the relative contribution of each remains elusive, scientists today understand that both nature and nurture play vital roles in forming who we are. In the Torah a verse from Parashat Noah alludes to environmental influences on a person's character:

אֵלֶּה תּוֹלְדֹת נֹחַ נֹחַ אִישׁ צַדִּיק תָּמִים הָיָה בְּדֹרֹתָיו אֶת הָאֱלֹהִים הִתְהַלֶּךְ נֹחַ: (בראשית ו, ט)

This is the line of Noah. Noah was a righteous man; he was blameless in his age; Noah walked with God. (Gen. 6:9)

In an effort to clarify why the verse states that Noah was "blameless in his age" rather than simply "blameless," Rashi comments:

בדורותיו: יש מרבותינו דורשים אותו לשבח, כל שכן שאלו היה בדור צדיקים היה צדיק יותר, ויש שדורשים אותו לגנאי, לפי דורו היה צדיק, ואלו היה בדורו של אברהם לא היה נחשב לכלום: (רש"י, שם)

in his age: Some of our sages interpret it [the word בְּדֹרֹתָיו] favorably: how much more so if he had lived in a generation of righteous people, he would have been even more righteous. Others interpret it negatively: in comparison with his generation he was righteous, but if he had been in Abraham's generation he would not have been considered of any importance. (Rashi, Gen. 6:9)

By explaining that had Noah lived in a generation of righteous people, he would have been even more righteous, Rashi implies that the Torah regards a person as being significantly affected by his or her environment. While some, such as Noah, may be able to withstand the corrosive effects of a negative environment, others may not be so fortunate.

Questions for Discussion

1. How do you believe your environment has helped shape your thoughts and actions?
2. Who do you know who comes closest to being "blameless in his age"? What qualities and actions has this person demonstrated to rise above his or her environment or situation?
3. What do you believe are the most important character traits to cultivate to help you (and perhaps others) rise above negative environmental influences?

❖ The Power of Persuasion

Words are themselves neutral—neither good nor bad. Like a hammer, they serve as a tool of those who use them, with the ability to create or destroy. The story of the Tower of Babel, built by Nimrod as a means of rebellion against God (see *Pirkei de-Rabbi Eliezer* 24), provides a cautionary tale of the destructive power of words.

הוּא הָיָה גִבֹּר צַיִד לִפְנֵי יְהוָה עַל כֵּן יֵאָמַר כְּנִמְרֹד גִּבּוֹר צַיִד לִפְנֵי יְהוָה: (בראשית י, ט)

He [Nimrod] was a mighty hunter by the grace of the Lord; hence the saying, "Like Nimrod a mighty hunter by the grace of the Lord." (Gen. 10:9)

The lack of any apparent connection between Nimrod's construction of the Tower of Babel and his being described as a "mighty hunter" led Rashi to comment:

גבור ציד: צד דעתן של בריות בפיו ומטען למרוד במקום: (רש"י, שם)

a mighty hunter: He ensnared people's minds with his speech and misled them to rebel against the Omnipresent. (Rashi, Gen. 10:9)

An orator par excellence, Nimrod was able to enlist support for his construction project through persuasion rather than compulsion. According to the midrash most people were won over by Nimrod's rhetoric and joined his rebellion (see *Pirkei de-Rabbi Eliezer* 24), but our Patriarch Abraham opposed Nimrod's enterprise. In modern times too, leaders in the image of Nimrod have risen to prominence due to the misplaced support of the masses, while other leaders in the image of Abraham have opposed them.

With the pendulum of world opinion swinging toward increased criticism of Israel—and by extension the Jews—it is important to remember Abraham's enduring influence in establishing monotheism in an idolatrous age. This is in fact why the Jews are called "Hebrews." The term "Hebrew" (Ivri, consisting of the Hebrew root letters ʿ v r) is derived from Abraham, who is referred to as Avram ha-Ivri (אברם העברי) since he came from the "other side" (עבר, consisting of the same Hebrew root letters ʿ-v-r) of the river (see Rashi, Gen. 14:13). Since Abraham

established monotheism in a world steeped in idolatry, he was given an appellation recalling that "the entire world was on one side, and he was on the other side" (*Bereshit Rabbah* 42:8). From Abraham we have the Jewish legacy of standing up for our beliefs, even when we stand alone.

Questions for Discussion

1. Today, who do you believe has risen to prominence due to the misplaced support of the masses (for example, a politician, religious figure, celebrity, or blogger)? Who do you believe has risen, in Abraham's image, in opposition?

2. Do you hold any beliefs about making a better society that seem to be at odds with other people's opinions? Have you asserted them?

3. Who is the most compelling speaker you have ever heard, and what have you learned from this person about communicating to others?

❖ United Nations

The United Nations (UN) was founded in 1945 to enable nations to "live together in peace with one another as good neighbours" (see Charter of the United Nations). While the UN has at best a mixed record with respect to achieving this goal, the midrash relates that Nimrod actually succeeded in uniting all the nations of the world when he directed their building of the Tower of Babel. However, instead of leading the nations, which were unified by a common language, to further the progress of humanity, Nimrod led them to build a tower to the heavens so they could wage war against God (see Rashi, Gen. 11:1). This quest failed miserably and resulted in the substitution of many languages for the one language that had united them.

עַל כֵּן קָרָא שְׁמָהּ בָּבֶל כִּי שָׁם בָּלַל יְהֹוָה שְׂפַת כָּל הָאָרֶץ וּמִשָּׁם הֱפִיצָם יְהֹוָה עַל פְּנֵי כָל הָאָרֶץ: (בראשית יא, ט)

That is why it was called Babel, because there the Lord confounded the speech of the whole earth; and from there the Lord scattered them over the face of the whole earth. (Gen. 11:9)

Rashi compares the punishment of those who built the Tower of Babel (called the generation of the dispersion because they were punished by being scattered across the globe), with those destroyed by the Flood in the days of Noah (the generation of the Flood):

ומשם הפיצם: וכי איזו קשה, של דור המבול או של דור הפלגה, אלו לא פשטו יד בעיקר, ואלו פשטו יד בעיקר כביכול להלחם בו, ואלו נשטפו, ואלו לא נאבדו מן העולם. אלא שדור המבול היו גזלנים והיתה מריבה ביניהם לכך נאבדו, ואלו היו נוהגים אהבה וריעות ביניהם, שנאמר שפה אחת ודברים אחדים. למדת ששנוי המחלוקת וגדול השלום: (רש״י, שם)

and from there [the Lord] scattered them: Now which [transgressions] were worse, those of the generation of the Flood or those of the generation of the dispersion? The former did not raise their hands against God, whereas the latter raised their hands against God to wage war against Him. [Nevertheless,] the former were drowned, while the latter did not perish from the world. That is because the generation of the Flood were robbers and there was strife between

them, and therefore they were destroyed. But these [the generation of the dispersion] conducted themselves with love and friendship, as it is said [Gen. 11:1]: "the same language and the same words." Thus you learn that strife is detested and peace is great. (Rashi, Gen. 11:9)

As Rashi explains, the generation of the dispersion, which was united in love, was allowed to live despite the fact that it rebelled against God. In contrast, the generation of the Flood, characterized by interpersonal conflict, was annihilated by the Flood. From this we learn both the destructive power of strife and the great blessings that may flow from peace.

Questions for Discussion

1. Describe a time when you experienced being united with others for a common purpose, honorable or dishonorable. What did you learn from that experience?
2. What life experiences come to mind when you think of Rashi's teaching, "Strife is detested and peace is great"?
3. What can be done to promote more togetherness or unity in your community, and how might you contribute to that?

LEKH LEKHA

❖ The Immigrant Experience

In the United States, where most citizens trace their roots to another country, there is nothing unusual about being descended from immigrants. However, most countries are populated by ethnic natives who have no collective memory of having lived anywhere else. As a people, Jews are largely unique in almost always tracing their lineage to a foreign land. In fact, Jewish history opens with perhaps the world's first recorded immigrant experience—the journey of Abram, the first Jew, from his native land to Israel. God's directive to Abram (whose name is later changed to Abraham) to immigrate to Israel is recorded in the opening verse of Parashat Lekh Lekha:

וַיֹּאמֶר יְהֹוָה אֶל אַבְרָם לֶךְ לְךָ מֵאַרְצְךָ וּמִמּוֹלַדְתְּךָ וּמִבֵּית אָבִיךָ אֶל הָאָרֶץ אֲשֶׁר אַרְאֶךָּ: (בראשית יב, א)

The Lord said to Abram, "Go forth from your native land and from your father's house to the land that I will show you." (Gen. 12:1)

In an effort to clarify why the verse says *lekh lekha* (literally, "Go to/for yourself") rather than simply *lekh* (Go), Rashi comments:

לֶךְ לְךָ: להנאתך ולטובתך, ושם אעשך לגוי גדול, וכאן אי אתה זוכה לבנים. ועוד שאודיע טבעך בעולם: (רש"י, שם)

Go forth: For your benefit and for your good, and there I will make you into a great nation, but here, you will not merit having children. Moreover, I will make your character known in the world. (Rashi, Gen. 12:1)

As Rashi explains, the additional word *lekha* (to/for yourself) is a reference to the benefit that will inure to Abram in complying with God's command to leave his native land. Rashi elaborates in his following comment that since such a journey—which in those days involved traveling for months in harsh desert conditions—has the effect of reducing one's wealth, social status, and ability to have children, God therefore promised Abram that in his new land he would be blessed in each of these three areas (see Rashi, Gen. 12:2).

Most American Jews are descended from Jews who immigrated to the United States between 1880 and 1920. In those years, new and would-be immigrants called America the *goldene medina* (Yiddish for "golden country"), perceiving it as a land of unbounded opportunity. While their aspirations for success in their new home would be fulfilled in many respects, this process usually involved great sacrifice.

Questions for Discussion

1. What was your family's experience of settling in America? Did your ancestors perceive it as a "golden country" before and after they immigrated?
2. What does a "golden country" mean to you? Do you think of America that way?
3. Implicit in the Lord's assurances to Abram is an understanding that the Patriarch was probably feeling considerable fear and anxiety about the prospect of journeying to somewhere completely unknown. Have you had to "go forth," whether to a destination or to something else you feared that required taking a huge leap of faith? What did you learn from the experience?

❖ Ladies First

The term "ladies first" has long been generally understood as a positive expression of deference toward women, but not everyone holds this view, as indicated by a recent *Vogue* article entitled "Modern Manners: Ladies First—Still Relevant or Hopelessly Outdated?" Today some people regard "ladies first" as a patronizing expression of a bygone era, yet an episode from Abraham's travels seems to exemplify the original intent of this term:

וַיַּעְתֵּק מִשָּׁם הָהָרָה מִקֶּדֶם לְבֵית אֵל וַיֵּט אָהֳלֹה
בֵּית אֵל מִיָּם וְהָעַי מִקֶּדֶם וַיִּבֶן שָׁם מִזְבֵּחַ לַיהוָה
וַיִּקְרָא בְּשֵׁם יְהוָה: (בראשית יב, ח)

From there he moved on to the hill country east of Bethel and pitched his tent, with Bethel on the west and Ai on the east; and he built there an altar to the Lord and invoked the Lord by name. (Gen. 12:8)

Rashi comments on the word *ohalo* (אָהֳלֹה, his tent), which is pronounced (consistent with its usual spelling) as if the last letter were a *vav* (the masculine possessive suffix meaning "his"), when in fact it is a *heh* (the feminine possessive suffix meaning "her"):

אהלה: אהלה כתיב, בתחלה נטה את אהל אשתו ואחר כך את
שלו: (רש"י, שם)

his tent: It is written אהלה [which can be read אָהֳלָה, "her tent"]. First he pitched his wife's tent and afterward his own. (Rashi, Gen. 12:8)

The Talmud advises that a man should honor his wife more than himself (*Bavli Sanhedrin* 76b). Abraham's pitching his wife's tent before his own was an expression of this value.

Today a variety of societal problems impose great tolls, in both human and economic terms, and elude simple solutions. Consequently, some people question whether today's movement away from "ladies first," and to some extent from other "traditional" values such as "honor" and "sacrifice," is really in society's best interests.

Questions for Discussion

1. What does the expression "ladies first" mean to you? Do you regard its implications for women as positive or negative?
2. Why do you think the concept of honor is not as valued today as it once was?
3. Do you believe that it is in contemporary society's best interests to uphold the values embodied in "ladies first," "honor," and "sacrifice"?

❖ Consider It Done

It's not uncommon for one person to remind another to complete something he or she promised but did not deliver. The subject of fulfilling one's commitments is raised in the parashah, when God promises to give the Land of Israel to Abraham's offspring:

בַּיּוֹם הַהוּא כָּרַת יְהוָה אֶת אַבְרָם בְּרִית לֵאמֹר לְזַרְעֲךָ נָתַתִּי אֶת הָאָרֶץ
הַזֹּאת מִנְּהַר מִצְרַיִם עַד הַנָּהָר הַגָּדֹל נְהַר פְּרָת: (בראשית טו, יח)

On that day the Lord made a covenant with Abram, saying, "To your offspring I assign this land, from the river of Egypt to the great river, the river Euphrates." (Gen. 15:18)

Noting that the verse states "I assign" rather than "I will assign"—even though Abram does not yet have any offspring—Rashi comments:

לְזַרְעֲךָ נָתַתִּי: אֲמִירָתוֹ שֶׁל הקב"ה כְּאִלּוּ הִיא עֲשׂוּיָה: (רש"י, שם)

To your offspring I assign: The word of the Holy One, blessed be He, is like an accomplished fact. (Rashi, Gen. 15:18)

While one may find it easy to regard a promise from God as a fait accompli (something decided on and thereby achieved from the outset), our own promises may not always be so reliable. Yet our credibility in others' eyes is largely a function of how well our actions accord with our words. It's a very human challenge to consistently deliver on every promise so that when we next pledge to accomplish something, the other person can consider it done.

Questions for Discussion

1. Are you someone who consistently fulfills your commitments to family members, friends, and colleagues? What helps you to meet those commitments, and what gets in the way?
2. Do you agree that our credibility in others' eyes is largely a function of how well our actions accord with our words? In your experience, what other qualities and behaviors influence how others see you?
3. What would it take for you to become so reliable that once you've pledged to accomplish something, another person considers it done?

VA-YERA'

❖ Healing without a Medical License

The mitzvah (commandment) to visit the sick (*bikur holim*) has been embraced by both Jews and non-Jews. Ronald McDonald House enables families to visit their sick children by providing low-cost accommodations adjacent to hospitals. Many Jewish communities have *bikur holim* organizations that facilitate volunteer visits to patients in local hospitals, and even provide Jewish patients with wine for *Kiddush* (prayer over wine) and candles for the Sabbath. In the opening verse of Parashat Va-yera', as explained by Rashi, God introduces the mitzvah of *bikur holim* by example:

וַיֵּרָא אֵלָיו יְהֹוָה בְּאֵלֹנֵי מַמְרֵא וְהוּא יֹשֵׁב פֶּתַח הָאֹהֶל כְּחֹם הַיּוֹם:
(בראשית יח, א)

The Lord appeared to him [Abraham] by the terebinths of Mamre; he was sitting at the entrance of the tent as the day grew hot. (Gen. 18:1)

In clarifying why God appeared to Abraham at this time, Rashi states:

וירא אליו: לבקר את החולה. אמר רבי חמא בר חנינא יום שלישי למילתו היה, ובא הקב"ה ושאל בשלומו: (רש"י, שם)

[The Lord] appeared to him: to visit the sick. Said Rabbi Chama the son of Chanina: It was the third day from his circumcision, and the Holy One, blessed be He, came and inquired about his welfare. (Rashi, Gen. 18:1)

The previous parashah (Lekh Lekha) ends with Abraham's circumcision, and this parashah begins with God's appearing before Abraham. Rashi therefore informs us that God visited Abraham to ask about his well-being—in effect, to demonstrate to Abraham that God cared for him.

From this perspective, practicing *bikur holim* can encompass many ways to help others heal: visiting patients in hospitals or nursing homes, engaging with neighbors who are home bound or recovering after medical treatment, and reaching out to people who are lonely or going through difficult times. Doctors or not, all of us can play a role in someone else's healing.

Questions for Discussion

1. Based on your experience either visiting someone who was sick or receiving a visitor when you were ill, how do you think practicing *bikur holim* affects the person receiving the visit?
2. From your experience, how can visiting the sick affect the person who is engaging in *bikur holim*?
3. Do you agree that all of us can play a role in someone else's healing?

❖ Learning by Doing

When one person delegates tasks to another, a natural tendency is to designate the relatively menial ones and keep the more important ones for oneself. However, the opposite pattern frequently holds true when parents delegate to their offspring.

Often parents assign them more challenging, value-laden tasks, hoping that the ensuing experiences will inform their children's knowledge and character. In the parashah Abraham delegates to his thirteen-year-old son the vital preparation of a calf as provision for the wayfarers whom he has just invited to join him for a meal:

וְאֶל הַבָּקָר רָץ אַבְרָהָם וַיִּקַּח בֶּן בָּקָר רַךְ וָטוֹב וַיִּתֵּן אֶל הַנַּעַר וַיְמַהֵר לַעֲשׂוֹת אֹתוֹ: (בראשית יח, ז)

Then Abraham ran to the herd, took a calf, tender and choice, and gave it to a servant-boy, who hastened to prepare it. (Gen. 18:7)

Rashi comments on who this "servant-boy" was:

אֶל הַנַּעַר: זֶה יִשְׁמָעֵאל לְחַנְּכוֹ בְּמִצְוֹת: (רש"י, שם)

to a servant-boy: This was Ishmael, to train him to perform mitzvot. (Rashi, Gen. 18:7)

Given that Abraham was then ninety-nine years old and recovering from his circumcision of three days before, one might think that he had delegated the calf's preparation to Ishmael out of necessity. Rashi tells us otherwise—that Abraham's decision was motivated by his desire to train Ishmael in mitzvot (commandments).

Today, when a parent asks a young child to help rake leaves or bake cookies, an otherwise relaxing activity may turn into a time-consuming project fraught with frustration. But if the child's development is the parent's primary consideration, he or she may deem the trade-off worthwhile.

Questions for Discussion

1. When delegating to others, do you typically designate the more menial tasks? Why or why not?

2. Have you ever found that in assigning a challenging task to someone, you may have helped shape his or her character? If yes, how so?

3. Under what circumstances would you consider it a worthwhile trade-off to delegate something important to you that you could do better yourself?

❖ Your Money or Your Life

Jack Benny, the mid-twentieth-century radio and television comedian, used to play a character known for his stinginess. In one routine a mugger accosts him, saying, "Don't make a move; this is a stickup. Now, come on. Your money or your life." Benny pauses, and the robber repeats his demand: "Look, bud! I said, 'Your money or your life!'" Benny then snaps back, "I'm thinking it over!" As the parashah relates, this punch line is reminiscent of a difficult decision Abraham's nephew Lot faced thirty-seven hundred years ago: whether or not to flee the city of Sodom before it was destroyed.

וַיִּתְמַהְמָהּ | וַיַּחֲזִיקוּ הָאֲנָשִׁים בְּיָדוֹ וּבְיַד אִשְׁתּוֹ וּבְיַד שְׁתֵּי בְנֹתָיו בְּחֶמְלַת יְהוָה עָלָיו וַיֹּצִאֻהוּ וַיַּנִּחֻהוּ מִחוּץ לָעִיר: (בראשית יט, טז)

Still he [Lot] delayed. So the men seized his hand, and the hands of his wife and his two daughters—in the Lord's mercy on him—and brought him out and left him outside the city. (Gen. 19:16)

Rashi explains why Lot hesitated from fleeing Sodom even after being informed it was about to be destroyed:

ויתמהמה: כדי להציל את ממונו: (רש"י, שם)

Still he delayed: in order to save his possessions. (Rashi, Gen. 19:16)

Lot's choice was stark—literally his money or his life—but the Jewish people's options throughout history have rarely been so clear. In 1492 Jews in Spain were given the choice either to leave the country (without money) or to convert to Christianity. While many Jews left, thousands remained and converted. Of those who converted, some continued to practice Judaism secretly, at peril to their lives. Even sincere converts could be suspected of heresy and killed at the hands of legal authorities or an enraged mob. In 2015, as a gesture of reconciliation, Spain enacted a law offering citizenship to Jews of Spanish descent (as long as they can overcome the law's many hurdles).

In 1930s Germany the Nazis enacted a series of laws that stripped Jews of basic civil rights. Some Jews fled the country, often abandoning all their possessions. Others remained, hoping conditions would improve and not recognizing the futility of their situation until it was too late to leave. In 1952 Germany agreed to pay the State of Israel reparations totaling three billion marks ($715 million in 1952 dollars, or $6.5 billion in 2017 dollars) over a period of fourteen years.

Questions for Discussion

1. Have you ever postponed taking an important action because you feared losing something vitally important to you?
2. Which of your "possessions" are most important for you to keep safe?
3. Do you believe acts of reparation serve a critical purpose? How do you feel about Germany's and Spain's deeds of reparation and reconciliation?

ḤAYYEI SARAH

❖ A Full Glass

Positive psychology is a new branch of psychology primarily concerned with understanding what makes people happy. While researchers believe that happiness depends on a combination of genetics, circumstances, and one's own perceptions, it is this last factor that has attracted the most attention in the popular press and in self-help literature. A person experiencing difficulties is often encouraged to see the glass as half-full rather than half-empty. A third possibility is to see the glass as full—without qualification—a perspective that can attributed to our Matriarch Sarah based on a verse from Parashat Ḥayyei Sarah.

וַיִּהְיוּ חַיֵּי שָׂרָה מֵאָה שָׁנָה וְעֶשְׂרִים שָׁנָה וְשֶׁבַע שָׁנִים שְׁנֵי חַיֵּי שָׂרָה:
(בראשית כג, א)

Sarah's lifetime—the span of Sarah's life—came to one hundred and twenty-seven years. (Gen. 23:1)

Explaining why the verse contains the seemingly superfluous phrase "the span of Sarah's life," Rashi states:

שני חיי שרה: כלן שוין לטובה: (רש"י, שם)

the span of Sarah's life: All of them [the years] equally good. (Rashi, Gen. 23:1)

To appreciate what Rashi is saying, it helps to know some details of Sarah's life. She immigrated to the Land of Israel at the age of sixty-five, was twice kidnapped by foreign kings, and remained infertile and childless until the age of ninety. After despairing of having children herself, she allowed her husband, Abraham, to have a child with her servant—a decision that led to many distressing consequences. Despite these challenges Sarah's life reflected great achievements. She influenced many people to accept monotheism, and at an advanced age she gave birth to the Patriarch Isaac. Through it all she remained cognizant of the ultimate goodness of her life's vicissitudes, thereby enabling all her years to be described as "equally good."

Questions for Discussion

1. Describe a difficulty you experienced and how you dealt with it.
2. In what ways have the challenges you have faced enabled you to become the person you are?
3. What would you describe as the happiest moments of your life? Do these moments have certain qualities in common?

❖ Woman of Valor

Before the traditional Sabbath evening meal, some people sing *Eshet Chayil* (Woman of Valor), a hymn from the book of Proverbs that extols the virtues of a Jewish wife, such as kindness, wisdom, industriousness, and good judgment. The quality of kindness emerges as paramount when Abraham's servant, whom Abraham has charged with finding a wife for his son Isaac, speaks to God about the criteria for a suitable candidate.

וְהָיָה הַנַּעֲרָה אֲשֶׁר אֹמַר אֵלֶיהָ הַטִּי נָא כַדֵּךְ וְאֶשְׁתֶּה וְאָמְרָה שְׁתֵה וְגַם גְּמַלֶּיךָ אַשְׁקֶה אֹתָהּ הֹכַחְתָּ לְעַבְדְּךָ לְיִצְחָק וּבָהּ אֵדַע כִּי עָשִׂיתָ חֶסֶד עִם אֲדֹנִי: (בראשית כד, יד)

[L]et the maiden to whom I say, "Please, lower your jar that I may drink," and who replies, "Drink, and I will also water your camels"—let her be the one whom You have decreed for Your servant Isaac. Thereby shall I know that You have dealt graciously with my master. (Gen. 24:14)

Rashi identifies the characteristic of Rebekah, the maiden who passed the test, that made her suitable for Isaac:

אותה הכחת: ראויה היא לו שתהא גומלת חסדים וכדאי ליכנס בביתו של אברהם: (רש"י, שם)

let her be the one whom You have decreed: She is worthy of him, for she will perform acts of kindness, and she is fit to enter the house of Abraham. (Rashi, Gen. 24:14)

During Rebekah's first encounter with Abraham's servant, she is described as being "very beautiful" (טֹבַת מַרְאֶה מְאֹד) (Gen. 24:16), but this quality was not a significant consideration in her being selected as Isaac's wife. Kindness alone defined her as a suitable wife for Isaac. In a similar vein *Eshet Chayil* minimizes the importance of appearance, stating, "Grace is deceptive, beauty is illusory" (שֶׁקֶר הַחֵן וְהֶבֶל הַיֹּפִי) (Prov. 31:30).

Questions for Discussion

1. What did your parents teach you about the most important qualities to seek out in a spouse? Do you agree with their criteria?

2. What criteria does popular culture regard as most important in choosing a spouse? Do you agree with these gauges?

3. What qualities do you think are most important in a spouse? How can you know, before marriage, that a prospective mate has these qualities?

❖ Leash Your Dog

Signs such as "Leash Your Dog" in public places put dog owners on notice that it is their legal responsibility to prevent their pets from injuring people or damaging property. Long before the dog was man's best friend, it was the camel—at least in the Middle East—that served in this capacity. Restraining one's animal from causing damage was a concern, as we see in this verse from the parashah that describes how Abraham's servant was welcomed at the house of Abraham's future daughter-in-law Rebekah.

וַיָּבֹא הָאִישׁ הַבַּיְתָה וַיְפַתַּח הַגְּמַלִּים וַיִּתֵּן תֶּבֶן וּמִסְפּוֹא לַגְּמַלִּים וּמַיִם לִרְחֹץ רַגְלָיו וְרַגְלֵי הָאֲנָשִׁים אֲשֶׁר אִתּוֹ (בראשית כד, לב)

So the man entered the house, and the camels were unloaded [alternatively, "unmuzzled"]. The camels were given straw and feed, and water was brought to bathe his feet and the feet of the men with him. (Gen. 24:32)

Rashi, who understands the word וַיְפַתַּח to mean "unmuzzled," explains why the camels were muzzled:

ויפתח: התיר זמם שלהם, שהיה סותם את פיהם שלא ירעו בדרך בשדות אחרים: (רש"י, שם)

and [the camels were] unmuzzled: He removed their muzzles, for he had muzzled them so that they would not graze along the way in fields belonging to others. (Rashi, Gen. 24:32)

Before the advent of the automobile, people relied on horses for transportation, and a horse grazing on the side of the road was a common sight. While one can understand that the owner of a field would be upset if passing animals ate his produce, the animal's behavior could presumably be justified as being the inevitable consequence of having fields along a public thoroughfare. Nevertheless, as Rashi points out, it was not acceptable for Abraham's camels to take such liberties.

In contemporary society we spend much of the day surrounded by and making use of other people's property. Additionally we may, like Abraham's servant, be responsible for others, such as pets or children, when they interact in someone else's domain.

Questions for Discussion

1. If you have owned a pet, what safeguards did you take to prevent it from hurting others or their property? Alternatively, what could pet owners do to be more respectful of others?
2. Describe a time you felt compelled to restrain a child due to a concern about damaging property or disturbing others. How do you balance the child's need for autonomy with consideration of others?
3. Describe a situation where it was not clear to you whether it was acceptable to make use of another person's property. How did you handle it, and would you make the same choice today?

TOLEDOT

❖ Rags to Riches

The United States is known universally as the "land of opportunity." Indeed the story of someone who starts with nothing and reaches the highest echelons of society is perhaps *the* quintessential and enduring American legend. In Parashat Toledot our Matriarch Rebekah provides a spiritual analogue for the rags-to-riches story:

וַיְהִי יִצְחָק בֶּן אַרְבָּעִים שָׁנָה בְּקַחְתּוֹ אֶת רִבְקָה בַּת בְּתוּאֵל הָאֲרַמִּי מִפַּדַּן אֲרָם אֲחוֹת לָבָן הָאֲרַמִּי לוֹ לְאִשָּׁה: (בראשית כה, כ)

Isaac was forty years old when he took to wife Rebekah, daughter of Bethuel the Aramean of Paddan-aram, sister of Laban the Aramean. (Gen. 25:20)

Rashi explains why this verse repeats information that has already been provided—that Rebekah is from Paddan-aram and is the daughter of Bethuel and the sister of Laban:

בת בתואל מפדן ארם אחות לבן: וכי עדיין לא נכתב שהיא בת בתואל ואחות לבן ומפדן ארם, אלא להגיד שבחה שהיתה בת רשע ואחות רשע ומקומה אנשי רשע, ולא למדה ממעשיהם: (רש"י, שם)

daughter of Bethuel the Aramean of Paddan-aram, sister of Laban: Was it not already written that she was the daughter of Bethuel and the sister of Laban and from Paddan-aram? Rather, this is to relate her praise, that she was the daughter

of a wicked man and the sister of a wicked man and her place was [inhabited by] wicked people, but she did not learn from their conduct. (Rashi, Gen. 25:20)

While being one of the Matriarchs of the Jewish people could itself be considered the crowning achievement of one's life, Rashi informs us that Rebekah's attainment was even greater, because she overcame very challenging obstacles. Surrounded by wickedness in both her family and community, she managed to avoid following in their ways and instead developed into a paradigm of virtue.

While excellence in many fields—professional, athletic, intellectual, personal, or otherwise—can generally be measured by objective standards, the adversity that a person surmounted to attain this distinction often remains hidden. Considering the circumstances that a person had to overcome may greatly enhance the significance of his or her achievements. The merit in overcoming adversity also seems to be acknowledged by the talmudic maxim: "In the place where *baalei teshuvah* [penitents] stand, even the completely righteous cannot stand" (*Bavli Berakhot* 34b).

Questions for Discussion

1. Describe someone you believe typifies the achievement of the American Dream. Are there factors in this person's background that cause you to hold this achievement in even higher regard?

2. Have you ever succeeded in something that required you to overcome obstacles others didn't face? How did these obstacles hinder your efforts, and what did you learn about facing obstacles as a result?

3. Why do you believe the Talmud teaches that even completely righteous people cannot stand with those who have become righteous through penitence? What lessons have

you learned the "hard way" that have made you more righteous in character?

....

❖ It's Not My Fault

The next time you hear a child who has done something wrong proclaim his or her innocence by asserting, "It's not my fault," consider that the child may be right. A verse describing Rebekah's pregnancy with the twins Jacob and Esau implies that a person's nature may be largely determined at birth.

וַיֹּאמֶר יְהֹוָה לָהּ שְׁנֵי גוֹיִם בְּבִטְנֵךְ וּשְׁנֵי לְאֻמִּים מִמֵּעַיִךְ יִפָּרֵדוּ וּלְאֹם מִלְאֹם יֶאֱמָץ וְרַב יַעֲבֹד צָעִיר: (בראשית כה, כג)

[A]nd the Lord answered her, "Two nations are in your womb, [t]wo separate peoples shall issue from your body; [o]ne people shall be mightier than the other, [a]nd the older shall serve the younger." (Gen. 25:23)

Rashi explains that the distress Rebekah experienced during her pregnancy resulted from a clash between two fetuses that were already on diametrically opposed paths:

ממעיך יפרדו: מן המעים הם נפרדים, זה לרשעו וזה לתומו: (רש"י, שם)

shall issue from your body: From the womb they are separated, this one [Esau] to his wickedness, and this one [Jacob] to his wholesomeness. (Rashi, Gen. 25:23)

While researchers are only beginning to understand why children from the same background can be so different, there is consensus that significant behavioral differences exist from birth. Given this fact, there would seem to be a gross injustice in applying the same expectations and standards to all children. Certain children may, for reasons beyond their control, find it difficult to do things that come easily to others. On the other hand, refusing to hold a child accountable for his or her conduct is not only unfair, but also exhibits a lack of concern for the child. An alternative approach is to assess the demonstrated abilities of a child and set one's expectations and standards for that child accordingly. This is consistent with the biblical directive, "Train a lad in the way he ought to go [דרכו, literally, "his path"]; he will not swerve from it even in old age" (Prov. 22:6).

Questions for Discussion

1. Describe any behavioral or personality differences between you and your siblings (or, if you don't have siblings, between you and your parents or cousins). How do you explain these differences?
2. Describe a quality or ability of yours that came naturally. How have you capitalized on this capacity to enhance your life?
3. How have your education and upbringing both addressed and failed to address your particular needs, capabilities, and interests?

....

❖ Death and Taxes

Benjamin Franklin, one of America's founders, once wrote, "Our new Constitution is now established, and has an appearance that promises permanency; but in this world nothing can be said to be certain, except death and taxes." The certainty of death has often served as a prompt to take action while it is still possible. We see an example of this in the parashah when Isaac, prompted by the following verse, decides to bless his son Jacob:

וַיֹּאמֶר הִנֵּה נָא זָקַנְתִּי לֹא יָדַעְתִּי יוֹם מוֹתִי: (בראשית כז, ב)

And he [Isaac] said, "I am old now, and I do not know how soon I may die." (Gen. 27:2)

In explaining why Isaac was concerned at that moment about his death, Rashi states:

לֹא ידעתי יום מותי: אמר רבי יהושע בן קרחה אם מגיע אדם לפרק אבותיו ידאג חמש שנים לפניהם וחמש לאחר כן, ויצחק היה בן מאה עשרים ושלש, אמר שמא לפרק אמי אני מגיע, והיא מתה בת מאה עשרים ושבע והריני בן חמש שנים סמוך לפרקה, לפיכך לא ידעתי יום מותי, שמא לפרק אמי, שמא לפרק אבא: (רש"י, שם)

I do not know how soon I may die: Rabbi Yehoshua ben Korchah said: If a person reaches the age of [the death of] his parents, he should worry five years beforehand and five years afterward, and Isaac was 123 years old. He said, "Perhaps I will reach the age of [the death of] my mother, and she died at 127, and I am thus within five years of her age; therefore, 'I do not know how soon I may die'; perhaps [I will die] at my mother's age and perhaps at my father's age [175]." (Rashi, Gen. 27:2)

As Rashi explains, the prospect of Isaac's impending death prompted him to summon his son so he could bless him. A natural human tendency is to postpone doing things—particularly those that are either difficult or not needed immediately—until,

with the passage of time, they become urgent. Then those absolutely necessary actions tend to demand our attention under less than ideal circumstances. It is generally better—and less stressful—to address such matters sooner rather than later.

Questions for Discussion

1. What important task have you been deferring? What is getting in your way, and what approach might enable you to accomplish it?
2. What action would you regret not having done if time did not permit you to at least attempt it?
3. What do you consider the most significant legacy left to you by your parents or grandparents? Did they leave you this legacy early or late in their lives?

VA-YETSE'

❖ Making a Difference

In last week's parashah Esau vowed to kill his brother Jacob, who had taken the paternal blessing intended for Esau, the firstborn. The opening verse of Parashat Va-yetse' records Jacob's flight from Beer-sheba to escape his vengeful brother.

וַיֵּצֵא יַעֲקֹב מִבְּאֵר שָׁבַע וַיֵּלֶךְ חָרָנָה: (בראשית כח, י)

Jacob left Beer-sheba, and set out for Haran. (Gen. 28:10)

Since we already know that Jacob lived in Beer-sheba, why does the verse state that he left Beer-sheba rather than simply state that he went to Haran? Rashi explains:

ויצא יעקב מבאר שבע: לא היה צריך לכתוב אלא וילך יעקב חרנה, ולמה הזכיר יציאתו, אלא מגיד שיציאת צדיק מן המקום עושה רושם, שבזמן שהצדיק בעיר הוא הודה הוא זיוה הוא הדרה, יצא משם פנה הודה פנה זיוה פנה הדרה: (רש"י, שם)

Jacob left Beer-sheba: The Torah had only to write: "And Jacob set out for Haran." Why did it mention his departure? Rather this tells [us] that the departure of a righteous man from a place makes an impression, for while the righteous man is in the city, he is its beauty, he is its splendor, he is its majesty. When he departs from there, its beauty has departed, its splendor has departed, its majesty has departed. (Rashi, Gen. 28:10)

As Rashi explains, Jacob's departure from Beer-sheba is mentioned to inform us of the tremendous void that his departure left in the city. Jacob's presence conferred glory and splendor on the city—a fact that was apparent to all once he had left.

Later in the Torah it is Jacob's son Joseph who, by example, demonstrated the positive impact a single individual can have on his environment. Anticipating the famine that was to afflict Egypt, Joseph orchestrated elaborate preparations by which Egypt was able to survive the ensuing devastation. During the famine, transcending his brothers' ill-treatment of him as a child, Joseph brought his extended family to Egypt to assure their well-being. They, in turn, developed into the Jewish people.

As with Jacob's departure from Beer-sheba, Joseph's departure from Egypt (as a result of his death) also had negative consequences—in this case for the Jewish people, who were then enslaved by the Egyptians.

Questions for Discussion

1. Describe a person who has had a positive impact on your city or community. What personal qualities do you think enabled him or her to have such an impact?

2. Name someone who has had a lasting, positive influence on society. To what extent was this person's legacy a function of personal character and to what extent a function of circumstances?

3. Describe something you have done (or have considered doing) that has benefited (or could benefit) your community or others around you.

❖ No Shirt, No Shoes, No Service

In beach communities one commonly sees establishments displaying the sign "No Shirt, No Shoes, No Service." Even in a casual setting, certain standards of conduct are expected. The parashah provides an example of the standards applicable to a place of sanctity, as Jacob unknowingly spends the night in the location of the future Temple.

וַיִּיקַץ יַעֲקֹב מִשְּׁנָתוֹ וַיֹּאמֶר אָכֵן יֵשׁ יְהֹוָה בַּמָּקוֹם הַזֶּה וְאָנֹכִי לֹא
יָדָעְתִּי: (בראשית כח, טז)

Jacob awoke from his sleep and said, "Surely the Lord is present in this place, and I did not know it!" (Gen. 28:16)

Answering the question of what was significant in Jacob's not knowing that God was in this place, Rashi comments:

ואנכי לא ידעתי: שאילו ידעתי לא ישנתי
במקום קדוש כזה: (רש"י, שם)

and I did not know it: For had I known, I would not have slept in such a holy place. (Rashi, Gen. 28:16)

A hallmark of any society is its standards of conduct in different settings, such as government offices and public spaces (libraries, theatres, etc.). Standards of behavior also inform how people interact with each other, and they can vary dramatically. For example, the protocol that applies to a meeting of heads of state is nothing like the decorum typical of a holiday party. Often these standards are unwritten.

In Jewish life too, standards of conduct affect how people relate to one another and act. For example, when the Torah is carried through the synagogue, congregants are expected to rise; and on the occasion of a *brit milah* (circumcision) or giving a daughter a Jewish name, the guests wish the parents a congratulatory *mazzal tov*.

Questions for Discussion

1. Is there a dress code or other established norms in your place of work or study? How does this affect your work or study environment?

2. In your experience, are the norms of interaction between parents and children different today than they were in previous generations? If so, in what ways are they better or worse than they used to be?

3. Are there consistent standards of conduct across the different facets of your life, or do they tend to vary widely? What standards of interaction with other people help you most to thrive?

❖ An Attitude of Gratitude

If you spend time around families with young children, you've likely heard a parent prompting a child to express appreciation for receiving a gift or compliment. The parent will ask, "Now what do you say?" and the child will respond, "Thank you." Gratitude is such a fundamental value in Judaism, the Hebrew term for Jew (*Yehudi*; literally, a member of the tribe of Judah) is derived from the word meaning "to give thanks" (לְהוֹדוֹת). The origin of this tribal name can be traced to a verse from the parashah in which our Matriarch Leah named her fourth son Judah:

וַתַּהַר עוֹד וַתֵּלֶד בֵּן וַתֹּאמֶר הַפַּעַם אוֹדֶה אֶת יְהוָה עַל כֵּן קָרְאָה שְׁמוֹ יְהוּדָה וַתַּעֲמֹד מִלֶּדֶת: (בראשית כט, לה)

She [Leah] conceived again and bore a son, and declared, "This time I will praise the Lord." Therefore she named him Judah. Then she stopped bearing. (Gen. 29:35)

Rashi explains why Leah was particularly thankful for this son:

הַפַּעַם אוֹדֶה: שֶׁנָּטַלְתִּי יוֹתֵר מֵחֶלְקִי, מֵעַתָּה יֵשׁ לִי לְהוֹדוֹת: (רש״י, שם)

This time I will praise: since I have taken more than my share. Consequently I must offer up thanks. (Rashi, Gen. 29:35)

Leah, one of Jacob's four wives, knew prophetically that her husband would have twelve sons. She therefore assumed that she would bear three (one-fourth) of them. When she had a fourth son, she felt inspired to thank God for giving her more than her fair share. She decided to give her son a name that would always recall her gratitude and thereby reinforce the value of gratitude through the legacy of her son.

His name, Judah (*Yehuda* in Hebrew), which derives from the same Hebrew root as the word for "acknowledge," was very fitting, for multiple reasons. Leah acknowledged God's kindness in giving her a fourth son, and Judah's brothers would later acknowledge him as the brother who was to become the family's leader, despite the fact that he was not the firstborn (see Gen. 49:8).

As the example with Leah illustrates, it is easier to feel a sense of gratitude when one has extraordinary success or experiences a windfall. However, it is harder to acknowledge just how blessed we are when we merely receive what we expected or, worse yet, do not receive our fair share. At such times it may be helpful to compare ourselves to others who are less fortunate, enabling ourselves to recognize that we are still far better off than many others.

Questions for Discussion

1. Jewish people are referred to as Jews, Hebrews, and Israelites. What does each of these terms conjure up for you?
2. Describe a time you received a memorable expression of gratitude from another person. Why did that "thank you" make such an impact?
3. What can you do to foster an attitude of gratitude in yourself? What would it take for you to bring that attitude into situations where you get what you expect, and even where you get less than your perceived "fair share"?

VA-YISHLAḤ

❖ Conflict Resolution

Parashat Va-yishlaḥ opens with Jacob's impending reunion with his brother Esau, who, twenty years later, still resents Jacob's having stolen their father's blessing from him. Esau approaches with a four-hundred-man army, and Jacob prepares for this ominous encounter by all available means, including dividing his camp into two.

וַיֹּאמֶר אִם יָבוֹא עֵשָׂו אֶל הַמַּחֲנֶה הָאַחַת וְהִכָּהוּ וְהָיָה הַמַּחֲנֶה הַנִּשְׁאָר לִפְלֵיטָה: (בראשית לב, ט)

Thinking, "If Esau comes to the one camp and attacks it, the other camp may yet escape." (Gen. 32:9)

Citing this verse and two others, Rashi explains what Jacob's preparedness for his meeting with Esau entailed:

והיה המחנה הנשאר לפליטה: על כרחו כי אלחם עמו. התקין עצמו לשלשה דברים לדורון, לתפלה ולמלחמה. לדורון (פסוק כב) ותעבור המנחה על פניו. לתפלה (פסוק י) אלהי אבי אברהם. למלחמה והיה המחנה הנשאר לפליטה: (רש"י, שם)

the other camp may yet escape: Against his [Esau's] will, for I will wage war with him. He [Jacob] prepared himself [by doing] three things: giving a gift, praying, and [preparing] for war. Giving a gift [as v. 22 states]: "And so the gift went on ahead." Praying [as his prayer in v. 10 begins]: "O God of my father Abraham." War [as this verse says]: "the other camp may yet escape [while the first camp is engaged in war]." (Rashi, Gen. 32:9)

To survive the dreaded encounter with his brother, Jacob took three actions: praying, giving gifts, and preparing for war. As he had hoped, the first two acts—prayer and appeasement—turned out to be sufficient to quell Esau's anger, and he therefore did not have to resort to war. We see from Jacob's example that appeasement—whether it takes the form of gifts or words of reconciliation—can be a valuable tool in resolving conflicts and avoiding violence.

The ability of gifts to influence the feelings (and even the behavior) of their recipients is well recognized. For example, pharmaceutical representatives are restricted in the degree of benefits they may confer on physicians because of concerns that such largesse could influence the physicians' drug prescriptions. In the field of international relations, countries spend billions of dollars on economic and military aid in an effort to influence the behavior of recipient countries. Appeasement in the form of gifts or words may not always work, but it remains a powerful tool for managing conflict, allying interests, and bringing people closer to one another.

Questions for Discussion

1. Describe a time you reconciled with someone after a falling-out in your relationship. Did either you or the other person use appeasement (gifts or words) to help reestablish the connection?
2. What preparedness advice would you give a child who is being bullied? What lessons in this parashah might or might not be applicable?

3. Have you received gifts unrelated to a birthday or similar customary occasion? If so, what do you think motivated the gift, and how did the gift affect you?

....

❖ Sweat Equity

Have you ever walked into a store or restaurant and seen a dollar bill prominently displayed on the wall behind the counter? Such a bill represents the first dollar the business ever earned and thus has great symbolic significance to the owner, even if its monetary value is trivial. In a similar vein, Rashi's commentary on the parashah alludes to objects that might appear trivial and yet have great symbolic value for Jacob:

וַיִּוָּתֵר יַעֲקֹב לְבַדּוֹ וַיֵּאָבֵק אִישׁ עִמּוֹ עַד עֲלוֹת
הַשָּׁחַר: (בראשית לב, כה)

Jacob was left alone. And a man wrestled with him until the break of dawn. (Gen. 32:25)

Jacob had just brought his family and possessions across a river on their way to the Land of Israel. Rashi explains why Jacob did not remain with them, but rather returned to the place he had left:

ויותר יעקב: שכח פכים קטנים וחזר עליהם: (רש״י, שם)

Jacob was left [alone]: He had forgotten some small jars and he returned for them. (Rashi, Gen. 32:25)

Jacob had amassed great wealth during his twenty-year sojourn working for his father-in-law, Laban, so the monetary value of the jars he left behind was not significant to him. Rather, their value derived from the fact that they were the result of his labors, and he was scrupulously honest in all his dealings with Laban. The sages of the Talmud comment on this episode: "to the righteous, their money is dearer to them than their bodies" because it represents the value they place on being honest in business (*Bavli Ḥullin* 91a).

Many objects of minimal monetary worth are nevertheless cherished by their owners because of the values or exertion they represent. Similarly, people sometimes treasure trinkets that remind them of people or experiences they have loved.

Questions for Discussion

1. If you had to leave your home suddenly without the ability to return and could bring along only what you could carry, what would you take?
2. What object of little monetary value do you cherish most because of what it represents?
3. Would you say that you have been as scrupulously honest as Jacob in the business (work or otherwise) you have conducted in your life? What do you believe it takes to achieve that level of righteousness?

....

❖ Who Is Wealthy?

Jacob returned home after having spent twenty grueling years abroad working for his father-in-law, Laban. En route he had a hostile encounter with his brother, Esau. Although this confrontation exacted a price, Jacob arrived at his destination unscathed, as related by a verse in the parashah:

וַיָּבֹא יַעֲקֹב שָׁלֵם עִיר שְׁכֶם אֲשֶׁר בְּאֶרֶץ כְּנַעַן בְּבֹאוֹ מִפַּדַּן אֲרָם וַיִּחַן אֶת פְּנֵי הָעִיר: (בראשית לג, יח)

Jacob arrived safely [שָׁלֵם] in the city of Shechem which is in the land of Canaan—having come thus from Paddan-aram—and he encamped before the city. (Gen. 33:18)

On his arrival in Shechem, Jacob is described as being *shalem* (שָׁלֵם), which literally means "whole." Rashi elaborates on this word:

שלם: שלם בגופו, שנתרפא מצלעתו. שלם בממונו, שלא חסר כלום מכל אותו דורון. שלם בתורתו, שלא שכח תלמודו בבית לבן: (רש"י, שם)

whole: Whole in his body, for he was cured of his limp [inflicted by Esau's angel (see Rashi, Gen. 32:25)]. Whole with his possessions for he was not lacking anything despite that entire gift [that he gave to Esau]. Whole in his Torah [knowledge], for he had not forgotten [any of] his learning in Laban's house. (Rashi, Gen. 33:18)

Despite the fact that Jacob gave hundreds of animals to his brother, Esau, Jacob is nevertheless described as "whole" with respect to his possessions. Since Jacob was worried that he and his family would be harmed, he must have been greatly relieved to have merely suffered a monetary loss in his encounter with Esau. Rashi's description of Jacob as "not lacking anything" calls to mind the talmudic maxim: "Who is wealthy? One who is happy with his lot" (*Pirkei Avot* 4:1).

Questions for Discussion

1. Describe a time you lost something of value or unexpectedly incurred a significant expense. Is there a way you can view this loss so it is easier to accept?
2. When in your life have you come closest to feeling *shalem* with regard to possessions and knowledge?
3. Do you know someone who epitomizes the talmudic maxim: "Who is wealthy? One who is happy with his lot"? What is it like to spend time with him or her?

VA-YESHEV

❖ WYSIWYG (What You See Is What You Get)

Parashat Va-yeshev opens by focusing on Jacob's special relationship with his son Joseph, as evidenced by the colorful coat Jacob gave only to Joseph and by how Joseph brought his father incriminating reports about his brothers. Joseph's behavior had the predictable effect of poisoning his relationship with his brothers, as described in the following verse:

וַיִּרְאוּ אֶחָיו כִּי אֹתוֹ אָהַב אֲבִיהֶם מִכָּל אֶחָיו וַיִּשְׂנְאוּ אֹתוֹ וְלֹא יָכְלוּ דַּבְּרוֹ לְשָׁלֹם: (בראשית לז, ד)

And when his [Joseph's] brothers saw that their father loved him more than any of his brothers, they hated him so that they could not speak a friendly word to him. (Gen. 37:4)

It would seem that Joseph's brothers also bore responsibility for the deterioration of the relationship, given that "they could not speak a friendly word to him." Nevertheless, Rashi finds something positive in their conduct:

ולא יכלו דברו לשלום: מתוך גנותם למדנו שבחם, שלא דברו אחת בפה ואחת בלב: (רש"י, שם)

they could not speak a friendly word to him: From what is stated to their discredit, we may learn something to their credit, that they did not say one thing with their mouth and think differently in their heart. (Rashi, Gen. 37:4)

Despite other shortcomings in their behavior, Rashi explains that the brothers exhibited integrity in their relationship with Joseph by letting him know exactly what they thought of him.

A hallmark of any authentic relationship is knowing where the parties stand with one another. This generally requires candid communication. If one party feels aggrieved, it is difficult for the relationship to be restored to health unless this grievance is carefully communicated to the other party. While this may be a sensitive process fraught with risk, it may also be the best way to rebuild a damaged relationship.

Questions for Discussion

1. If you have siblings, has your relationship been characterized by sibling rivalry? If yes, how so? Did you or your siblings feel that either you or they had a special relationship with your parents? Have those perceptions changed over the years?
2. Describe an instance where you made a conscious decision to communicate candidly with another about a difficult issue, despite the possible discomfort and risks it entailed for you.
3. Do you agree with Rashi that it is to a person's credit to "not say one thing with their mouth and think differently in their heart"?

❖ Favoritism

Fraternal strife is a familiar theme in the book of Genesis. We see it in three successive generations of brothers: Isaac and Ishmael,

Jacob and Esau, and Joseph and his brothers. In this last case, after Jacob contributes to the fraternal animosity by singling out Joseph to receive a special garment, his brothers later strip him of the garment and use it as evidence to convince their father that Joseph is dead:

וַיְהִי כַּאֲשֶׁר בָּא יוֹסֵף אֶל אֶחָיו וַיַּפְשִׁיטוּ אֶת יוֹסֵף אֶת כֻּתָּנְתּוֹ אֶת כְּתֹנֶת הַפַּסִּים אֲשֶׁר עָלָיו: (בראשית לז, כג)

When Joseph came up to his brothers, they stripped Joseph of his tunic, the ornamented tunic that he was wearing. (Gen. 37:23)

Identifying this tunic, Rashi explains how it might have contributed to the brothers' attack on Joseph:

אֶת כְּתֹנֶת הַפַּסִּים: הוא שהוסיף לו אביו יותר על אחיו: (רש״י, שם)

the ornamented tunic: This is an additional one that his father gave him in excess of what was given to his brothers. (Rashi, Gen. 37:23)

Rashi points out that even though their father gave clothing to his other sons, he showed favoritism toward Joseph by giving him an additional fine garment. This gift seems to have confirmed the brothers' suspicion that their father loved Joseph most of all.

Even though it may be appropriate for parents to relate differently to each of their children, the children may nevertheless regard this differential treatment as an expression of favoritism. It therefore falls on parents to exercise great care to avoid having even their legitimate behavior be mistaken for favoritism.

Questions for Discussion

1. Why do you think fraternal strife is such a repetitive theme in the book of Genesis? What might be the purpose of conveying so many similar, yet different stories of sibling discord?

2. If you have siblings, did your parents ever give a unique, valuable gift to one of you that led to feelings of favoritism? Do you regard the gifting experience any differently now?

3. What advice would you offer parents to avoid contributing to a perception of favoritism while also addressing the unique needs of each child?

❖ An Observant Jew

Joseph's brothers sold him to merchants bound for Egypt, and he was later imprisoned in Egypt. In this verse from the parashah, Joseph notices that two of his fellow prisoners—Pharaoh's cupbearer and baker—appear distressed:

וַיָּבֹא אֲלֵיהֶם יוֹסֵף בַּבֹּקֶר וַיַּרְא אֹתָם וְהִנָּם זֹעֲפִים: (בראשית מ, ו)

When Joseph came to them [the cupbearer and baker] in the morning, he saw that they were distraught. (Gen. 40:6)

Rashi defines the unusual word *zoafim* (זֹעֲפִים):

זֹעֲפִים: עצבים: (רש״י, שם)

distraught: זֹעֲפִים: sad. (Rashi, Gen. 40:6)

When Joseph inquired why the two prisoners looked dis-traught, they responded that they wanted to have their dreams interpreted but could find no one to do this. Joseph volunteered to interpret their dreams, and the events in their lives unfolded exactly as he had interpreted, with the cupbearer being returned to his former post and the baker executed. When Pharaoh subse-quently had a dream that no one could interpret, the cupbearer recommended that Pharaoh consult with Joseph. This set in motion a series of events that ended with Joseph becoming the vizier of Egypt. The starting point for all this was when Joseph noticed that something was amiss with his fellow prisoners. Had Joseph failed to observe the distress of his fellow prisoners and inquire about their welfare, he might have languished in prison indefinitely.

People tend to notice the things that are important to them. For example, upon entering a house, a builder will instinctively take note of the quality of construction, while an interior deco-rator's eye will naturally be drawn to the furnishings and finish. Joseph observed people, and as a result Jewish history has been irrevocably altered.

Questions for Discussion

1. Name something you tend to notice more than other peo-ple do because of your particular strengths or interests. Conversely, what do other people seem to notice that you do not?
2. Have you ever inquired about someone else's welfare and later seen that the inquiry made a difference in that per-son's or your life?
3. Do you believe it is possible to have a more positive im-pact on other people by being more observant of them? If so, what steps might you take to become more observant?

MIKKETS

❖ Who Is Powerful?

The acclaimed 1990s film *Schindler's List* told the story of how German businessman Oskar Schindler saved more than one thousand Jews during the Holocaust. In a memorable scene Schindler informs a Nazi commander that an emperor who pardons—rather than executes—a convicted thief exercises true power. An encounter in Parashat Mikkets recalls this notion of power. Joseph, now vizier of Egypt, sees his brothers for the first time since they sold him into slavery more than twenty years ago:

וַיַּכֵּר יוֹסֵף אֶת אֶחָיו וְהֵם לֹא הִכִּרֻהוּ: (בראשית מב, ח)

For though Joseph recognized his brothers, they did not recognize him. (Gen. 42:8)

Since the fact that Joseph recognized his brothers is already known from the previous verse, Rashi provides a midrashic interpretation of this verse:

והם לא הכרהו: ומדרש אגדה ויכר יוסף את אחיו כשנמסרו בידו הכיר שהם אחיו ורחם עליהם, והם לא הכירוהו כשנפל בידם לנהוג בו אחוה: (רש"י, שם)

they did not recognize him: The midrashic explanation: "For though Joseph recognized his brothers"—when they were delivered into his hands, he recognized that they were his brothers and he had pity on them. "They did not recognize

him" when he fell into their hands, to behave toward him with brotherhood. (Rashi, Gen. 42:8)

Here Rashi compares how Joseph and his brothers treat each other. Twenty years earlier Joseph's brothers seized him and sold him as a slave without regard to the fate that might befall him—surely not behaviors of brotherhood. By contrast, two decades later when the brothers arrive at court during a great famine to ask Joseph for food, Joseph not only recognizes his brothers, but also recognizes his obligation to treat them with brotherhood. Joseph proceeds to provide them with sustenance and even returns the money they tender as payment.

One might expect Joseph to use the power of his position to avenge his brothers' treachery. Instead Joseph exercises true power by recognizing his duty to treat them with compassion, consistent with the talmudic maxim: "Who is powerful? One who conquers his inclination" (*Pirkei Avot* 4:1).

Questions for Discussion

1. Do you agree that true power is the ability to restrain oneself from acting on a less noble inclination?
2. Describe a time that you exercised true power according to the definition offered in *Pirkei Avot*.
3. In your opinion, what political or other leader has been most able to exercise this conception of true power and why?

❖ BFF (Best Friends Forever)

Joseph's brothers seek sustenance in Egypt, which because of Joseph's visionary planning is the only place where food is available.

They pay him for their food, but Joseph secretly returns the money to them. This verse from the parashah describes the brothers' discovery of the money as they return to the Land of Israel:

וַיִּפְתַּח הָאֶחָד אֶת שַׂקּוֹ לָתֵת מִסְפּוֹא לַחֲמֹרוֹ בַּמָּלוֹן וַיַּרְא אֶת כַּסְפּוֹ וְהִנֵּה הוּא בְּפִי אַמְתַּחְתּוֹ: (בראשית מב, כז)

As one of them was opening his sack to give feed to his ass at the night encampment, he saw his money right there at the mouth of his bag. (Gen. 42:27)

Based on the word *ha-echad* (הָאֶחָד), which can mean "the lone one," Rashi identifies which of the brothers discovered his money in his bag:

ויפתח האחד: הוא לוי שנשאר יחיד משמעון בן זוגו: (רש"י, שם)

As one of them was opening: That was Levi, who was left alone, without [his brother] Simeon, his companion. (Rashi, Gen. 42:27)

Rashi alludes to the special relationship between Simeon and Levi (see Rashi, Gen. 49:5). When the brothers previously purchased food from Joseph, he required that Simeon remain in Egypt to guarantee that they would return with Benjamin—the one brother who did not come to Egypt. Levi felt alone without Simeon. Sometimes one's sibling is one's closest companion.

Questions for Discussion

1. Who was your closest companion from childhood? Share a memory of your time together.

2. Who do you consider to be your closest friend today and why?

3. Describe a time you missed someone during a period of separation. What did you do to remain in contact or to handle any feelings of aloneness?

❖ The Choice Is Yours

After Jacob's family consumes the food the brothers have brought home from Egypt, Jacob instructs his sons to return to buy more. His son Judah insists that Benjamin, the youngest brother, accompany them, as Joseph had stipulated. However, Jacob believes that Joseph is dead and is reluctant to send Benjamin, the only other remaining son from his beloved wife, Rachel. A verse from the parashah records Judah's response to his father, Jacob (also known as Israel):

וַיֹּאמֶר יְהוּדָה אֶל יִשְׂרָאֵל אָבִיו שִׁלְחָה הַנַּעַר אִתִּי וְנָקוּמָה וְנֵלֵכָה וְנִחְיֶה וְלֹא נָמוּת גַּם אֲנַחְנוּ גַם אַתָּה גַם טַפֵּנוּ: (בראשית מג, ח)

Then Judah said to his father Israel, "Send the boy in my care, and let us be on our way, that we may live and not die—you and we and our children." (Gen. 43:8)

Rashi explains how Judah succeeds in convincing his father to let Benjamin go:

ולא נמות: ברעב. בנימין ספק יתפש ספק לא יתפש, ואנו כלנו מתים ברעב אם לא נלך, מוטב שתניח את הספק ותתפוש את הודאי: (רש"י, שם)

and not die: of hunger. As for Benjamin, we are not sure whether he will be seized or he will not be seized, but all of us will [certainly] die of hunger if we do not go. Better that you release that which is doubtful and take hold of that which is certain. (Rashi, Gen. 43:8)

As Rashi explains, Judah urged his father to deal with the certainty they faced—that they would all starve unless they bought more food—and overlook the possibility that something might befall Benjamin. Jacob accepted this reasoning.

A defining quality of human beings is their ability to make choices of consequence. Making appropriate decisions is also largely a learnable skill. Effective decision-making typically entails knowing the goal one seeks to achieve, acquiring information, assessing the risk of different options, and choosing what appears to be the best course of action. Sometimes, though, the true best course of action in a given situation becomes apparent only in hindsight. And sometimes, when even more time has passed, we may look back on a decision we once regretted and come to realize it was for the best.

A major goal of parenting is teaching children to make good decisions. However, if parents are overzealous in preventing their children from making mistakes, they may not give their children the necessary autonomy to develop decision-making skills. Instead, parents can give children opportunities to make choices and bear their consequences.

Questions for Discussion

1. Describe a choice you made that had far-reaching consequences. What considerations did you address or fail to address in making this choice?
2. With the benefit of hindsight, describe a decision that now you would have made differently. What did you learn from your choice?
3. When you were growing up, how did your parents balance the tension between asserting and relinquishing their authority over you? Did they ever give you the autonomy to make a choice with which they disagreed?

VA-YIGGASH

❖ When Honesty Is Not the Best Policy

In last week's parashah the Egyptian vizier Joseph frames his brother Benjamin for the theft of a prized goblet. Now, as Benjamin faces the prospect of remaining in Egypt as a slave, his brother Judah confronts Joseph in Benjamin's defense. Imploring Joseph (whom the brothers still do not recognize) to free Benjamin, Judah explains that Benjamin is Rachel's only remaining son:

וַנֹּאמֶר אֶל אֲדֹנִי יֶשׁ לָנוּ אָב זָקֵן וְיֶלֶד זְקֻנִים קָטָן וְאָחִיו מֵת וַיִּוָּתֵר הוּא לְבַדּוֹ לְאִמּוֹ וְאָבִיו אֲהֵבוֹ: (בראשית מד, כ)

We told my lord [Joseph], "We have an old father, and there is a child of his old age, the youngest [Benjamin]; his full brother [Joseph] is dead, so that he alone is left of his mother, and his father dotes on him." (Gen. 44:20)

Rashi justifies why Judah, who had to be uncertain of the fate that had befallen Joseph, stated with surety that he was dead:

ואחיו מת: מפני היראה היה מוציא דבר שקר מפיו. אמר אם אומר לו שהוא קיים, יאמר הביאוהו אצלי: (רש"י, שם)

his full brother is dead: Out of fear he made a false statement. He said [to himself], "If I tell him that he is alive, he will say, 'Bring him to me.'" (Rashi, Gen. 44:20)

During their first meeting with the vizier, the brothers had told Joseph that their youngest brother, Benjamin, had remained at home. Joseph then imprisoned one of the brothers and stipulated that his freedom was contingent on their bringing back Benjamin. Now, at their second meeting, Judah feared that if they told Joseph that they had yet another brother, Joseph would demand that they produce this brother too—an impossible task since they didn't know his whereabouts. To preclude any such demand, Judah therefore stated that Joseph was dead.

While the Torah demands honesty, as indicated by the verse, "Keep far from a false charge" (Exod. 23:7) (מִדְּבַר שֶׁקֶר תִּרְחָק), it also recognizes circumstances where truth must yield to other considerations. In this encounter between Judah and Joseph, the family's safety took precedence over the primacy of truth. Knowing when to allow exceptions to such a fundamental value requires astuteness and maturity.

Questions for Discussion

1. Growing up, what messages did you receive about the importance of honesty? What consequences (if any) did you face as a result of dishonesty?
2. When a situation arises in which honesty is in conflict with another fundamental value, how can (or do) you decide which value should be given precedence?
3. Give an example of an instance where you believe another person expressed astuteness and maturity in not being truthful.

❖ Grandparents

In the following verse, Jacob journeys to be reunited at last with his son Joseph:

וַיִּסַּע יִשְׂרָאֵל וְכָל אֲשֶׁר לוֹ וַיָּבֹא בְּאֵרָה שָּׁבַע וַיִּזְבַּח זְבָחִים לֵאלֹהֵי אָבִיו יִצְחָק: (בראשית מו, א)

So Israel [Jacob] set out with all that was his, and he came to Beer-sheba, where he offered sacrifices to the God of his father Isaac. (Gen. 46:1)

Rashi explains why the verse states that Jacob offered sacrifices only to the God of his father, Isaac, and not also to the God of his grandfather, Abraham, even though both men had worshiped the same God:

לאלהי אביו יצחק: חייב אדם בכבוד אביו יותר מבכבוד זקנו לפיכך תלה ביצחק ולא באברהם: (רש"י, שם)

to the God of his father Isaac: One is required to honor his father more than his grandfather. Therefore [the sacrifices] are associated with Isaac and not with Abraham. (Rashi, Gen. 46:1)

Rashi addresses the relative respect due to different members of one's family. If one has to choose between honoring parents and grandparents, esteeming one's parents takes precedence.

Questions for Discussion

1. How would you define the differences between the roles of parents and grandparents in raising children?

2. Why do you believe that "one is required to honor his father more than his grandfather"?

3. Give an example of how you have honored a parent and a grandparent.

❖ Jewish Continuity

In the parashah, Jacob makes preparations before relocating his family to Egypt, including sending his son Judah ahead of the rest of the family:

וְאֶת יְהוּדָה שָׁלַח לְפָנָיו אֶל יוֹסֵף לְהוֹרֹת לְפָנָיו גֹּשְׁנָה וַיָּבֹאוּ אַרְצָה גֹּשֶׁן: (בראשית מו, כח)

He [Jacob] had sent Judah ahead of him to Joseph, to point the way before him to Goshen. So when they came to the region of Goshen, . . . (Gen. 46:28)

Rashi offers a midrashic interpretation of the phrase *lihorot lifanav* (לְהוֹרֹת לְפָנָיו), which literally means "to point the way before him":

לפניו: קודם שיגיע לשם. ומדרש אגדה להורות לפניו לתקן לו בית תלמוד שמשם תצא הוראה: (רש"י, שם)

before him: Before he [Jacob] would arrive there. The midrashic interpretation of *lihorot lifanav* is to establish for him a house of study, from which [Torah] teaching would emanate. (Rashi, Gen. 46:28)

In our era, a family's move to a new place usually involves extensive planning: finding a home, securing jobs for the parents, selecting schools for the children, and more. Jacob's move, however, was considerably more complex. He was relocating with his extended family of seventy people and immigrating to a foreign land with an unfamiliar language and culture.

With all he faced, Jacob's primary concern was to assure that his new home would sustain his family's Jewish identity. While he might have approached this in any number of ways—by establishing a synagogue, a *mikveh* (ritual bath), or even a Jewish Community Center—he chose to establish a house of study.

Questions for Discussion

1. What role did Jewish considerations play in your choice to move to or live in your current neighborhood?
2. If you were to move to a new locale, what preparations would you choose to attend to first, and why?
3. What elements from your upbringing had the greatest impact in shaping your Jewish identity? When you think about passing on Jewish identity to your children or to a new generation, what elements from your childhood would you retain and what new elements would you introduce?

VA-YEḤI

❖ A Final Request

Jacob spends the final seventeen years of his life in Egypt under the protective care of his son Joseph. In Parashat Va-yeḥi when Jacob becomes aware of his impending death, he summons Joseph to make a final request:

וַיִּקְרְבוּ יְמֵי יִשְׂרָאֵל לָמוּת וַיִּקְרָא | לִבְנוֹ לְיוֹסֵף וַיֹּאמֶר לוֹ אִם נָא מָצָאתִי חֵן בְּעֵינֶיךָ שִׂים נָא יָדְךָ תַּחַת יְרֵכִי וְעָשִׂיתָ עִמָּדִי חֶסֶד וֶאֱמֶת אַל נָא תִקְבְּרֵנִי בְּמִצְרָיִם: (בראשית מז, כט)

And when the time approached for Israel [Jacob] to die, he summoned his son Joseph and said to him, "Do me this favor, place your hand under my thigh as a pledge of your steadfast loyalty [literally, "kindness and truth"]: please do not bury me in Egypt." (Gen. 47:29)

Rashi explains why Jacob described his burial request as "kindness and truth" (חֶסֶד וֶאֱמֶת):

חסד ואמת: חסד שעושין עם המתים הוא חסד של אמת, שאינו מצפה לתשלום גמול: (רש"י, שם)

kindness and truth: Kindness that is done with the dead is true kindness since he expects nothing in return. (Rashi, Gen. 47:29)

In Judaism, actions performed for the deceased, such as arranging for burial, are regarded as acts of true kindness because the beneficiary cannot repay the favor. Moreover, Judaism has particularly high regard for people who occupy themselves with the mitzvah (commandment) of burying the dead. For example, a *kohen* (priest) is normally prohibited from being in proximity to a corpse unless the person was an immediate family member. But if a Jewish corpse needs to be buried and no one else is available to do this mitzvah, a *kohen* must perform the burial.

Questions for Discussion

1. What do you know about how the Jewish burial society (*hevra kadisha*) operates in your community? Have you ever been involved with a *hevra kadisha*? Is that something you would like to do?
2. Where are your relatives buried? Have you thought about where you would like to be buried?
3. Describe something another person has done for you that you feel is beyond your ability to repay.

❖ The Evil Eye

Joseph brings his sons, Manasseh and Ephraim, to visit his ailing father, Jacob. Jacob then bestows the following blessing on his grandsons:

הַמַּלְאָךְ הַגֹּאֵל אֹתִי מִכָּל רָע יְבָרֵךְ אֶת הַנְּעָרִים וְיִקָּרֵא בָהֶם שְׁמִי וְשֵׁם אֲבֹתַי אַבְרָהָם וְיִצְחָק וְיִדְגּוּ לָרֹב בְּקֶרֶב הָאָרֶץ: (בראשית מח, טז)

The Angel who has redeemed me from all harm—[b]less the lads. In them may my name be recalled, [a]nd the names of my fathers Abraham and Isaac, [a]nd may they be teeming multitudes upon the earth. (Gen. 48:16)

Rashi explains the Torah's usage of the uncommon verb *vi-yidgu* (וְיִדְגּוּ), which contains the word for fish (דג):

וידגו: כדגים הללו שפרים ורבים ואין עין הרע שולטת בהם: (רש"י, שם)

[a]nd may they be teeming: like these fish that proliferate and multiply, and are unaffected by the evil eye. (Rashi, Gen. 48:16)

Rashi explains that the blessing Jacob bestowed on his grandsons was twofold. First, his grandchildren would have abundant offspring. Second, these offspring would not arouse jealousy in others that could jeopardize this blessing ("the evil eye").

Jacob demonstrated great sensitivity in his blessing. His words were meant to fulfill his grandsons' aspirations for their families, while simultaneously not arousing envy in others.

By drawing attention to one's good fortune, one may cause someone less fortunate to feel jealousy, thereby having one's benefit result in another's detriment.

Jacob's blessing, which according to Rashi contains an allusion to the evil eye, was specifically intended for the children of Joseph. As a servant in the house of Potiphar, Joseph adamantly avoided the persistent attempts by his master's wife to seduce him, thereby establishing himself as the paradigm of one who does not covet that which is not his. Joseph thereby bequeathed to his progeny an immunity from the evil eye: even though they may possess admirable qualities, they will not arouse jealousy in others (see *Bavli Berakhot* 20a).

Questions for Discussion

1. The world's Jewish population is just over fourteen million—roughly equivalent to the population of Zimbabwe. Do you believe Jacob's blessing that his offspring will be "teeming multitudes" has been fulfilled? Why or why not?

2. What blessing do you have that is not shared by others? Do you feel that your good fortune carries any obligation toward others?

3. What personal blessing would you like to give to someone else, based on your own life experience?

❖ Blessing Children

According to the Torah, our forefathers, Abraham, Isaac, and Jacob, serve as role models for us. We see an example of this in the following verse, which describes the blessing Jacob bestowed on his grandsons:

וַיְבָרֲכֵם בַּיּוֹם הַהוּא לֵאמוֹר בְּךָ יְבָרֵךְ יִשְׂרָאֵל לֵאמֹר יְשִׂמְךָ אֱלֹהִים כְּאֶפְרַיִם וְכִמְנַשֶּׁה וַיָּשֶׂם אֶת אֶפְרַיִם לִפְנֵי מְנַשֶּׁה: (בראשית מח, כ)

So he blessed them that day, saying, "By you shall Israel invoke blessings, saying: God make you like Ephraim and Manasseh." Thus he put Ephraim before Manasseh. (Gen. 48:20)

Rashi explains how Jacob's blessing serves as a paradigm to all future generations:

בְּךָ יְבָרֵךְ יִשְׂרָאֵל: הבא לברך את בניו, יברכם בברכתם ויאמר איש
לבנו ישימך אלהים כאפרים וכמנשה: (רש"י, שם)

By you shall Israel invoke blessings: Whoever wishes to bless his sons, will bless them with their blessing, and a man will say to his son, "God make you like Ephraim and Manasseh." (Rashi, Gen. 48:20)

In the more than three thousand years since Jacob first uttered this blessing, it has been repeated billions of times in an unbroken chain from father to son, extending to the present day. The corresponding blessing for daughters is "May God make you like Sarah, Rebekah, Rachel, and Leah." Traditionally parents give these blessings to their children each week before Sabbath dinner.

Questions for Discussion

1. Who do you regard as a role model? What have you learned from this person that you attempt to apply in your life?
2. Did you grow up with the custom of parents blessing the children for Shabbat? Do you practice this in your household, or would you like to?
3. If you were to compose your own blessing for your child, what would it be?

Exodus

SHEMOT

❖ Name-Calling

As every successful politician knows, addressing someone by name evokes feelings of warmth and closeness. Parashat Shemot (Names) begins by recounting the names of Jacob's sons who accompanied him to Egypt.

וְאֵלֶּה שְׁמוֹת בְּנֵי יִשְׂרָאֵל הַבָּאִים מִצְרָיְמָה אֵת יַעֲקֹב אִישׁ וּבֵיתוֹ בָּאוּ: (שמות א, א)

These are the names of the sons of Israel [Jacob] who came to Egypt with Jacob, each coming with his household. (Exod. 1:1)

Given that the names of Jacob's sons were previously mentioned, Rashi explains why they are repeated here:

ואלה שמות בני ישראל: אף על פי שמנאן בחייהן בשמותן, חזר ומנאן במיתתן, להודיע חבתן שנמשלו לכוכבים, שמוציאן ומכניסן במספר ובשמותם, שנאמר (ישעיהו מ, כו) המוציא במספר צבאם לכולם בשם יקרא: (רש"י, שם)

These are the names of the sons of Israel: Although [God] counted them in their lifetime by their names, He counted them again after their death, to let us know how precious they were [to Him], because they were likened to the stars, which He takes out and brings in by number and by their names, as it states (Isa. 40:26): "He who sends out their host by count, who calls them each by name." (Rashi, Exod. 1:1)

By repeating the names of Jacob's sons, Rashi tells us that God focused attention on and thereby expressed affection for each son individually.

In today's wired age most of us do not have to remember friends' phone numbers and birthdays, as people once did. Moreover, in a single session, with just a few clicks, we can arrange to send all our friends birthday e-cards for the year. We have also become accustomed to having full conversations with people (via text or e-mail) without ever using their names. Perhaps, now more than ever, addressing another person by name can amplify our shared sense of connection.

Questions for Discussion

1. Have you ever felt a sense of connection to someone in part because that person remembered or repeated your name?
2. Do you ever have difficulty remembering people's names? What methods do you use to help remember them?
3. Do you think using online communication causes people to feel more or less connected to other people (or both)? If it can cause people to feel anonymous, what can be done to minimize this phenomenon?

❖ Growing Up

At the time Moses was born, the Egyptians had enslaved the Jews, and Pharaoh had decreed that all Jewish baby boys were to be killed at birth. When Moses reached three months of age, his parents, unable to conceal him any longer, decided to send him down the Nile River in a basket. Pharaoh's daughter found him and raised him as her own son. A verse from the parashah recounts Moses's first experience as an adult:

וַיְהִי | בַּיָּמִים הָהֵם וַיִּגְדַּל מֹשֶׁה וַיֵּצֵא אֶל אֶחָיו וַיַּרְא בְּסִבְלֹתָם וַיַּרְא אִישׁ מִצְרִי מַכֶּה אִישׁ עִבְרִי מֵאֶחָיו: (שמות ב, יא)

Some time after that, when Moses had grown up, he went out to his kinsfolk and witnessed their labors. He saw an Egyptian beating a Hebrew, one of his kinsmen. (Exod. 2:11)

Rashi explains why the Torah repeats that Moses grew up (וַיִּגְדַּל), after having already stated in the preceding verse that he grew up (וַיִּגְדַּל):

ויגדל משה: והלא כבר כתיב ויגדל הילד (פסוק י). אמר רבי יהודה ברבי אלעאי הראשון לקומה והשני לגדולה, שמינהו פרעה על ביתו: (רש"י, שם)

when Moses had grown up: Was it not already written: "When the child grew up" (Exod. 2:10)? Rabbi Judah the son of Rabbi Ilai said: The first reference is to height, and the second is to greatness, because Pharaoh had appointed him over his house. (Rashi, Exod. 2:11)

Rashi distinguishes between the two meanings of the word *vayigdal* (וַיִּגְדַּל): "grew up" and "became great." First, Moses grew up. Then, having been placed in charge of Pharaoh's palace, he became great.

While growing older is inevitable, the passage of years doesn't necessarily bring with it maturity. Sometimes maturity develops in accordance with how people handle responsibilities. If they deal effectively with circumstances, they may develop readiness for greater challenges. Moses's responsibility for Pharaoh's palace prepared him for his future role as leader of the Jewish people.

Questions for Discussion

1. Describe the first time you experienced a sense of autonomy from your family. How did that episode change you?
2. Which experiences do you believe have best—and worst—prepared you for maturity in adulthood?
3. What great challenges do you currently feel unprepared to tackle? What steps might you take to develop readiness for them?

❖ Courage of Conviction

After killing an Egyptian who was beating a Jew, Moses is sentenced to death. He flees Egypt and settles in the land of Midian, where, as the parashah relates, he meets one of its leading families:

וּלְכֹהֵן מִדְיָן שֶׁבַע בָּנוֹת וַתָּבֹאנָה וַתִּדְלֶנָה וַתְּמַלֶּאנָה אֶת הָרְהָטִים לְהַשְׁקוֹת צֹאן אֲבִיהֶן: (שמות ב, טז)

Now the priest of Midian [Jethro] had seven daughters. They came to draw water, and filled the troughs to water their father's flock. (Exod. 2:16)

Rashi comments on the verse's description of Jethro as the Midianite *kohen* (כֹּהֵן, priest):

ולכהן מדין: רב שבהן ופירש לו מעבודה זרה ונידוהו מאצלם:
(רש״י, שם)

the priest of Midian: The most prominent among them [the Midianites]. He [Jethro] had abandoned idolatry, so they [the Midianites] banished him. (Rashi, Exod. 2:16)

Rashi indicates that the word *kohen* should not be understood in its usual sense of "priest," since Jethro was no longer a Midianite priest. In this instance, *kohen* refers to Jethro's status as Midian's most prominent citizen. Rashi adds that because Jethro had rejected the Midianites' idolatrous religion, they expelled him from their community.

Jethro stands as a paradigm of someone who had the courage of his convictions. The sages teach that Jethro was familiar with every sort of idolatrous practice but rejected them all in favor of the true God (see *Mekhilta de-Rabbi Yishmael, Yitro*). As a result, he was rejected by his own people.

Questions for Discussion

1. Describe a time you mustered the courage to act on your convictions.
2. Describe a decision you made that resulted in separating you from those around you. Is there anything you did or could do to mitigate that breach?
3. Does your Jewish identity separate you from others or compel you to act in courageous ways? Explain.

VA-'ERA'

❖ Family Matters

Choosing a spouse may be the most important decision a person makes. While describing the genealogy of Moses's brother, Aaron, a verse from Parashat Va-'era' offers some advice on this subject.

וַיִּקַּח אַהֲרֹן אֶת אֱלִישֶׁבַע בַּת עַמִּינָדָב אֲחוֹת נַחְשׁוֹן לוֹ לְאִשָּׁה וַתֵּלֶד לוֹ
אֶת נָדָב וְאֶת אֲבִיהוּא אֶת אֶלְעָזָר וְאֶת אִיתָמָר: (שמות ו, כג)

Aaron took to wife Elisheba, daughter of Amminadab and sister of Nahshon, and she bore him Nadab and Abihu, Eleazar and Ithamar. (Exod. 6:23)

Given that the verse names Elisheba's father, Amminadab, there is no need to also mention her brother's name, since the Torah states elsewhere (Num. 7:12) that Nahshon was the son of Amminadab (and thus the brother of Elisheba). Rashi explains this seeming redundancy:

אחות נחשון: מכאן למדנו הנושא אשה צריך לבדוק באחיה:
(רש"י, שם)

sister of Nahshon: From here we learn that one who [contemplates] marrying a woman should [first] investigate her brothers. (Rashi, Exod. 6:23)

Until recent generations, it was customary for Jews to arrange the marriages of their children (with their consent, of course). In contemporary society, parents are usually no longer involved in their children's choice of spouse. Within the Orthodox Jewish community, and especially in its more traditional segments, however, parents and matchmakers retain an important role; it is common to make inquiries into a prospective spouse's family background before or during the dating process.

Questions for Discussion

1. How did you meet your spouse (or, if you have not been married, how did your parents meet)? What input (if any) did your parents have in the courtship?
2. What relevant information can be learned by inquiring about a prospective spouse's family background? How do you account for the possibility that a person may differ in significant ways from his or her family?
3. If you were investigating the suitability of a potential spouse for your child, what would you want to know about that person's family?

❖ Showing Gratitude

Moses, who has returned to Egypt at God's behest, demands that Pharaoh free his Jewish slaves, but Pharaoh defiantly refuses. In response, God dispatches Moses to initiate this first plague against the Egyptians:

וַיֹּאמֶר יְהוָה אֶל מֹשֶׁה אֱמֹר אֶל אַהֲרֹן קַח מַטְּךָ וּנְטֵה יָדְךָ עַל מֵימֵי
מִצְרַיִם עַל נַהֲרֹתָם | עַל יְאֹרֵיהֶם וְעַל אַגְמֵיהֶם וְעַל כָּל מִקְוֵה
מֵימֵיהֶם וְיִהְיוּ דָם וְהָיָה דָם בְּכָל אֶרֶץ מִצְרַיִם וּבָעֵצִים וּבָאֲבָנִים:
(שמות ז, יט)

And the Lord said to Moses, "Say to Aaron: Take your rod and hold out your arm over the waters of Egypt—its rivers, its canals, its ponds, all its bodies of water—that they may turn to blood; there shall be blood throughout the land of Egypt, even in vessels of wood and stone." (Exod. 7:19)

Rashi addresses why God specified that Aaron, rather than Moses, be the one to use the staff to turn the water into blood:

אמר אל אהרן: לפי שהגין היאור על משה כשנשלך
לתוכו, לפיכך לא לקה על ידו לא בדם ולא
בצפרדעים, ולקה על ידי אהרן: (רש"י, שם)

Say to Aaron: Since the Nile River protected Moses when he was cast into it, it therefore was not struck by him, neither with blood nor with frogs, but was struck by Aaron. (Rashi, Exod. 7:19)

Rashi explains that Moses owed the Nile a debt of gratitude because, as a baby, he escaped Pharaoh's decree of infanticide by being floated down the river. Since it was not appropriate for him to turn the Nile's waters into blood, this task was delegated to Aaron.

This episode encourages mindfulness of the entities deserving of our gratitude, regardless of who or what they are. If Moses is required to recognize and demonstrate his appreciation to the Nile—an inanimate body of water—how much more so must we express thankfulness to those people to whom we owe a debt of gratitude?

Questions for Discussion

1. Is there someone you regard as having "saved your life" (either literally or figuratively)? What have you done to express your gratitude to this person?

2. Have you ever had a situation where you felt compelled to take an action that could be detrimental to a close friend or other person to whom you felt a sense of loyalty? How did you resolve this dilemma?

3. Do you believe you have "saved someone else's life"? If so, what did you do? Has that person expressed gratitude?

❖ Peaceful Coexistence

The parashah concludes with a description of the seventh plague, the plague of hail:

וַיְהִי בָרָד וְאֵשׁ מִתְלַקַּחַת בְּתוֹךְ הַבָּרָד כָּבֵד מְאֹד אֲשֶׁר לֹא הָיָה כָמֹהוּ
בְּכָל אֶרֶץ מִצְרַיִם מֵאָז הָיְתָה לְגוֹי: (שמות ט, כד)

The hail was very heavy—fire flashing in the midst of the hail—such as had not fallen on the land of Egypt since it had become a nation. (Exod. 9:24)

Rashi comments on the composition of the hail, as it consisted of the seemingly incompatible elements of fire and ice:

מתלקחת בתוך הברד: נס בתוך נס, האש והברד מעורבין, והברד
מים הוא, ולעשות רצון קונם עשו שלום ביניהם: (רש"י, שם)

Flashing in the midst of the hail: [This was] a miracle within a miracle. The fire and hail intermingled, even though hail is water. To do the will of their Maker, they made peace between themselves [the hail did not extinguish the fire, and the fire did not melt the hail]. (Rashi, Exod. 9:24)

According to Rashi, this hailstorm, coming on cue from Moses, was an unprecedented miracle, made all the more spectacular through the presence of fire in the hail. Fire and ice, whose natures are to consume one another, were able to coexist in order to perform as their Maker required. Perhaps this conveys the message that even the fiercest of adversaries can reach a modicum of peace when they prioritize pursuit of a common goal over parochial interests.

The transformative impact of shared commitment is powerfully illustrated in modern Israel. The population in Israel is divided between Ashkenazim (Jews from Europe) and Sephardim (Jews from North Africa and Asia), religious and secular, native-born Israelis and immigrants, Jews and Arabs, rich and poor, political hawks and doves. Despite these and other deep-seated divisions, Israel has created a flourishing democracy. At critical junctures, Israelis have consistently demonstrated the ability to focus on what unites rather than what divides them, with nothing short of miraculous results.

Questions for Discussion

1. How do or might you find common ground with fellow Jews whose religious practices are different from yours?
2. Share an experience of working together with an adversary or competitor to achieve a larger goal, including what you learned from the encounter.
3. Do you believe it is possible for Israel to live peacefully with its neighbors? Why or why not?

BO'

❖ Know Your Audience

Despite nine plagues that devastate Egypt, Pharaoh continues to enslave the Jewish nation. In Parashat Bo', Moses appears before Pharaoh a final time to warn him about the last of the Ten Plagues—the death of the firstborn.

וַיֹּאמֶר מֹשֶׁה כֹּה אָמַר יְהֹוָה כַּחֲצֹת הַלַּיְלָה אֲנִי יוֹצֵא בְּתוֹךְ מִצְרָיִם:
(שמות יא, ד)

Moses said, "Thus says the Lord: Toward midnight I will go forth among the Egyptians." (Exod. 11:4)

Rashi explains why Moses used the term *ka-chatzot ha-laila* ("toward midnight," preceded by the letter *kaf* [כ]), rather than the more typical phrasing of *ba-chatzot ha-laila* ("at midnight," preceded by the letter *bet* [ב]):

כחצת הלילה: ורבותינו דרשוהו כמו כבחצי הלילה ואמרו שאמר משה כחצות, שמשמע סמוך לו או לפניו או לאחריו, ולא אמר בחצות, שמא יטעו אצטגניני פרעה, ויאמרו משה בדאי הוא, אבל הקב"ה יודע עתיו ורגעיו אמר בחצות: (רש"י, שם)

Toward midnight: Our Rabbis interpreted it [*ka-chatzot ha-laila*, כַּחֲצֹת הַלַּיְלָה] like [*k'ba-chatzi ha-laila*, כְּבַחֲצִי הַלַּיְלָה, at about midnight], and they said that Moses used the word כַּחֲצֹת [*ka-chatzot*], which implies at about [midnight] (either [slightly] before or after it), but he did not say בַּחֲצֹת

[*ba-chatzot*, at midnight] lest Pharaoh's astrologers err [in calculating the exact moment of midnight] and say, "Moses is a liar," but God, who knows His [exact] times and moments, said בַּחֲצֹת [*ba-chatzot*, at midnight]. (Rashi, Exod. 11:4)

As Rashi explains, Moses chooses his words carefully. He even goes so far as to alter the time God specified from "at midnight" to "about midnight," taking into account that any imprecision in the astrologers' calculation of time would likely be used as a pretext for defaming Moses (and, by extension, God). In other words, understanding his audience's agenda enables him to develop and deliver an appropriate message to Pharaoh.

Today as well, when we reach out to other people, their biases and limitations in comprehension may cause them—inadvertently or deliberately—to distort our messages. If we seek understanding and agreement, we are similarly challenged to understand others' shortcomings and viewpoints and to develop appropriate means to connect with them.

Questions for Discussion

1. Do you know someone who chooses his or her words with great care? Can you give an example that illustrates this?
2. Describe a time you spoke to someone who was antagonistic to what you had to say. What impact did this have on how you delivered your message?
3. If a listener already has convictions concerning a certain issue, how can someone presenting a contrary viewpoint successfully challenge these preconceptions? Is it possible to convince a person of something that he or she does not want to hear?

❖ Private Display of Protection

On the eve of their departure from Egypt, the Jews are instructed to slaughter the paschal sacrifice and place its blood on their houses, as this verse from the parashah describes:

וְהָיָה הַדָּם לָכֶם לְאֹת עַל הַבָּתִּים אֲשֶׁר אַתֶּם שָׁם וְרָאִיתִי אֶת הַדָּם
וּפָסַחְתִּי עֲלֵכֶם וְלֹא יִהְיֶה בָכֶם נֶגֶף לְמַשְׁחִית בְּהַכֹּתִי בְּאֶרֶץ מִצְרָיִם:
(שמות יב, יג)

And the blood on the houses where you are staying shall be a sign for you: when I see the blood I will pass over you, so that no plague will destroy you when I strike the land of Egypt. (Exod. 12:13)

Rashi explains the seemingly superfluous word *lachem* (לָכֶם, for you), without which the meaning of the verse would remain unchanged:

והיה הדם לכם לאת: לכם לאות ולא לאחרים לאות. מכאן שלא
נתנו הדם אלא מבפנים: (רש"י, שם)

And the blood [on the houses where you are staying] shall be a sign for you: For you a sign, but not a sign for others. From here, it is derived that they put the blood only on the inside. (Rashi, Exod. 12:13)

The blood would seem to have been a sign directed outward, so that Jewish homes would be spared the death of the firstborn. However, as Rashi explains in his next comment, God carried out this plague, and God certainly had no need for signage identifying Jewish homes. Rather, the blood inside the house served as a sign to the Jewish residents that they were being spared from the plague. It was a private display of protection.

Perhaps, at its essence, this bloody symbol was a reminder of the precariousness of life. Within a short time, Egypt—the most powerful nation on earth—was devastated by its leader's obstinacy in refusing to emancipate the Jews: in every Egyptian household, the firstborn male died. There is also reason to be believe that the Egyptians themselves were ready to free the Jews—Pharaoh's servants had urged him before the eighth plague: "Let the [Jewish] men go to worship the Lord their God! Are you not yet aware that Egypt is lost?" (Exod. 10:7). By ignoring their pleas, Pharaoh demonstrated that the fate of his people would be subject to the capriciousness of his rule.

Huddled in their houses, the Jews might also have recognized how their fate was determined by their Ruler—the blood serving as a graphic sign of their Ruler's beneficence toward them.

Questions for Discussion

1. Pharaoh repeatedly refused to free the Jews because God had strengthened his resolve not to capitulate to Moses's demands (see Exod. 9:12, 10:20,27). The Egyptian people, by contrast, were under no such compulsion and would thus be more inclined to free the Jews as life became unbearable. Under the circumstances, how would you compare the morality of Pharaoh's conduct with that of his people's?

2. Describe any experience you have had that caused you to appreciate the fleeting nature of life. Do you do anything differently as a result?

3. Modern history is replete with examples of societies that experienced financial and military ruin under a despotic

ruler. Yet it is impossible for any leader—wicked, benign, or otherwise—to have significant impact without the assistance of many others. Cite an example of a tyrannical ruler and regime. To what extent do you believe that the society's citizens were responsible for malicious acts perpetrated under this regime? Were all citizens equally responsible?

❖ Holy Days

The following verse from the parashah describes the observance of Passover and teaches us about the Jewish conception of a holy day:

וּבַיּוֹם הָרִאשׁוֹן מִקְרָא קֹדֶשׁ וּבַיּוֹם הַשְּׁבִיעִי מִקְרָא קֹדֶשׁ יִהְיֶה לָכֶם כָּל מְלָאכָה לֹא יֵעָשֶׂה בָהֶם אַךְ אֲשֶׁר יֵאָכֵל לְכָל נֶפֶשׁ הוּא לְבַדּוֹ יֵעָשֶׂה לָכֶם: (שמות יב, טז)

You shall celebrate a sacred occasion on the first day, and a sacred occasion on the seventh day; no work at all shall be done on them; only what every person is to eat, that alone may be prepared for you. (Exod. 12:16)

Rashi comments on the term *mikra kodesh* (מִקְרָא קֹדֶשׁ, sacred occasion):

מקרא קדש: מקרא שם דבר, קרא אותו קדש לאכילה ושתייה וכסות: (רש"י, שם)

sacred occasion: The word *mikra* [מִקְרָא, occasion] is a noun—you must proclaim [the day's] holiness by means of eating, drinking, and [special] clothing. (Rashi, Exod. 12:16)

Rashi explains that Passover's status as a holy day requires Jews to eat well, drink wine, and dress in a festive manner. While the word "holy" is often associated with asceticism—abstinence from the pleasures of this world—as if a religious ideal requires rejecting the physical in favor of the spiritual, the Torah's conception of holiness contains no such dichotomy. Rather, Jews are directed to observe Pesach and other holidays in ways that bring physical pleasure.

Questions for Discussion

1. In what ways do you believe physical pleasures such as eating, drinking wine, and dressing festively can enhance holiness?
2. If you were to formulate the menu for the holiest Passover seder ever, what foods and drinks would you include?
3. A Greek philosophy called Epicureanism is associated with the hedonistic principle "eat, drink, and be merry, for tomorrow we die." In what ways is this different from the eating and drinking that constitute the observance of Jewish holidays such as Passover?

BE-SHALLAḤ

❖ The Heart That Sings

Parashat Be-shallaḥ recounts the climactic Exodus from Egypt: the Jews miraculously pass through the sea while their Egyptian pursuers drown. Gratefully the Jews sing God's praises in the epic Song at the Sea, introduced by the following verse:

אָז יָשִׁיר מֹשֶׁה וּבְנֵי יִשְׂרָאֵל אֶת הַשִּׁירָה הַזֹּאת לַיהֹוָה וַיֹּאמְרוּ לֵאמֹר אָשִׁירָה לַיהֹוָה כִּי גָאֹה גָּאָה סוּס וְרֹכְבוֹ רָמָה בַיָּם: (שמות טו, א)

Then Moses and the Israelites sang this song to the Lord. They said: I will sing to the Lord, for He has triumphed gloriously; [h]orse and driver He has hurled into the sea. (Exod. 15:1)

This verse begins with the word *az* (אָז, then), denoting an event that occurred in the past. However, *az* is followed immediately by the word *yashir* (יָשִׁיר, will sing), which is in the future tense. Rashi comments on this inconsistency:

אז ישיר משה: אז כשראה הנס עלה בלבו שישיר שירה, וכן (יהושע י, יב) אז ידבר יהושע, וכן (מלכים א' ז, ח) ובית יעשה לבת פרעה, חשב בלבו שיעשה לה, אף כאן ישיר, אמר לו לבו שישיר, וכן עשה, ויאמרו לאמר אשירה לה'. וכן ביהושע, כשראה הנס אמר לו לבו שידבר וכן עשה (יהושע י, יב) ויאמר לעיני ישראל, וכן שירת הבאר שפתח בה (במדבר כא, יז) אז ישיר ישראל, פירש אחריו עלי באר ענו לה. (מלכים א' יא, ז) אז יבנה שלמה במה, פירשו בו חכמי

ישראל שבקש לבנות ולא בנה. למדנו שהיו"ד על שם המחשבה נאמרה, זהו ליישב פשוטו: (רש"י, שם)

Then Moses sang: Then, when he [Moses] saw the miracle, [the impulse] arose in his heart to sing a song. Similarly, "Then Joshua spoke" [אָז יְדַבֵּר יְהוֹשֻׁעַ] (Josh. 10:12); and, similarly, "and the house [which] he would make [יַעֲשֶׂה] for Pharaoh's daughter" (1 Kings 7:8), [which means] he thought in his heart to make it for her. Here, too, יָשִׁיר [in the future tense means] his heart told him that he should sing, and so he did: "They said: I will sing to the Lord." . . . We [thus] learn that the prefix letter *yud* may serve to express intention. (Rashi, Exod. 15:1)

Rashi explains that the miracle of the splitting of the sea inspired Moses and the Jewish people to burst out singing. The power of the moment was so great, and the divine providence so overwhelming, an impulse arose in the hearts of the Jews that they could only express through spontaneous song.

Questions for Discussion

1. Describe a time you impulsively expressed relief, gratitude, or joy for a "miracle" in your life. What is your natural, spontaneous way to express happiness?
2. When you experience life's "miracles," do you tend to praise God for them?
3. What (if any) kinds of singing or music express your deep feelings of joy?

❖ A Voice of Their Own

The Song at the Sea begins with Moses leading the men in song and concludes with his sister, Miriam, leading the women:

וַתַּעַן לָהֶם מִרְיָם שִׁירוּ לַיהוָה כִּי גָאֹה גָּאָה סוּס וְרֹכְבוֹ רָמָה בַיָּם:
(שמות טו, כא)

And Miriam chanted for them: Sing to the Lord, for He has triumphed gloriously; [h]orse and driver He has hurled into the sea. (Exod. 15:21)

Rashi explains the words of Miriam, which are virtually identical to those spoken by her brother Moses in the opening stanza (Exod. 15:1) of the Song at the Sea:

ותען להם מרים: משה אמר שירה לאנשים, הוא אומר והם עונין אחריו, ומרים אמרה שירה לנשים: (רש"י, שם)

And Miriam chanted for them: Moses sang the song for the men—he would say it and they would respond after him—and Miriam sang the song for the women [and they too repeated it]. (Rashi, Exod. 15:21)

As Rashi explains, Moses led the men in song, and Miriam led the women in song. The sages comment on this episode: "A maidservant saw at the sea more than Ezekiel and the other prophets" (*Mekhilta de-Rabbi Yishmael*, Exod. 15:2). At this moment of sublime experience of the Divine, the Jews expressed themselves in two parallel voices—that of Moses and that of Miriam.

Questions for Discussion

1. Moses begins his song, "I will sing to the Lord, for He has triumphed gloriously; [h]orse and driver He has hurled into the sea" (Exod. 15:1), and Miriam begins her song, "Sing to the Lord, for He has triumphed gloriously; [h]orse and driver He has hurled into the sea" (Exod. 15:21). Given that these songs are virtually identical, why do you think the men and women sang separately rather than together? What message might this have for contemporary society?

2. Do you think that men and women provide different types of leadership? If so, how? Does it follow that males may be more effective in leading men, and females may be more effective in leading women?

3. Discuss what you regard as the most important roles in Jewish life and whether gender should be relevant for who fulfills them.

❖ Honor the Student

The parashah concludes with the first confrontation between the Jews and their perennial enemy: the nation of Amalek, whom the Jews are commanded to destroy (see Deut. 25:19):

וַיֹּאמֶר מֹשֶׁה אֶל יְהוֹשֻׁעַ בְּחַר לָנוּ אֲנָשִׁים וְצֵא הִלָּחֵם בַּעֲמָלֵק מָחָר אָנֹכִי נִצָּב עַל רֹאשׁ הַגִּבְעָה וּמַטֵּה הָאֱלֹהִים בְּיָדִי: (שמות יז, ט)

Moses said to Joshua, "Pick some men for us, and go out and do battle with Amalek. Tomorrow I will station myself

on the top of the hill, with the rod of God in my hand."
(Exod. 17:9)

Rashi comments on why Moses, the leader of the Jewish people and mentor of Joshua, said "Pick some men for us" rather
than "for me":

בחר לנו: לי ולך, השוהו לו, מכאן אמרו יהי כבוד תלמידך חביב
עליך כשלך: (רש"י, שם)

Pick [some men] for us: for me and for you. He [Moses]
equated him [Joshua] to himself. From here [the sages]
stated: "The honor of your student should be as dear to
you as your own" (*Pirkei Avot* 4:15). (Rashi, Exod. 17:9)

Rashi explains that Moses's choice of words conferred honor
on his disciple, Joshua. Moses did not cast himself as being su-
perior to his disciple; rather, he treated Joshua as an equal. In
this way, he also served as a paradigm of humility.

Moses's actions also serve as a model for effective pedagogy
in and beyond the classroom. A teacher's success in educating
students is as much a function of the students' receptiveness to
learn as the teacher's mastery of the material and the educational
approach. Since the student-teacher relationship can greatly influence students' openness to learn, teachers who go out of their
way to treat students with respect can make a big difference in
their learning. And, when the circumstances are appropriate, what
could be more respectful than treating a student as a colleague?

Questions for Discussion

1. Who was your favorite teacher and why? In what ways did
   this teacher treat you with respect?

2. Describe a time you taught someone else, whether in a
   classroom setting or informally. What challenges did you
   encounter, and how did you attempt to establish rapport?

3. If students behave disrespectfully toward their teacher, is
   it possible for the teacher to still treat the students with respect? Must respect be earned? Can it be lost?

YITRO

❖ First Person

After Moses's father-in-law, Jethro, hears about the miraculous Exodus from Egypt and the Jews' subsequent victory over the nation of Amalek, he comes to see Moses, who relates all that happened:

וַיְסַפֵּר מֹשֶׁה לְחֹתְנוֹ אֵת כָּל אֲשֶׁר עָשָׂה יְהוָה לְפַרְעֹה וּלְמִצְרַיִם עַל אוֹדֹת יִשְׂרָאֵל אֵת כָּל הַתְּלָאָה אֲשֶׁר מְצָאָתַם בַּדֶּרֶךְ וַיַּצִּלֵם יְהוָה: (שמות יח, ח)

Moses then recounted to his father-in-law everything that the Lord had done to Pharaoh and to the Egyptians for Israel's sake, all the hardships that had befallen them on the way, and how the Lord had delivered them. (Exod. 18:8)

Since Jethro's visit to Moses had been prompted by Jethro's hearing about the Exodus and the war with Amalek (see Rashi, Exod. 18:1), it is not clear why Moses repeated these same events to Jethro. Rashi comments:

ויספר משה לחתנו: למשוך את לבו לקרבו לתורה: (רש"י, שם)

Moses then recounted to his father-in-law: to draw his heart, to bring him closer to the Torah. (Rashi, Exod. 18:8)

Rashi explains that Moses was not simply informing Jethro of what had happened to the Jewish people, as Jethro already knew

that. It is true that Moses alone would have known and been able to share certain details of the Exodus. But, more importantly, Jethro's hearing about the Jews' salvation from his son-in-law would necessarily have affected him more strongly than hearing about it from another source. In essence, Moses was telling the story of God's miraculous salvation of the Jews in a way that would penetrate Jethro's heart, thereby bringing Jethro, a convert, closer to the Torah.

Hearing a dramatic story secondhand rarely compares to hearing it from a participant in the drama. Firsthand, the details and emotions make a powerful impression. The listener's memory of the story often becomes inextricably linked to the person who related it.

Questions for Discussion

1. What dramatic story of your life do you enjoy recounting to others?
2. Relate a story you heard that has made a lasting impression on you. What is it about that story that "penetrates your heart"?
3. What story has become part of your family lore and why?

❖ National Unity

The highlight of this parashah—and perhaps of the Bible's entire narrative—is the Jews' receiving the Torah at Mount Sinai. The Torah relates some details of the days leading up to this momentous experience:

וַיִּסְעוּ מֵרְפִידִים וַיָּבֹאוּ מִדְבַּר סִינַי וַיַּחֲנוּ בַּמִּדְבָּר וַיִּחַן שָׁם יִשְׂרָאֵל נֶגֶד הָהָר: (שמות יט, ב)

Having journeyed from Rephidim, they entered the wilderness of Sinai and encamped in the wilderness. Israel encamped there in front of the mountain. (Exod. 19:2)

Rashi addresses why the second instance of the word "encamped" is in the singular (וַיִּחַן) while its first instance is in the plural (וַיַּחֲנוּ), even though both refer to the Jewish people:

ויחן שם ישראל: כאיש אחד בלב אחד, אבל שאר כל החניות
בתרעומת ובמחלוקת: (רש"י, שם)

Israel encamped there: As one person with one heart. But all the other encampments were with resentment and dissension. (Rashi, Exod. 19:2)

As Rashi explains, this encampment was unique because the Jewish people were unified. The Jews had gathered as one for a purpose unprecedented in human history: to hear God address an entire nation. At such a momentous time, matters of common dissension—"He has a better seat than I do," "I don't like her attire," "His tone was offensive"—would have seemed laughably trivial. As the Jews prepared to encounter God, all tendencies toward divisiveness evaporated.

The pre-Sinai experience is a paradigm of peace and a potent, pertinent reminder that it is possible to unify the many factions of the Jewish people.

Questions for Discussion

1. Why do you believe Jews are so divided?
2. Have you ever experienced a time when the Jewish community put aside individual differences to unite around one event or cause? If so, what made this possible?
3. What can be done to unify the Jewish people? Are there any steps you yourself can take?

❖ Be Prepared

The early Zionist thinker Ahad Ha'am wrote, "More than the Jews have kept the Sabbath, the Sabbath has kept the Jews." This parashah contains the Ten Commandments, which include the mitzvah of keeping the Sabbath:

זָכוֹר אֶת יוֹם הַשַּׁבָּת לְקַדְּשׁוֹ: (שמות כ, ח)

Remember the sabbath day and keep it holy. (Exod. 20:8)

Rashi comments on the word "remember" (זָכוֹר), which is not vowelized in the usual manner of a word in the imperative:

זכור: זכור לשון פעול הוא, כמו (ישעיה כב, יג)
אכול ושתו, (שמואל ב ג, טז) הלוך ובכה, וכן פתרונו
תנו לב לזכור תמיד את יום השבת, שאם נזדמן לך
חפץ יפה תהא מזמינו לשבת: (רש"י, שם)

Remember: [The word] *zachor* [זָכוֹר, remember] [which is vowelized with a *kametz* under the letter *zayin* rather than a *shva* (זְכוֹר), the usual form of the imperative] is in the פָּעוֹל verb form [denoting an ongoing action], like אָכוֹל וְשָׁתוֹ [engage in eating and drinking] (Isa. 22:13), [and] הָלוֹךְ וּבָכֹה [walking and weeping] (2 Sam. 3:16), and this is the explanation [of זָכוֹר אֶת יוֹם הַשַּׁבָּת]: pay attention to always remember the Sabbath day, so that if you chance upon a beautiful thing, you shall prepare it for the Sabbath. (Rashi, Exod. 20:8)

Rashi explains that we are directed to constantly keep the Sabbath in mind. If we come across a lovely item during the week, we are to purchase it for the purpose of making the Sabbath more beautiful and special. The Sabbath, then, is much more than another day of the week—it is *the* point of reference by which time is reckoned.

Our liturgy too makes this apparent. The concluding psalm of the daily morning prayer service refers to the relationship between each day and the Sabbath, for example, "Today is the first day toward Sabbath" (for Sunday), "Today is the second day toward Sabbath" (for Monday), and so forth. The hymn *Lekhah Dodi*, recited as part of the Friday evening *Kabbalat Shabbat* (Sabbath eve prayer service), states: "Last in deed but first in thought" (סוֹף מַעֲשֶׂה בְּמַחֲשָׁבָה תְּחִלָּה), meaning that even though the Sabbath was the last act of Creation, it was conceived of at the very start of Creation.

Rashi teaches us that the quality of one's Sabbath experience is a function of the effort invested in it (which is true of many other undertakings as well). Preparing for the Sabbath throughout the week has the potential to elevate the days leading up to it and then, all the more so, the Sabbath day itself.

Questions for Discussion

1. Do you have any memories of celebrating the Sabbath growing up? How are those different from or similar to how you mark the Sabbath today?

2. Have you found that the effort you invest in preparing for an experience can have a marked effect on the quality of that experience? Provide an example.

3. Have you ever found that preparing earlier in the week for the Sabbath makes the Sabbath experience more beautiful? If so, in what ways?

MISHPATIM

❖ Criminal Treatment

The Torah provides a comprehensive blueprint for Jewish living. Parashat Mishpatim covers a range of conduct relating to both civil and criminal law, including slavery.

כִּי תִקְנֶה עֶבֶד עִבְרִי שֵׁשׁ שָׁנִים יַעֲבֹד וּבַשְּׁבִעֵת יֵצֵא לַחָפְשִׁי חִנָּם:
(שמות כא, ב)

When you acquire a Hebrew slave, he shall serve six years; in the seventh year he shall go free, without payment. (Exod. 21:2)

Since the verse does not specify the circumstances under which a Jew would be sold into servitude, Rashi elaborates:

כי תקנה: מיד בית דין שמכרוהו בגנבתו כמו שנאמר
(שמות כב, ב) אם אין לו ונמכר בגנבתו: (רש"י, שם)

When you acquire: from the hand of the court that sold him [into servitude] because of his theft, as it says (Exod. 22:2): "If he [the thief] lacks the means [to repay what he stole], he shall be sold for his theft." (Rashi, Exod. 21:2)

Rashi explains that a Jew who has stolen must make restitution to his victim. If the thief lacks the means to repay, the court requires him to be sold for a six-year term of servitude, with the proceeds of that sale providing restitution to the victim.

The Torah's approach to punishing a convicted thief is radically different from punishment in contemporary society, which relies principally on incarceration.

Incarceration has a number of deficiencies. The re-incarceration rate is about 50 percent, an indication that the current prison system does not rehabilitate prisoners. Incarcerating a thief provides no restitution to his victim and thus lacks an essential element of justice. In addition, imprisoning thieves is costly to the state.

The Torah's framework for thieves without the means to reimburse their victims addresses all three of these shortcomings: (1) it costs the state nothing because there is no incarceration; (2) it places the criminal in a family setting where he may gain useful skills and exposure to role models, which may prevent his lapsing into his criminal ways after release; and (3) it provides restitution to the victim from the funds paid for the convict's services.

The Torah's system of Hebrew servitude bore little resemblance to the popular conception of slavery. The Torah imposed on the master extensive obligations concerning the care and maintenance of his servant. For example, if the master ate bread made from fine flour, he was not to feed the servant bread made from coarse flour; and if the master drank aged wine, he could not give the servant new wine. The onerous nature of the master's duties toward his servant led the Talmud to state, "One who buys a Jewish servant has essentially acquired a master for himself" (*Bavli Kiddushin* 20a).

Questions for Discussion

1. What is your opinion about incarceration as a means of punishing thieves?

2. Should rehabilitation be a primary goal of the criminal justice system? If so, how might it better achieve this goal?
3. Do you believe it is ever appropriate for a person to be sold into servitude?

❖ Charity Begins at Home

The Jewish community has a long history of providing for the poor. The origins of this practice can be traced back to this week's parashah:

אִם כֶּסֶף | תַּלְוֶה אֶת עַמִּי אֶת הֶעָנִי עִמָּךְ לֹא תִהְיֶה לוֹ כְּנֹשֶׁה לֹא תְשִׂימוּן עָלָיו נֶשֶׁךְ: (שמות כב, כד)

If you lend money to My people, to the poor among you, do not act toward them as a creditor; exact no interest from them. (Exod. 22:24)

Rashi explains that important principles concerning priorities in charitable giving are derived from the beginning of this verse:

אֶת עַמִּי: עַמִּי וְגוֹי, עַמִּי קוֹדֵם. עָנִי וְעָשִׁיר, עָנִי קוֹדֵם. עֲנִיֵּי עִירְךָ וַעֲנִיֵּי עִיר אַחֶרֶת, עֲנִיֵּי עִירְךָ קוֹדְמִין: (רש"י, שם)

to My people: [If you are faced with a choice of lending money (אִם כֶּסֶף תַּלְוֶה) to one of] My people [i.e., a Jew] or a gentile, then "My people" [אֶת עַמִּי] has priority; [if the choice is between] a poor person and a rich person, the poor person [אֶת הֶעָנִי] has priority; [if the choice is between] the poor of your city [i.e., "among you"] and the poor of another city, the poor of your city [עִמָּךְ] have priority. (Rashi, Exod. 22:24)

Rashi advises that, foremost, we are to prioritize helping people of limited means rather than those of means. But we may have to choose among many people of inadequate means who need help. In contemporary society, more than ever before, we may know as much about deprivation that exists in a remote location on the other side of the world as we know about the pressing needs on the other side of town. How are we to allocate our limited charitable funds among seemingly unlimited demands? The Torah's perspective is that charity begins at home.

Questions for Discussion

1. What charities do you support and why?
2. How do you decide how to allocate your giving among the various charitable requests you receive?
3. How do you or might you assist organizations or people in need in nonmonetary ways?

❖ Robin Hood

The enduring appeal of Robin Hood, who took from the rich and gave to the poor, is testament to the popular sentiment that the poor—particularly if they have been victimized by the powerful—may be justified in seeking recompense from the wealthy. While the Torah is concerned with providing for the poor, it rejects such approaches to redistribution of wealth—and even prohibits judges from considering the socioeconomic circumstances of litigants in ruling on their claims:

וְדָל לֹא תֶהְדַּר בְּרִיבוֹ: (שמות כג, ג)

Nor shall you show deference to a poor man in his dispute. (Exod. 23:3)

Rashi explains why a judge might favor the poor:

לא תהדר: לא תחלוק לו כבוד לזכותו בדין ולומר דל הוא, אזכנו ואכבדנו: (רש"י, שם)

Nor shall you show deference: Do not bestow honor on him by deciding in his favor in the lawsuit, saying, "He is a poor man; I will decide in his favor and honor him." (Rashi, Exod. 23:3)

Rashi notes that a litigant's lack of means should not influence a judge's ruling because this would unfairly prejudice the rights of the other litigant. While compassion is to be encouraged, when it is expressed inappropriately it can be destructive and even hurt the very people it is intended to benefit.

Questions for Discussion

1. Do you agree that litigants' socioeconomic circumstances should not be considered when adjudicating disputes?
2. Today wealthy litigants may have inherent advantages, such as the ability to hire top-of-the-line attorneys and firms. Under these conditions, would it ever be fair to show favoritism toward a poor litigant?
3. Do you believe Robin Hood was a hero? What real or mythic figure who championed the poor is a hero to you?

TERUMAH

❖ Collective Responsibility

Parashat Terumah centers on the Tabernacle (*mishkan*), the portable sanctuary where the Jews congregated to worship during their journey through the wilderness to the Land of Israel. Describing the Tabernacle's construction, the parashah specifies the required building materials:

וְזֹאת הַתְּרוּמָה אֲשֶׁר תִּקְחוּ מֵאִתָּם זָהָב וָכֶסֶף וּנְחֹשֶׁת: (שמות כה, ג)

And these are the gifts that you shall accept from them: gold, silver, and copper. (Exod. 25:3)

Rashi comments on how the building materials were provided:

זהב וכסף ונחשת וגו׳: כולם באו בנדבה, איש איש מה שנדבו לבו, חוץ מן הכסף שבא בשוה מחצית השקל לכל אחד: (רש״י, שם)

gold, silver, and copper, etc.: They were all given voluntarily, each person according to how his heart moved him, except for the silver, which was given by everyone equally, a half-shekel by each person. (Rashi, Exod. 25:3)

Rashi explains that all construction materials were donated according to the benefactor's generosity, with the exception of a half-shekel of silver, given equally by all.

It is understandable that the people's support of the Tabernacle varied according to both their means and their desire to contribute. Why, then, was it necessary to require a minimum contribution from each person? An answer is that the Tabernacle, the focal point of the Jews' relationship with God, served all members of the Jewish nation—irrespective of wealth, piety, or standing within the community. The stipulation that all Jews contribute to it was therefore a reflection of each Jew's connection with the Tabernacle.

Maimonides states that the weight of the biblical half-shekel is 160 grains of barley (see *Mishneh Torah, Hilkhot Shekalim* 1:5). This is equivalent to about eight grams—worth around five dollars at silver's current value. This seems to have been an insignificant sum for the typical person, and thus represented a symbolic gesture by which each Jew joined in supporting the Tabernacle's construction. The choice of a half-shekel can therefore be understood to signify that the Jewish community remains incomplete—unable to reach its full potential—without each and every member's participation.

Questions for Discussion

1. If you are affiliated with a synagogue, is there a minimum level of support or involvement that is expected of you? How would you describe your contribution to it?
2. When you are choosing how much to give to a charity or an individual, do you decide "according to how your heart moves you"? What factors influence your decision?
3. Describe a cause for which you have extended yourself or your support generously. Why is this important to you?

❖ I Don't Know

The Tabernacle had an inner room, known as the Holy of Holies, which housed the Ark of the Covenant (אָרוֹן), a decorative gold box. A verse from the parashah discusses the purpose of the ark.

וְנָתַתָּ אֶת הַכַּפֹּרֶת עַל הָאָרֹן מִלְמָעְלָה וְאֶל הָאָרֹן תִּתֵּן אֶת הָעֵדֻת אֲשֶׁר אֶתֵּן אֵלֶיךָ: (שמות כה, כא)

Place the cover on top of the Ark, after depositing inside the Ark the Pact that I will give you. (Exod. 25:21)

Rashi questions the repetition of a directive that had already been given:

ואל הארן תתן את העדות: לא ידעתי למה נכפל, שהרי כבר נאמר (פסוק טז) ונתת אל הארון את העדות: (רש"י, שם)

after depositing inside the Ark the Pact: I do not know why it was repeated, for it already said (v. 16): "And deposit in the Ark [the tablets of] the Pact." (Rashi, Exod. 25:21)

Here Rashi, the biblical commentator par excellence who possessed an unsurpassed mastery of Jewish sources, is not sure how to interpret the repetition of instructions to place the tablets of the Pact in the ark. He says, "I do not know." Afterward, however, he does offer a possible rationale.

Rashi thereby teaches us that there is no shame in acknowledging when one does not know something; rather, such an admission attests to one's integrity. Moreover, even when one does not know something, one should still strive to understand the matter to the best of one's abilities.

Questions for Discussion

1. Describe a time you acknowledged you did not know something and how you felt in making that admission.
2. How does Rashi's admission that he did not know the reason for a verse influence your view of Rashi and how he worked?
3. The emphasis in education seems to be on acquiring knowledge. Does such a system cultivate students who may be reluctant to admit their ignorance? If so, is this a problem?

❖ Visual Aids

When most people hear the word "menorah," they think of the familiar nine-branched candelabrum Jews light for Hanukkah. When the Torah mentions the menorah, however, it refers to the Tabernacle's seven-branched candelabrum, crafted more than one thousand years before the events of Hanukkah. A verse from the parashah describes the instructions given to Moses concerning this menorah.

וּרְאֵה וַעֲשֵׂה בְּתַבְנִיתָם אֲשֶׁר אַתָּה מָרְאֶה בָּהָר: (שמות כה, מ)

Note well, and follow the patterns for them [the components of the menorah] that are being shown you on the mountain. (Exod. 25:40)

Rashi explains why Moses received both a detailed description of the menorah and then a pattern of it:

וראה ועשה: ראה כאן בהר תבנית שאני מראה אותך, מגיד
שנתקשה משה במעשה המנורה, עד שהראה לו הקב"ה מנורה של
אש: (רש"י, שם)

Note well, and follow: See here on the mountain the pattern that I am showing you. This informs us that Moses had difficulties with the construction of the menorah until God showed him a [model] menorah made of fire. (Rashi, Exod. 25:40)

As Rashi explains, Moses did not understand how to make the menorah until God showed him an image of it—in other words, a visual aid. Today, a student-centered approach to learning called differentiation considers each child's learning needs, preferences, social and emotional behaviors, musical abilities, and gross and fine motor skills in order to optimize his or her education. Differentiation proponents also contend that instruction encompassing multiple senses (sight, touch, taste, smell, and sound) increases stimulation to the brain and thus creates an optimized learning environment.

Questions for Discussion

1. Describe how you found a visual (or other) aid helpful in either learning something or teaching something to others.
2. What subject in school do or did you find most challenging? Do you think you would have understood it better or more easily with a different pedagogical approach? If so, please explain.
3. What kind of learner would you say you are? Do you learn best by seeing (visual), hearing (auditory), touching (sensory), or other senses? Do you try to apply this awareness when you seek to learn new things?

TETSAVVEH

❖ Good to the First Drop

Parashat Tetsavveh begins with a description of the oil used for kindling the menorah (the Tabernacle's seven-branched candelabrum):

וְאַתָּה תְּצַוֶּה | אֶת בְּנֵי יִשְׂרָאֵל וְיִקְחוּ אֵלֶיךָ שֶׁמֶן זַיִת זָךְ כָּתִית לַמָּאוֹר לְהַעֲלֹת נֵר תָּמִיד: (שמות כז, כ)

You shall further instruct the Israelites to bring you clear oil of beaten olives for lighting, for kindling lamps regularly. (Exod. 27:20)

Rashi elaborates on the special process for making the oil:

כתית: הזיתים היה כותש במכתשת, ואינו טוחנן בריחים, כדי שלא יהו בו שמרים, ואחר שהוציא טפה ראשונה מכניסן לריחים וטוחנן, והשמן השני פסול למנורה וכשר למנחות, שנאמר כתית למאור, ולא כתית למנחות: (רש"י, שם)

beaten: He must crush the olives in a mortar, but he may not grind them in a mill, so that they will not contain sediment. After he has extracted the first drop [of oil], he places them [the olives] into a mill and grinds them. The [resulting] second oil is unfit for the menorah but is fit for meal offerings, as it states: "beaten [olives] for lighting," but not beaten for meal offerings. (Rashi, Exod. 27:20)

Rashi explains that only the purest oil was suitable for the menorah. Not only was the oil to be extracted using a mortar rather than a mill (which would result in sediment), but only the first drop of oil from each olive could be used. Given that the menorah contained seven lamps, each holding half a *log* (about ten ounces or 4,800 drops) of oil (see Rashi, v. 21), the daily consumption of seventy ounces required 33,600 olives! This arduous process for producing the oil was testament to the importance of its purpose: kindling the menorah.

People tend to exert themselves in the areas of life—such as relationships, health, intellect, and religion—important to them. We may be able to gain insight into what we value by examining where we invest our time and effort to the utmost.

Questions for Discussion

1. Describe a time you invested considerable effort to achieve something unique. What purpose or value motivated your actions?
2. What are your three most time-consuming activities each week? Do these accurately reflect what is most important to you? If not, how do you hope to spend your time in the future?
3. Rashi explains that only the purest of oil befitted the sacred task of kindling the menorah. Can you relate to the idea of purity in service of sanctity?

❖ Always on My Mind

The parashah describes the clothing and sacrifices accompanying the inauguration of the priests (*kohanim*). Aaron was the first

High Priest (*Kohen Gadol*). He and all his successors wore eight garments, among them a golden frontlet.

וְהָיָה עַל מֵצַח אַהֲרֹן וְנָשָׂא אַהֲרֹן אֶת עֲוֹן הַקֳּדָשִׁים אֲשֶׁר יַקְדִּישׁוּ בְּנֵי יִשְׂרָאֵל לְכָל מַתְּנֹת קָדְשֵׁיהֶם וְהָיָה עַל מִצְחוֹ תָּמִיד לְרָצוֹן לָהֶם לִפְנֵי יְהֹוָה: (שמות כח, לח)

It [the golden frontlet] shall be on Aaron's forehead, that Aaron may take away any sin arising from the holy things that the Israelites consecrate, from any of their sacred donations; it shall be on his forehead at all times, to win acceptance for them [the consecrated offerings] before the Lord. (Exod. 28:38)

Since the golden frontlet is to be worn only while performing the priestly duties, Rashi is bothered by the requirement that it be on Aaron's forehead "at all times" (תָּמִיד):

והיה על מצחו תמיד: אי אפשר לומר שיהא על מצחו תמיד, שהרי אינו עליו אלא בשעת העבודה, אלא תמיד לרצות להם, אפילו אינו על מצחו, שלא היה כהן גדול עובד באותה שעה. ולדברי האומר (יומא ז ב) עודהו על מצחו מכפר ומרצה, ואם לאו אינו מרצה, נדרש על מצחו תמיד, מלמד שממשמש בו בעודו על מצחו, שלא יסיח דעתו ממנו: (רש"י, שם)

it shall be on his forehead at all times: It is impossible to say that it should always be on his forehead, for it was not on him except at the time of the [priestly] service. . . . "[O]n his forehead at all times" is interpreted to mean that he must touch it [the golden frontlet] while it is on his forehead so as to not take his mind off it. (Rashi, Exod. 28:38)

As Rashi explains, the High Priest would touch the golden frontlet to remind himself of the responsibilities he bore while wearing the priestly garments. This external reminder helped him focus his thoughts.

Judaism has many examples of external reminders to keep an idea in the forefront of one's mind. Affixing a mezuzah, an encased parchment inscribed with the verses of the *Shema* (Deut. 6:4–9), to the doorway of one's house serves to remind us of the Oneness of God as we leave and return home. Fringes (tzitzit) attached to each corner of a four-cornered garment serve as a reminder of the Torah's 613 commandments—the letters of the Hebrew word tzitzit (צִיצִית) have a numerical value (*gematria*) of 600 (90 [צ] + 10 [י] + 90 [צ] + 10 [י] + 400 [ת]), and each fringe includes eight strings and five knots (600 + 8 + 5 = 613) (see Rashi, Num. 15:39). The Jewish practice of leaving a small, unfinished area on the wall inside one's house serves as a graphic reminder of the destruction of the Temple in Jerusalem.

Questions for Discussion

1. What Jewish symbols do you have in your house? What do they remind you of?

2. Are you ever challenged by distraction during an activity that requires mental focus? What can you do to better focus your attention?

3. How might you use external reminders to help you dwell on an important idea or principle?

❖ From My Perspective

After receiving instructions on how to make the priestly garments, Moses is charged with inaugurating his brother, Aaron, and Aaron's sons as priests:

וְהִלְבַּשְׁתָּ אֹתָם אֶת אַהֲרֹן אָחִיךָ וְאֶת בָּנָיו אִתּוֹ וּמָשַׁחְתָּ אֹתָם וּמִלֵּאתָ אֶת יָדָם וְקִדַּשְׁתָּ אֹתָם וְכִהֲנוּ לִי: (שמות כח, מא)

Put these on your brother Aaron and on his sons as well; anoint them, and ordain them and consecrate them to serve Me as priests. (Exod. 28:41)

Rashi explains the term "ordain them" (וּמִלֵּאתָ אֶת יָדָם), which literally means "and fill their hands":

ומלאת את ידם: כל מלוי ידים לשון חנוך, כשהוא נכנס לדבר להיות מוחזק בו מאותו יום והלאה הוא מלוי, ובלשון לעז כשממנין אדם על פקידת דבר, נותן השליט בידו בית יד של עור שקורין גנ"ט בלעז, ועל ידו הוא מחזיקו בדבר, וקורין לאותו מסירה ריוישטי"ר בלעז והוא מלוי ידים: (רש"י, שם)

and ordain them: Every [mention of] "filling the hands" is an expression of installation. . . . In Old French, when a person is appointed to any position [in government], the ruler puts in his hand a leather glove called *gant*, and thereby establishes him in that position. This transmission is called *revestir* in Old French, and that is [the expression of] "filling the hands." (Rashi, Exod. 28:41)

Having lived in France, Rashi often provides French equivalents for difficult Hebrew words or expressions, as he does here for "filling the hands" (מלוי ידים). And, to clarify a Hebrew term, he also occasionally refers to a practice or custom in his time (nearly one thousand years ago), thereby providing a familiar point of reference. We too can enhance our understanding of the Torah by drawing on our life experiences and contemporary phenomena that reflect its concepts and ideas.

Questions for Discussion

1. Have you ever been elected or appointed to a position? If so, describe any ceremony that marked your installation, and whether you feel that it helped establish you in the position.
2. Rashi recounts that in his day officials were inaugurated by receiving a leather glove from the ruler. What would be the equivalent ritual today, and what does that reflect about our society?
3. Name an expression that continues to be used today even though the circumstances that gave rise to it are no longer universal human experiences (e.g., "take the reins" [of a horse], which means to assume control)?

KI TISSA'

❖ Age of Majority

"Old enough to fight, old enough to vote" was a common slogan in the Vietnam War era. Protesters called out the injustice of eighteen-year-olds being subject to the draft yet being unable to vote because U.S. voters had to be at least twenty-one years old. This gave impetus to the passage of the Twenty-Sixth Amendment, in 1971, which lowered the voting age to eighteen. In the Torah as well, age is used as a basis for assuming responsibilities and conferring legal rights, as we see in this verse from Parashat Ki Tissa' in which a census counts each person via the donation of half a silver shekel.

כֹּל הָעֹבֵר עַל הַפְּקֻדִים מִבֶּן עֶשְׂרִים שָׁנָה וָמָעְלָה יִתֵּן תְּרוּמַת יְהֹוָה:
(שמות ל, יד)

Everyone who is entered in the records, from the age of twenty years up, shall give the Lord's offering. (Exod. 30:14)

Rashi explains why the census began at the age of twenty:

מבן עשרים שנה ומעלה: למדך כאן, שאין פחות מבן עשרים יוצא לצבא ונמנה בכלל אנשים: (רש"י, שם)

from the age of twenty years up: It teaches you here that no one under twenty years old goes out [to serve] in the army or is counted among men. (Rashi, Exod. 30:14)

The twenty-year-old minimum age for military service is just one of a number of age-related milestones in Judaism. Most familiar to us are the ages when a Jew becomes obligated to observe the commandments (mitzvot)—age twelve for girls (bat mitzvah) and thirteen for boys (bar mitzvah) (*Bavli Yoma* 82a). The Torah also specifies that the Levites who were responsible for carrying various components of the Tabernacle as it was transported were to be thirty to fifty years old, the ages when they were in the prime of their strength (see Rashi, Num. 4:2). The Talmud mentions that an eighteen-year-old is suitable for marriage (*Pirkei Avot* 5:25).

Questions for Discussion

1. What is the most significant age-related milestone you have had, and how did it influence your life? Do you feel you were ready for it at that age?

2. What is the next major age-related milestone you face? What meaning does it have for you?

3. Did you have a bar or bat mitzvah? If so, what impact (if any) did it have on your relationship to Judaism? Do you think the bar or bat mitzvah could be invested with greater meaning? If so, how?

❖ Paradigm Shift

After providing detailed plans for the Tabernacle, the Torah designates Bezalel with the responsibility to supervise its construction:

וָאֲמַלֵּא אֹתוֹ רוּחַ אֱלֹהִים בְּחָכְמָה וּבִתְבוּנָה וּבְדַעַת וּבְכָל מְלָאכָה:
(שמות לא, ג)

I have endowed him [Bezalel] with a divine spirit of skill, ability, and knowledge in every kind of craft. (Exod. 31:3)

Rashi explains the differences between Bezalel's various qualities as mentioned in the verse:

בחכמה: מה שאדם שומע מאחרים ולמד; ובתבונה: מבין דבר מלבו מתוך דברים שלמד: (רש"י, שם)

skill: what a person hears from others and learns; **ability**: with his intellect he understands other things based on what he learned. (Rashi, Exod. 31:3)

Rashi distinguishes between two types of knowledge: *chokhmah* (חָכְמָה), which refers to information, and *tevunah* (תְּבוּנָה), which refers to deriving insights based on information.

Today, in the "Information Age," the Internet puts virtually unlimited amounts of data at everyone's fingertips. Therefore, the ability to merely provide information may not be as significant as it once was. However, the capability to process information through the application of judgment and insight remains as valuable a skill as ever.

These technological developments may call for a paradigm shift in education to help students thrive in the modern world. Because of the easy access to information, teaching students to regurgitate facts, for example, "When was the U.S. Civil War?" is not as valuable as teaching them how to think critically and solve problems, for example, "What does the Civil War teach us about how a country should respond to a separatist movement?"

Questions for Discussion

1. What life experiences have helped you to be able to derive insights from information?
2. Who do you regard as particularly insightful? Share something memorable you learned from this person.
3. Do you aspire to gain insight into a particular area? If so, in what area? How might you achieve it?

❖ Accentuate the Positive

The parashah contains what may be the low point in Jewish history—the Israelites worshiping the Golden Calf. Despite God's readiness to destroy the Jewish people after this episode, Moses succeeds in obtaining atonement for them. In the process God teaches Moses the Thirteen Attributes of Mercy, an appeal to God's mercy that will always serve as a way for the Jewish nation to achieve repentance. The following verse contains the second half of the Thirteen Attributes of Mercy:

נֹצֵר חֶסֶד לָאֲלָפִים נֹשֵׂא עָוֹן וָפֶשַׁע וְחַטָּאָה וְנַקֵּה לֹא יְנַקֶּה פֹּקֵד | עֲוֹן אָבוֹת עַל בָּנִים וְעַל בְּנֵי בָנִים עַל שִׁלֵּשִׁים וְעַל רִבֵּעִים: (שמות לד, ז)

Extending kindness to the thousandth generation, forgiving iniquity, transgression, and sin; yet He does not remit all punishment, but visits the iniquity of parents upon children and children's children, upon the third and fourth generations. (Exod. 34:7)

Rashi explains this verse:

ועל רבעים: דור רביעי, נמצאת מדה טובה מרובה על מדת פורענות
אחת לחמש מאות, שבמדה טובה הוא אומר נוצר חסד לאלפים:
(רש"י, שם)

and fourth generations: the fourth generation. Thus, [God's] attribute of good [i.e., reward] exceeds [His] attribute of retribution five-hundredfold, for regarding [His] attribute of good it states, "He preserves kindness for [two] thousand [generations]." (Rashi, Exod. 34:7)

As Rashi explains, God preserves a person's kindness five hundred times longer than his transgressions. This emphasis on compassion brings to mind the talmudic dictum, "One should always push away with the left hand, and draw close with the right hand" (*Bavli Sotah* 47a). When teaching a child right from wrong, parents are to act predominantly with kindness. The stronger (right) hand caringly encourages the child. When discipline is necessary, it is moderated, associated with the weaker (left) hand.

This accentuating the positive is similar to a popular modern approach to parenting that emphasizes catching the child being good and then praising the child to encourage his or her continued good behavior. While this approach does not explicitly address negative conduct, the intention is that focusing on desirable conduct will reduce the child's inclination to engage in less desirable behavior.

Questions for Discussion

1. Do you think our society emphasizes consequences or compassion? Explain. Is this approach best for society? Why or why not?

2. How did your parents discipline you? Was it effective? Was it coming from kindness? Would you choose to perpetuate it?

3. Do you believe a child's good behavior should be incentivized? Why or why not? If yes, under what circumstances?

VA-YAK'HEL

❖ TGIF

The notion of our working lives being divided into weekly segments punctuated by a day (or two) off is so ingrained in Western society, it is difficult to conceive of life without it. Both Jews and non-Jews may say, "Thank God it's Friday," though for Jews TGIF has added significance: the Sabbath is approaching. In Parashat Va-yak'hel, which describes the construction of the Tabernacle, we discover the origins of this weekly respite:

שֵׁשֶׁת יָמִים תֵּעָשֶׂה מְלָאכָה וּבַיּוֹם הַשְּׁבִיעִי יִהְיֶה לָכֶם קֹדֶשׁ שַׁבַּת שַׁבָּתוֹן לַיהֹוָה כָּל הָעֹשֶׂה בוֹ מְלָאכָה יוּמָת: (שמות לה, ב)

On six days work may be done, but on the seventh day you shall have a sabbath of complete rest, holy to the Lord; whoever does any work on it shall be put to death. (Exod. 35:2)

Since in the previous verse Moses had assembled the Jews for the ostensible purpose of collecting materials for the Tabernacle (whose construction is described in subsequent verses), Rashi is compelled to address why the Torah interrupts the narrative with a reference to the Sabbath:

ששת ימים: הקדים להם אזהרת שבת לצווי מלאכת המשכן לומר שאינה דוחה את השבת: (רש"י, שם)

On six days: He [Moses] prefaced [the discussion of the details of] the work of the Tabernacle with the warning to keep the Sabbath, to inform [them] that [the work of the Tabernacle] does not supersede the Sabbath. (Rashi, Exod. 35:2)

As Rashi explains, the timing of this warning to keep the Sabbath—given when all the Jews had been assembled to build the Tabernacle—indicates that keeping the Sabbath was so important it took precedence even over building the Tabernacle, God's dwelling place on earth.

The Torah, however, does not specify what constitutes Sabbath observance. The sages derived these rules from analyzing the juxtaposition of the obligation to keep the Sabbath with the directive to build the Tabernacle—concluding that on the Sabbath one may not do any of the thirty-nine activities (*melakhot*) involved in constructing the Tabernacle (see *Mishnah Shabbat 7:2*).

The Sabbath therefore does not require "rest" in the colloquial sense—though rest was likely a consequence of ceasing the Tabernacle work and a further distinction between Shabbat and the other days of the week.

Questions for Discussion

1. Almost all Jews are descended from families that, until a handful of generations ago, observed the traditional Sabbath by refraining from the thirty-nine *melakhot*. Describe how your family's Sabbath observance resembles or differs from this earlier standard.
2. Have you ever experienced a traditional Sabbath? If so, what was that experience like for you? What Sabbath experience has been most meaningful to you and why?
3. What does the Sabbath mean to you? How do you relate to the conception of its being a day of rest?

❖ Pedigree

As this parashah relates, Bezalel and his assistant, Oholiab, were to direct the Tabernacle's construction:

וּלְהוֹרֹת נָתַן בְּלִבּוֹ הוּא וְאָהֳלִיאָב בֶּן אֲחִיסָמָךְ לְמַטֵּה דָן: (שמות לה, לד)

And to give directions. He and Oholiab son of Ahisamach of the tribe of Dan. (Exod. 35:34)

Rashi comments on the appointment of two people from such different backgrounds to supervise the construction:

ואהליאב: משבט דן, מן הירודין שבשבטים מבני השפחות, והשוהו המקום לבצלאל למלאכת המשכן, והוא מגדולי השבטים, לקיים מה שנאמר (איוב לד, יט) ולא נכר שוע לפני דל: (רש"י, שם)

and Oholiab: of the tribe of Dan, from the lowliest of the tribes, one of the sons of [Jacob's] maidservants. Yet God made him [Oholiab] equal to Bezalel for the work of the Tabernacle, and he [Bezalel] was from the greatest of the tribes, to fulfill what is stated, "The noble are not preferred to the wretched" (Job 34:19). (Rashi, Exod. 35:34)

Rashi contrasts the ancestry of Bezalel and Oholiab. Bezalel was the grandson of Hur (חור), who assisted Moses and Aaron in leading the Jews to victory against the nation of Amalek (see Exod. 17:10). Hur had perhaps the most illustrious lineage among all Jews. His mother was Moses's sister, Miriam. His father was Caleb, son of Jephunneh, distinguished leader of the tribe of Judah (see Rashi, Exod. 24:14); and Judah was the son of Jacob's wife Leah and the forebear of the kings of Israel. By contrast, Oholiab was descended from Jacob's maidservant Bilhah. Nevertheless, God appointed them both to build God's house on earth.

In other words, when it comes to assuming responsibility at even the highest of levels, eminently qualified people of unexceptional lineage are also to be selected—and, as Rashi indicates, treated as equals during the course of the endeavor.

Questions for Discussion

1. How far back can you trace your ancestry? What do you know about your family's lineage?
2. Until a few generations ago, quotas and other barriers impeded Jews' entry into elite universities and prestigious professions. How did your forebears, or others you know of, face up to these challenges and endeavor to overcome them?
3. Do you believe everyone has equal opportunities today, regardless of differences in race, ethnicity, gender, religious background, and so forth?

❖ Name Recognition

Babe Ruth's impact on the New York Yankees was so great that Yankee Stadium, the baseball stadium built during his tenure with the Yankees, also came to be known as "The House that Ruth Built." A verse from the parashah relates a similar phenomenon concerning the ark, the decorative gold box located in the Tabernacle's inner sanctum.

וַיַּעַשׂ בְּצַלְאֵל אֶת הָאָרֹן עֲצֵי שִׁטִּים אַמָּתַיִם וָחֵצִי אָרְכּוֹ וְאַמָּה וָחֵצִי רָחְבּוֹ וְאַמָּה וָחֵצִי קֹמָתוֹ: (שמות לז, א)

Bezalel made the ark of acacia wood, two and a half cubits long, a cubit and a half wide, and a cubit and a half high. (Exod. 37:1)

Rashi explains why Bezalel is singled out as the person who made the ark, despite the fact that others also worked on it:

ויעש בצלאל: לפי שנתן נפשו על המלאכה יותר משאר חכמים,
נקראת על שמו: (רש"י, שם)

Bezalel made: Since he devoted himself to the work more than the other wise men, it is called by his name. (Rashi, Exod. 37:1)

As Rashi states, Bezalel is credited with having built the ark because he distinguished himself by the effort he invested in its construction. Notably, Rashi describes Bezalel's contribution with the term (שנתן נפשו), which literally means, "he gave his life." Not only did Bezalel have a unique impact in magnitude, he also exerted himself to a greater degree than anyone else. In other words, even if Bezalel was the most skilled of all the artisans working on the Tabernacle, he did not let this advantage diminish his effort. As Thomas Edison famously said: "Genius is one percent inspiration, ninety-nine percent perspiration."

Questions for Discussion

1. If you could have people associate you with one accomplishment, what would it be and why? Did you devote your full effort to it?
2. Have you ever contributed to an initiative in which one person exerted him or herself to a greater degree than everyone else? What (if anything) happened as a result?
3. Who do you admire most for his or her tenacity? If you were to develop this type of persistence, what difference might it make in your life?

PEKUDEI

❖ Public Accounting

In the Jewish community, charitable causes abound. Parashat Pekudei, which concludes the construction of the Tabernacle, offers insights that can benefit individuals and organizations seeking donations:

אֵלֶּה פְקוּדֵי הַמִּשְׁכָּן מִשְׁכַּן הָעֵדֻת אֲשֶׁר פֻּקַּד עַל פִּי מֹשֶׁה עֲבֹדַת הַלְוִיִּם בְּיַד אִיתָמָר בֶּן אַהֲרֹן הַכֹּהֵן: (שמות לח, כא)

These are the records of the Tabernacle, the Tabernacle of the Pact, which were drawn up at Moses' bidding—the work of the Levites under the direction of Ithamar son of Aaron the priest. (Exod. 38:21)

Rashi clarifies the meaning of *pekudei* (פְּקוּדֵי), from the Hebrew root letters *p-k-d* (פקד), which means either "appoint" or "count":

אלה פקודי: בפרשה זו נמנו כל משקלי נדבת המשכן, לכסף ולזהב ולנחשת, ונמנו כל כליו לכל עבודתו: (רש"י, שם)

These are the records: In this parashah all the weights of the donations for the Tabernacle are counted—the silver, the gold, and the copper. And all its implements for all its work are [also] counted. (Rashi, Exod. 38:21)

As Rashi explains, the parashah details the contributions of gold, silver, and copper. The fundraising process to build the Tabernacle included: (1) clearly articulating the purpose and necessity of the fundraising campaign at the outset, (2) specifying the amount of funds required and how they would be spent, and, (3) in this parashah, recording and disclosing the contributions received and how they were used. Nonprofits have found that this approach engenders the trust of benefactors, thereby helping to secure their continued support in the future.

Questions for Discussion

1. How do you know whether the funds you (and others) contribute to charitable organizations you support are actually reaching the intended beneficiaries?
2. If you were to start a charitable organization, what need would it address and why?
3. Many institutions recognize their benefactors by naming buildings or seats in their honor, or otherwise publicly acknowledging their contributions. What do you think about public recognition of personal philanthropy?

❖ Check Out Your Assumptions

If you received a baby announcement stating that the newborn infant weighed "7 pounds, 18 ounces," you might scratch you head and ask yourself, "Shouldn't it instead read '8 pounds, 2 ounces?'" The parashah similarly describes the quantity of silver contributed to the Tabernacle:

וְכֶסֶף פְּקוּדֵי הָעֵדָה מְאַת כִּכָּר וְאֶלֶף וּשְׁבַע מֵאוֹת וַחֲמִשָּׁה וְשִׁבְעִים שֶׁקֶל בְּשֶׁקֶל הַקֹּדֶשׁ: (שמות לח, כה)

The silver of those of the community who were recorded came to 100 talents and 1,775 shekels by the sanctuary weight. (Exod. 38:25)

At a time when everyone knew 1,500 shekels equaled a standard talent, the expressed weight of the silver would have seemed amiss. Shouldn't it have been written as 101 talents and 275 shekels (1,775 shekels minus 1,500 = 275)? Rashi clarifies:

כבר: ששים מנה, ומנה של קדש כפול היה, הרי הכבר מאה ועשרים מנה, והמנה עשרים וחמשה סלעים, הרי כבר של קדש שלושת אלפים שקלים, לפיכך מנה בפרוטרוט כל השקלים שפחותין במנינם משלושת אלפים שאין מגיעין לכבר: (רש"י, שמות לח, כד)

talents: [The weight of the sanctuary talent (3,000 shekels) was twice that of the standard talent (1,500 shekels).] . . . Therefore [the text] counted out in [shekel] units all the shekels whose sum was less than 3,000 since they did not amount to a talent. (Rashi, Exod. 38:24)

As Rashi explains, because the sanctuary weights were twice that of standard weights, the sanctuary talent weighed 3,000—rather than 1,500—shekels. With this understanding, 100 talents and 1,775 shekels becomes the natural measurement.

When something does not make sense, it may be due to an incorrect assumption. Even if our assumptions are generally reasonable and accurate, at times our usual assumptions will not apply. By questioning our assumptions, we may be able to determine the reason for the confusion.

Questions for Discussion

1. What do you believe is an incorrect assumption held by many people? Would they be open to reconsidering this misperception? If yes, what might help them to do so?
2. Describe a time you initially believed that another person had acted improperly or wrongly, but you later realized that the problem was your own misunderstanding. What did you learn from this experience?
3. What behavior modifications could you adopt to "check out your assumptions"?

❖ Just Do It (Right)

The iconic television program *Mister Rogers' Neighborhood* featured a song with the refrain "I like to take my time and do it right." The parashah alludes to a similar approach when describing the conclusion of the Tabernacle's construction:

וַתֵּכֶל כָּל עֲבֹדַת מִשְׁכַּן אֹהֶל מוֹעֵד וַיַּעֲשׂוּ בְּנֵי יִשְׂרָאֵל כְּכֹל אֲשֶׁר צִוָּה יְהֹוָה אֶת מֹשֶׁה כֵּן עָשׂוּ: (שמות לט, לב)

Thus was completed all the work of the Tabernacle of the Tent of Meeting. The Israelites did so; just as the Lord had commanded Moses, so they did. (Exod. 39:32)

Since the verse states that the Israelites "did so" (וַיַּעֲשׂוּ), Rashi addresses the seeming repetition in the words "so they did" (עָשׂוּ):

ויעשו בני ישראל: את המלאכה ככל אשר צוה ה' וגו': (רש"י, שם)

The Israelites did so: the work, [and they did it] according to all that God commanded, etc. (Rashi, Exod. 39:32)

Rashi explains that the Israelites not only did the required tasks, but were meticulous in performing them precisely as they had been commanded.

Especially in a time like ours, where "ASAP" and "multitasking" have become part of everyday parlance, such careful attention to detail cannot be taken for granted. Yet the way we accomplish a task—rather than the mere fact of our having done it—may make an enduring impression.

Questions for Discussion

1. When do you work in a meticulous fashion? Does the result justify the effort? If so, why might other people not do it that way? If not, what drives you to act so carefully?

2. When you don't work as meticulously, what gets in your way? If you would like to "do it right," what might help you to get there?

3. If you think "good enough" work is sufficient, but the person you're reporting to expects exemplary work, how can you ensure that everyone is satisfied with the outcome?

Leviticus

VA-YIKRA'

❖ Terms of Endearment

Parashat Va-yikra' describes the various types of offerings the Jews were instructed to bring to the Temple. The Hebrew word for offering is *korban* (קָרְבָּן), from the Hebrew root letters *k-r-v* (קרב), meaning "to bring close," which suggests a *korban* is meant to bring the one who offers it close to God. Even before the offerings were instituted, another mechanism was in place that fostered closeness between God and Moses, as alluded to in the parashah's opening verse:

וַיִּקְרָא אֶל מֹשֶׁה וַיְדַבֵּר יְהֹוָה אֵלָיו מֵאֹהֶל מוֹעֵד לֵאמֹר: (ויקרא א, א)

The Lord called to Moses and spoke to him from the Tent of Meeting, saying. (Lev. 1:1)

Since the verse states that the Lord "spoke to [Moses] . . . saying," Rashi explains the significance of the seemingly superfluous phrase, "The Lord called to Moses," which introduces the verse:

ויקרא אל משה: לכל דברות ולכל אמירות ולכל צוויים קדמה
קריאה, לשון חבה, לשון שמלאכי השרת משתמשים בו, שנאמר
(ישעיה ו, ג) וקרא זה אל זה: (רש"י, שם)

The Lord called to Moses: Every [time God communicated with Moses, whether it was represented by the expression] "And He spoke" [וַיְדַבֵּר], "and He said" [וַיֹּאמֶר],

or "and He commanded" [וַיְצַו], it was always preceded by [God's] calling [Moses by name], an expression of love, an expression that the ministering angels use, as it says, "And one would call to the other" (Isa. 6:3). (Rashi, Lev. 1:1)

Rashi's comment is based on the *Sifra* (the halakhic midrash to the book of Leviticus), which states that God prefaced communications with Moses by calling out, "Moses, Moses," to which Moses would respond, "Here I am!" God's addressing Moses by name demonstrated affection and connection.

Similarly when two people are not well acquainted, addressing the other person by name can create a sense of closeness by communicating that one is making the effort to learn that person's name and thereby continue the relationship.

When a close relationship exists, prefacing a conversation with the other person's name can help focus the listener's attention—a necessary condition for effective communication—and help build rapport and ongoing connection.

Questions for Discussion

1. Have you been called by an affectionate term or nickname? What was its origin, and how do you feel when you are called by it?
2. Do you ever have difficulty remembering other people's names? If so, does it feel different to address a person whose name you can't recall? Why?
3. When you write e-mails, do you start with the recipient's name? Why or why not?

❖ Time to Reflect

While the term "parashah" is commonly used to refer to the weekly Torah reading, the correct term is actually *sidrah*. A parashah is a paragraph in the Torah, and there are two types: "closed" (*setumah*), which are separated from the previous paragraph by a nine-letter-long space, and "open" (*petuchah*), which begin on a new line. A verse from the *sidrah* provides insight into the significance of these paragraph breaks.

וְאִם מִן הַצֹּאן קָרְבָּנוֹ מִן הַכְּשָׂבִים אוֹ מִן הָעִזִּים לְעֹלָה זָכָר תָּמִים
יַקְרִיבֶנּוּ: (ויקרא א, י)

If his offering for a burnt offering is from the flock, of sheep or of goats, he shall make his offering a male without blemish. (Lev. 1:10)

Rashi questions why this verse starts a new parashah (paragraph), even though it continues with the subject matter of the previous parashah, and even begins with the Hebrew letter *vav* (and), thereby connecting it grammatically to the previous parashah:

ואם מן הצאן: וי"ו מוסיף על ענין ראשון. ולמה הפסיק, ליתן ריוח
למשה להתבונן בין פרשה לפרשה: (רש"י, שם)

If . . . from the flock: [The paragraph beginning with] the Hebrew letter *vav* [and] is a continuation of the previous subject. Why [then] was there a paragraph break? In order to give Moses a pause, so that he could contemplate between one passage and the next. (Rashi, Lev. 1:10)

Rashi explains that the paragraph break gave Moses the opportunity to reflect on what he had been told in the previous parashah before he directed his attention toward the next parashah.

In our era, people are bombarded with information—e-mails, texts, tweets, posts, and so forth—as well as responsibilities, activities, and sensory inputs. Often there is little time to digest the day's events, let alone think about issues beyond the hubbub of life. Moses's directed practice to pause and reflect before focusing on a new matter is possibly even more essential for us today.

Questions for Discussion

1. Do you find that over the years you have had more, less, or about the same amount of time to engage in introspection? If this has changed in your life, what accounts for the change?
2. Do you feel you have adequate downtime during which you can simply think? If so, when do you do this? If not, how might you make this time for yourself?
3. What was the last thing you read that required you to pause to comprehend or digest the material? Was your effort rewarding? If so, what did you learn?

❖ Leadership

Former chief rabbi of Great Britain Jonathan Sacks commented after meeting the Lubavitcher Rebbe, "Good leaders create followers; great leaders create leaders." Another quality found in great leaders is discussed in this week's parashah in a passage on the offerings brought by a Jewish king.

אֲשֶׁר נָשִׂיא יֶחֱטָא וְעָשָׂה אַחַת מִכָּל מִצְוֺת יְהֹוָה אֱלֹהָיו אֲשֶׁר לֹא
תֵעָשֶׂינָה בִּשְׁגָגָה וְאָשֵׁם: (ויקרא ד, כב)

In case it is a chieftain who incurs guilt by doing unwittingly any of the things which by the commandment of the Lord his God ought not to be done, and he realizes his guilt— . . . (Lev. 4:22)

Rashi explains why the verse begins with the word *asher* (אֲשֶׁר, in case), rather than a more typical word for this context such as "if" (אם):

אשר נשיא יחטא: לשון אשרי, אשרי הדור שהנשיא
שלו נותן לב להביא כפרה על שגגתו, קל וחומר
שמתחרט על זדונותיו: (רש"י, שם)

In case it is a chieftain who incurs guilt: [*Asher* (אֲשֶׁר) is] an expression reminiscent of [the dictum from the *Sifra* starting with the word] *ashrei* [אַשְׁרֵי, fortunate is], namely: "Fortunate is the generation whose leader is concerned with bringing atonement for his inadvertent transgression—how much more will he experience remorse for his intentional transgressions!" (Rashi, Lev. 4:22)

Rashi explains that the verse uses the word association between *asher* (אֲשֶׁר) and *ashrei* (אַשְׁרֵי) to teach us that a great leader will express remorse for his (or her) accidental wrongdoings—and even more remorse for intentional transgressions. Moreover, that leader's integrity—as exhibited by making amends for mistakes of all kinds—has significant bearing on the populace.

Recent history provides numerous examples of leaders who were regarded as effective in their public roles, yet made errors in judgment in their personal lives. Making a dichotomy between professional and personal conduct undermines a basic premise of integrity. The Torah does not make a distinction between these two spheres of life, but rather provides a uniform standard of conduct for both public and private affairs.

Questions for Discussion

1. Name a leader who breached the public's trust. Why do you think this person acted in that way? What were the consequences? How did it affect the public? What lessons can you learn from that episode?

2. What leader do you admire, and why? Does this person appear to exhibit a uniform standard of conduct in both professional and personal matters?

3. Have you ever atoned for inadvertent wrongdoings? If yes, what did you do? If not, why did you choose not to address the matter?

TSAV

❖ Change of Clothes

Discussing the offerings brought in the Tabernacle, Parashat Tsav focuses on the role of Moses's brother, Aaron, and his sons, who served as the priests.

וּפָשַׁט אֶת בְּגָדָיו וְלָבַשׁ בְּגָדִים אֲחֵרִים וְהוֹצִיא אֶת הַדֶּשֶׁן אֶל מִחוּץ לַמַּחֲנֶה אֶל מָקוֹם טָהוֹר: (ויקרא ו, ד)

He [the priest] shall then take off his vestments and put on other vestments, and carry the ashes outside the camp to a clean place. (Lev. 6:4)

Rashi elaborates on the priest's change of clothing:

וּפשט את בגדיו: אין זו חובה אלא דרך ארץ, שלא ילכלך בהוצאת הדשן בגדים שהוא משמש בהן תמיד. בגדים שבשל בהן קדרה לרבו אל ימזוג בהן כוס לרבו, לכך ולבש בגדים אחרים פחותין מהן: (רש"י, שם)

He shall then take off his vestments: This is not an obligation, but proper practice, that in taking out the ashes he not soil the garments in which he always officiates. [An analogy:] The clothes worn [by a servant] while cooking a pot [of food] for his master, he should not wear when he pours a glass [of wine] for his master. Therefore [the verse continues], "and put on other vestments," inferior to those. (Rashi, Lev. 6:4)

Rashi explains that it would not be appropriate for the priest to officiate over the sacrifices in the same clothing that may have been soiled as he disposed of the ashes from the altar.

While dressing for the occasion remains a value today, both the clothing we wear and the societal approach to attire have evolved over time. A century ago men typically wore suits and hats, and women donned long dresses or blouses and skirts. The 1960s era encouraged nonconformity in many facets of society, including how to present oneself in dress. Since then, clothing styles have become even less formal, a trend reinforced by the prevalence of telecommuting from home rather than working in an office setting.

Questions for Discussion

1. What do your clothes tend to communicate about you? Is this a conscious message you wish to convey?
2. Name an occasion for which how much you dress up or what you wear has changed over time. What does that imply about you and society?
3. Based on your understanding of how attire has evolved in (or out of) step with society, what changes in people's dress do you think we are likely to see in the next generation?

❖ Environmental Impact

The term "environmental impact" generally denotes the impact of human activity on the environment. This parashah concerning Aaron, the High Priest, might prompt reflection on a different sort of environmental impact—the impact the environment has on us.

כָּל זָכָר בִּבְנֵי אַהֲרֹן יֹאכְלֶנָּה חָק עוֹלָם לְדֹרֹתֵיכֶם מֵאִשֵּׁי יְהוָה כֹּל אֲשֶׁר יִגַּע בָּהֶם יִקְדָּשׁ: (ויקרא ו, יא)

Only the males among Aaron's descendants may eat of it [the meal offering], as their due for all time throughout the ages from the Lord's offerings by fire. Anything that touches these shall become holy. (Lev. 6:11)

Rashi explains the meaning of the concluding word in this verse:

יקדש: להיות כמוה, שאם פסולה יפסלו, ואם כשרה יאכלו כחומר המנחה: (רש"י, שם)

shall become holy: to become like it [the meal offering]. If it is invalid, then [offerings of lesser sanctity or unsanctified food that touch it] will become invalid; and if it [the meal offering] is valid, they will have to be eaten under the same stringent conditions as the meal offering [namely, within the Tabernacle's courtyard and during the day and the following night]. (Rashi, Lev. 6:11)

As Rashi explains, if the meal offering came into contact with other foods, its status—whether valid or invalid—would be transferred to them. This offering therefore had the ability to change other foods merely by its proximity to them.

Inherent in this phenomenon is the broader principle that all of us are influenced by our environment. This understanding can be empowering. For example, if someone wants to become a person who is concerned with the plight of others, he or she could spend time helping those who are less fortunate. If someone hopes to influence children to think in a certain way, she

or he could seek out or create an environment that reflects the desired qualities.

This same insight also implies to exposure to negative environmental influences, which may impede our becoming the people we aspire to be.

Questions for Discussion

1. Name a few societal influences in your life. Which ones have had a positive impact, which ones a negative impact, and which have had both? Does identifying these influences as being positive, negative, or both have the potential to change how you relate to them?

2. Have you ever sought out an environment expressly to influence your own character? If so, what happened? If not, is this something you would consider? Why or why not?

3. Describe a positive influence you believe you have had on another person. Has this been deliberate or incidental or both?

❖ Reframing Language

The parashah concludes with Moses instructing the priests regarding their required duties and hinting at the consequence should they fail to do as instructed.

וּפֶתַח אֹהֶל מוֹעֵד תֵּשְׁבוּ יוֹמָם וָלַיְלָה שִׁבְעַת יָמִים וּשְׁמַרְתֶּם אֶת מִשְׁמֶרֶת יְהוָה וְלֹא תָמוּתוּ כִּי כֵן צֻוֵּיתִי: (ויקרא ח, לה)

You [the priests] shall remain at the entrance of the Tent of Meeting day and night for seven days, keeping the Lord's charge—that you may not die—for so I have been commanded. (Lev. 8:35)

Rashi states a rule that can be inferred from the verse's phrasing:

ולא תמותו: הא אם לא תעשו כן, הרי
אתם חייבים מיתה: (רש"י, שם)

[so] that you may not die: But if you do not do so, you incur the death penalty. (Rashi, Lev. 8:35)

Rashi draws attention to the fact that the priests will "not die" (וְלֹא תָמוּתוּ) if they do as required. But if the purpose of the biblical verse was to put the priests on notice that they will die if they fail to do as required, wouldn't it have been better to state that directly?

Moses made this announcement during the inauguration of the Tabernacle—a joyous event for the Jewish nation. Perhaps this phrasing was specifically chosen to avoid uttering "you will die" (תָמוּתוּ), and thereby detracting from the festive character of the occasion.

The way a person chooses to convey information can make an important difference in how it is received. A popular approach to interpersonal communication advocates making "I" statements rather than "you" statements when delivering a message that the listener may regard as a criticism. For example, if a teenager is annoyed that his parents are constantly reminding him to do his homework, instead of responding, "Lay off me!" he could reply, "I feel frustrated by these reminders to do my homework. I am mature enough to complete my homework without the prompting of others." This approach has two advantages: (1) not using the accusatory "you" may avoid making the listener defensive and thereby unreceptive to the expressed concerns; and (2) when people explain their perceptions and feelings from a place of "I," others are generally inclined to understand and accept them as valid even when those points of view are different from their own.

Questions for Discussion

1. Describe how a typical interaction that includes a critical comment might be converted to an "I" statement of feeling and explanation. What difference do you think recasting the statement might make?

2. In the above verse and more generally, there is often reluctance to speak about death. Do you ever experience discomfort discussing this topic? If so, how do you understand this unease?

3. How has language changed in the past decades specifically to avoid offending people? Do you speak differently than you used to? If so, how? And how have those changes influenced your perceptions of and actions toward other people?

SHEMINI

❖ Drinking Responsibly

Parashat Shemini (literally, "Eighth") takes its name from the opening verse, which recounts the events of the eighth and final day of the Tabernacle's inauguration. On what should have been a wholly glorious day, Nadab and Abihu, two of Aaron's four sons, brought an offering that God had not commanded, and perished as a result. Immediately following this tragedy, God delivered instructions to Aaron, the High Priest:

יַיִן וְשֵׁכָר אַל תֵּשְׁתְּ | אַתָּה | וּבָנֶיךָ אִתָּךְ בְּבֹאֲכֶם אֶל אֹהֶל מוֹעֵד וְלֹא תָמֻתוּ חֻקַּת עוֹלָם לְדֹרֹתֵיכֶם: (ויקרא י, ט)

Drink no wine or other intoxicant, you or your sons, when you enter the Tent of Meeting, that you may not die. This is a law for all time throughout the ages. (Lev. 10:9)

Rashi comments on why the verse refers to two beverages (יַיִן וְשֵׁכָר):

יין ושכר: יין דרך שכרותו: (רש"י, שם)

wine or other intoxicant: Wine in a manner that intoxicates. (Rashi, Lev. 10:9)

Rashi explains that this verse prohibits the priests from entering the Tent of Meeting while inebriated. In his commentary on verse 2, Rashi cites the placement of this prohibition immediately after the deaths of Nadab and Abihu as proof that their deaths resulted from their entering the Tabernacle while intoxicated.

While some religions, such as Islam and Mormonism, prohibit consuming alcohol, Judaism condones drinking alcoholic beverages—and, even more so, requires drinking wine on certain occasions. For example, Sabbath is marked by reciting a blessing over wine at both its entry (*Kiddush*) and its departure (*Havdalah*); and Passover, the holiday when Jews transmit the fundamentals of our history and faith to the next generation, involves drinking four cups of wine, corresponding to the four different verbs used in Exodus 6:6–8 to express God's promise to redeem the Jews from Egypt. Judaism recognizes that alcohol has the ability to enhance life when used within prescribed guidelines and the potential to destroy life when it is not, as illustrated by the incident of Nadab and Abihu.

Questions for Discussion

1. When do you tend to consume alcohol today? Do you agree that it has the ability to both enhance and destroy life?

2. Although there are expressions of asceticism in Judaism (e.g., "Such is the way of Torah: You shall eat bread with salt, you shall drink water in small measure, and you shall sleep on the ground; live a life of deprivation and toil in Torah" [*Pirkei Avot* 6:4]), they are the exception rather than the rule. How do you feel about Judaism's teaching that (moderated) physical pleasure can enhance spiritual life? Do you find this to be true in your life as well?

3. The government tries to curtail alcohol use by prohibiting driving while intoxicated, banning the consumption of alcohol in many outdoor spaces, and outlawing purchases

of alcohol by those below the minimum legal age. Do you think these restrictions are justified? Why or why not?

....

❖ Humility

The concluding day of the Tabernacle's inauguration was the first day of the Hebrew month of Nisan (see Rashi, Lev. 9:1), and thus required an offering for the new month (Rosh Hodesh). While Aaron, as High Priest, would normally partake of the Rosh Hodesh offering, he refrained from eating it on this occasion because his sons remained unburied (thus giving him the status of an *onen*, one awaiting the burial of one of seven close relatives—father, mother, brother, sister, son, daughter, or spouse). In the meantime the offering became defiled, and Moses was upset with Aaron for not having eaten it before it was defiled. However, upon further consideration, Moses approved of Aaron's conduct, as the following verse relates:

וַיִּשְׁמַע מֹשֶׁה וַיִּיטַב בְּעֵינָיו: (ויקרא י, כ)

And when Moses heard this, he approved. (Lev. 10:20)

Rashi explains what caused Moses to change his mind about Aaron's behavior:

וייטב בעיניו: הודה ולא בוש לומר לא שמעתי: (רש"י, שם)

he approved: [Moses] admitted [that Aaron was correct] and [Moses] was not ashamed, [for Moses could have covered up by] saying, "I have not heard [of the law that an *onen* may not

eat from . . . the Rosh Hodesh offering." Rather, he said, "I heard it and forgot." (*Bavli Zevachim* 101a)]. (Rashi, Lev. 10:20)

As Rashi explains, Aaron correctly refrained from partaking of the Rosh Hodesh offering because of his status as an *onen*. After hearing Aaron's explanation, Moses admitted that Aaron was correct.

Notably, even though Moses was the acknowledged expert in the sacrificial service, he gave Aaron the opportunity to explain himself. Once he heard Aaron's explanation, Moses realized he had erred in expressing anger toward Aaron. Then Moses publicly acknowledged that Aaron had been correct, risking his own possible humiliation in the process.

This incident reflects Moses's great humility, to which the Torah attests, stating, "Now Moses was a very humble man, more so than any other man" (וְהָאִישׁ מֹשֶׁה עָנָיו מְאֹד מִכֹּל הָאָדָם) (Num. 12:3).

Questions for Discussion

1. How do you understand the difference between genuine modesty and false modesty? Can a particularly accomplished person recognize his or her own greatness and still be modest? Why or why not?
2. Recall a time when you came to recognize and acknowledge that you were wrong and another person was correct. Did admitting your mistake affect the relationship?
3. Can you describe an act of humility that you find inspiring?

....

❖ Creatures as Teachers

The parashah concludes with a discussion of kosher and non-kosher animals, including the many birds that are not kosher.

וְאֵת הַחֲסִידָה הָאֲנָפָה לְמִינָהּ וְאֶת הַדּוּכִיפַת וְאֶת הָעֲטַלֵּף: (ויקרא יא, יט)

The stork; herons of every variety; the hoopoe, and the bat. (Lev. 11:19)

Rashi explains the meaning of the word *hasidah* (חֲסִידָה), translated as "stork":

החסידה: זו דיה לבנה ציגוני"ה. ולמה נקרא שמה חסידה, שעושה חסידות עם חברותיה במזונות: (רש"י, שם)

The stork: This is a white *dayah*, [called] *cigogne* [in Old French]. And why is it called *hasidah* [חֲסִידָה]? Because it does kindness [*hasidut*, חֲסִידוּת] with its fellow birds [by sharing] its food. (Rashi, Lev. 11:19)

Rashi explains that because the *dayah* bird shares its food with others, it is also called *hasidah*, derived from the word *hesed* (kindness).

Jewish tradition makes mention of other animals that exhibit positive traits. For example, the Talmud states, "If the Torah had not been given, we could have learned modesty from the cat [which relieves itself in private], honesty from the ant [which doesn't steal the food of another ant], and fidelity from the dove [which is monogamous]" (see Rashi, *Bavli Eruvin* 100b).

Questions for Discussion

1. Have you ever owned a pet? If so, what have you learned from him or her?
2. What positive character trait that is often associated with an animal do you aspire to achieve?
3. Do you believe that exemplary behaviors exhibited by animals can be considered "moral" in the same sense they would be if performed by a person? Why or why not?

TAZRIA'

❖ Revealing Wrongdoing

Parashat Tazria' discusses an affliction of the skin called *tzara'at*, which, despite not having an English equivalent, has often been translated as "leprosy." While both *tzara'at* and leprosy are characterized by skin lesions, otherwise there is little commonality between the two conditions. *Tzara'at*, unlike leprosy, afflicts clothing and buildings in addition to people. Leprosy is caused by a bacterial infection, while *tzara'at* is a spiritual malady with physical manifestations that can be caused by one's involvement in slander, murder, false oaths, incest, arrogance, robbery, or greed (see *Bavli Arakhin* 16a). The parashah details the physical manifestations of *tzara'at* and specifies the procedure by which the priest (kohen) is to determine whether a person suffers from this affliction.

וְאִם בַּהֶרֶת לְבָנָה הִוא בְּעוֹר בְּשָׂרוֹ וְעָמֹק אֵין מַרְאֶהָ מִן הָעוֹר וּשְׂעָרָה
לֹא הָפַךְ לָבָן וְהִסְגִּיר הַכֹּהֵן אֶת הַנֶּגַע שִׁבְעַת יָמִים: (ויקרא יג, ד)

But if it is a white discoloration on the skin of his body which does not appear to be deeper than the skin and the hair in it has not turned white, the priest shall isolate the affected person for seven days. (Lev. 13:4)

Rashi elaborates on the isolation requirement:

והסגיר: יסגירנו בבית אחד ולא יראה עד סוף השבוע, ויוכיחו
סימנים עליו: (רש"י, שם)

shall isolate: He [the kohen] shall confine him to one house, and the person shall not be seen [by the kohen] until the end of the week, [at which point] the signs [of his lesion] will demonstrate [whether or not he is afflicted with *tzara'at*]. (Rashi, Lev. 13:4)

As Rashi explains, during a weeklong period of confinement the skin lesion may develop further. Then the kohen will be able to see and determine whether it is indeed a case of *tzara'at*.

The phenomenon of a person's misdeeds being reflected in his appearance has no parallel in contemporary society. In earlier times, however, *tzara'at* was seen as serving an important function: revealing an errant person's offenses and forcing him or her to confront them. Without such a mechanism, a person could avoid accepting individual responsibility for behavior and thereby prolong any damage one may be causing to both self and others.

Questions for Discussion

1. How do you determine whether someone you know has committed a minor or major transgression?
2. A mechanism intended to uphold justice may itself, upon later understanding, be unjust (e.g., the "scarlet letter" or corporal punishment in schools). What example comes to mind in society today? How might it be rectified?
3. Can you think of any fair, yet uncommon means for encouraging people to acknowledge individual responsibility for wrongdoing?

❖ 20/20

If asked to identify a job that requires perfect vision, many people would rightly answer "air force pilot." The U.S. Air Force does have vision standards—only candidates with vision correctable to 20/20 are accepted into its flight-training program. This parashah identifies a role in the Jewish community that also had vision requirements.

וְאִם פָּרֹוחַ תִּפְרַח הַצָּרַעַת בָּעֹור וְכִסְּתָה הַצָּרַעַת אֵת כָּל עֹור הַנֶּגַע מֵרֹאשֹׁו וְעַד רַגְלָיו לְכָל מַרְאֵה עֵינֵי הַכֹּהֵן: (ויקרא יג, יב)

If the eruption spreads out over the skin so that it covers all the skin of the affected person from head to foot, wherever the priest [*kohen*] can see. (Lev. 13:12)

Rashi explains the reference to the priest's vision:

לכל מראה עיני הכהן: פרט לכהן שחשך מאורו: (רש"י, שם)

wherever the priest can see: [This phrase] comes to exclude a priest whose eyesight has dimmed [i.e., a priest with one blind eye or with impaired vision in both eyes may not rule on the status of lesions]. (Rashi, Lev. 13:12)

As Rashi explains, only priests who do not have a vision impairment are qualified to determine whether a person with lesions suffers from *tzara'at*.

Until the invention of eyeglasses in thirteenth-century Italy, people's daily lives were affected in significant ways by visual deficiencies. For example, individuals who were farsighted—even if literate—could not read, and those who were nearsighted probably could not hunt. Today, since poor vision can generally be corrected with glasses or surgery, there are fewer practical constraints on account of eyesight. We are fortunate to live in a time when vision and certain other health-related problems have largely been addressed.

Medical improvements and the accompanying increase in life expectancy have created issues that were not prevalent in earlier generations. Some older adults who remain in excellent physical health find the traditional retirement age of sixty-five to be neither desirable nor financially feasible. Typically they are the most experienced workers in the company and can often continue to make significant contributions to their employers if they remain on the workforce past age sixty-five.

Sometimes senior employees will start to experience the effects of aging in ways that negatively affect their job performance. If there is mutual respect and interest, the employer and employee can find ways to accommodate disabilities such as reduced visual and auditory acuity and loss of mobility, with results that benefit both parties.

Questions for Discussion

1. Has aging had any impact on your professional performance? If so, describe the impact and how you have dealt with it. If not, what impact might it have in the future, and how would you try to address it?

2. Do you think reasonable accommodations should be made for older employees who desire to continue to work despite some moderate age-related disability? If so, at what point do these accommodations cease being "reasonable"? Should this determination be made by the employer, or should it be subject to government regulation?

3. Incredible advances in health care have enabled people to have longer, more productive, and more comfortable lives.

At the same time that people are living longer, health-care costs constitute an escalating share of societal expenditures. Do you believe that society should be more responsible for the health care of its citizens than it is today or less so? Should health care be rationed (and, if so, how?) or expanded (and, if so, how should society pay for it?)?

....

❖ Sticks and Stones

If the priest (*kohen*) determines that a person afflicted with a skin lesion does indeed have *tzara'at*, the parashah specifies the protocol to be followed:

כָּל יְמֵי אֲשֶׁר הַנֶּגַע בּוֹ יִטְמָא טָמֵא הוּא בָּדָד יֵשֵׁב מִחוּץ לַמַּחֲנֶה מוֹשָׁבוֹ: (ויקרא יג, מו)

He shall be unclean as long as the disease is on him. Being unclean, he shall dwell apart; his dwelling shall be outside the camp. (Lev. 13:46)

Rashi elaborates on the requirement that the individual dwell in isolation:

בדד ישב: שלא יהיו שאר טמאים יושבים עמו. ואמרו רבותינו מה נשתנה משאר טמאים לישב בדד, הואיל והוא הבדיל בלשון הרע בין איש לאשתו ובין איש לרעהו, אף הוא יבדל: (רש"י, שם)

he shall dwell apart: [meaning] that other impure people [not stricken with *tzara'at*] shall not dwell with him. Our sages said: "Why is he different from other impure people,

that he must remain isolated? Since, with his evil speech [*lashon ha-ra*, לְשׁוֹן הָרַע], he separated man from his wife, and man from his fellow, he too shall be separated [from society]." (Rashi, Lev. 13:46)

A person can become spiritually impure (*tame*) in a variety of ways, for example, through contact with a human corpse or a dead animal. As Rashi explains, however, only a person whose spiritual impurity (*tumah*) is caused by *tzara'at* is required to dwell in isolation. Acts causing *tzara'at* also include murder and false oaths, but here Rashi focuses on the *tzara'at* of harmful speech, perhaps because speaking ill of others is the most common of such misdeeds. He explains that serious consequences ensue when someone speaks of others in an injurious way: the speaker has temporarily forfeited his right to enjoy other people's company.

The Jewish concept of *lashon ha-ra* (evil speech) is different from slander. Slander encompasses only false defamatory statements; *lashon ha-ra*, by contrast, consists of true statements that cause harm to others. For example, certain popular magazines are dedicated to publicizing the details of famous people's lives. Little, if any, of their content would legally constitute defamation—the magazines' lawyers make sure of that—but it may nevertheless be damaging to the celebrities themselves and would thus constitute *lashon ha-ra*. *Lashon ha-ra* is one of many examples where the protections afforded by Jewish law are broader than those of secular law.

Questions for Discussion

1. Many disciplinary approaches, such as "bedroom time," seek to punish a child by isolating him or her from others. Have you had experience with this approach? Do you think an isolation strategy is effective?

2. Can you give an example of speech that is common despite being potentially harmful to others? Why do you think people engage in it?

3. Hate speech—speech that may incite violence against a protected individual or group—is illegal in many European countries, but is allowed in the United States, under the First Amendment. Would you want your government, workplace, or school to regulate hate speech? If yes, why and how? If not, why not?

METSORA'

❖ Twitter

Twitter founder, Jack Dorsey, said he named his 140-character-maximum social networking and microblogging service Twitter because the word's definition, "birdlike chatter," perfectly described sending "a short burst of inconsequential information." This definition is relevant to an issue raised in Parashat Metsora', which addresses the purification process for a person afflicted with *tzara'at*, the skin lesion, in this case resulting from improper speech:

וְצִוָּה הַכֹּהֵן וְלָקַח לַמִּטַּהֵר שְׁתֵּי צִפֳּרִים חַיּוֹת טְהֹרוֹת וְעֵץ אֶרֶז וּשְׁנִי תוֹלַעַת וְאֵזֹב: (ויקרא יד, ד)

The priest shall order two live clean birds, cedar wood, crimson stuff, and hyssop to be brought for him who is to be cleansed. (Lev. 14:4)

Rashi elaborates on the birds' role as part of the purification process:

טהרות: פרט לעוף טמא. לפי שהנגעים באין על לשון הרע, שהוא מעשה פטפוטי דברים, לפיכך הוזקקו לטהרתו צפרים, שמפטפטין תמיד בצפצוף קול: (רש"י, שם)

clean [birds]: [L]esions of *tzara'at* come as a result of derogatory speech [לְשׁוֹן הָרָע], which is an action [involving] chattering. Therefore, a requirement for his purification are birds that twitter constantly with chirping sounds. (Rashi, Lev. 14:4)

As Rashi explains, birds are required for purifying the person with *tzara'at* because his birdlike chattering caused his affliction. One should be mindful of how one "tweets" both on- and off-line, and perhaps maintain as safe a distance from such activity as necessary.

Questions for Discussion

1. Have you ever tweeted or posted information about someone or something that you later regretted? How did you handle it?
2. For historical reasons the written word is typically accorded more credibility than the spoken word. Consequently, from the perspective of *tzara'at*, should a person exercise even greater discretion in written communication than in verbal communication? Explain.
3. Do you think adults and children have different capacities to exercise judgment when talking about others on social media? If so, would you restrict or monitor your children's involvement online? Are there ways to do this while still giving them privacy?

....

❖ *Die Goldene Medina*

More than two million Jews immigrated to the United States from 1880 to 1924, drawn in large part by the perception that America was *die goldene medina*—the "golden country." Needless to say, those who expected to find the streets paved with gold were greatly disappointed. This week's parashah, however, alludes to a much earlier episode of Jewish immigration in which the Jews did in fact find gold awaiting them.

כִּי תָבֹאוּ אֶל אֶרֶץ כְּנַעַן אֲשֶׁר אֲנִי נֹתֵן לָכֶם לַאֲחֻזָּה וְנָתַתִּי נֶגַע צָרַעַת
בְּבֵית אֶרֶץ אֲחֻזַּתְכֶם: (ויקרא יד, לד)

When you enter the land of Canaan that I give you as a possession, and I inflict an eruptive plague upon a house in the land you possess. (Lev. 14:34)

Rashi explains why a house would be afflicted with *tzara'at*:

ונתתי נגע צרעת: בשורה היא להם שהנגעים באים עליהם, לפי
שהטמינו אמוריים מטמוניות של זהב בקירות בתיהם כל ארבעים שנה
שהיו ישראל במדבר, ועל ידי הנגע נותץ הבית ומוצאן: (רש"י, שם)

and I inflict an eruptive plague: This is an announcement to them [the Jews] that lesions will come upon them [the houses] because the Amorites hid treasures of gold inside the walls of their houses throughout the forty years that the Israelites were in the desert, and, on account of the lesion, [the Israelite] will demolish the house and find them. (Rashi, Lev. 14:34)

Rashi explains that by afflicting the houses with *tzara'at*, God provided a means for the Jews to discover the treasures hidden by the houses' previous owners. What had thus begun as a curious growth on the Jewish owner's house ended up being the source of an unexpected windfall, demonstrating that within adversity often lies opportunity.

Questions for Discussion

1. Did your ancestors leave their ancestral home in the nineteenth or twentieth century and settle in a new land? If so, describe what you know about their experience. What do you think were their greatest challenges and most satisfying achievements?
2. Describe an experience you had that at the time seemed to be a failure or a disaster, but later proved to be the genesis of a future success. What did you learn from this?
3. If you were to discover abundant gold hidden in your house, what would you do with your windfall? Would it change your life in a significant way?

❖ Flipper

For some readers, the title of this essay may bring back memories of the dolphin Flipper that starred in a 1960s television program by the same name. For others, it may bring to mind a person who buys, renovates, and sells homes. In flipping the house, the flipper may throw out perfectly functional furnishings, appliances, and fixtures that don't fit with the new décor. The issue of preserving a home's contents is raised in a verse from the parashah concerning a house suspected of having *tzara'at*.

וְצִוָּה הַכֹּהֵן וּפִנּוּ אֶת הַבַּיִת בְּטֶרֶם יָבֹא הַכֹּהֵן לִרְאוֹת
אֶת הַנֶּגַע וְלֹא יִטְמָא כָּל אֲשֶׁר בַּבָּיִת וְאַחַר כֵּן יָבֹא
הַכֹּהֵן לִרְאוֹת אֶת הַבָּיִת: (ויקרא יד, לו)

The priest shall order the house cleared before the priest enters to examine the plague, so that nothing in the house may become unclean; after that the priest shall enter to examine the house. (Lev. 14:36)

While the verse expresses concern that the contents of the house not become "unclean" (*tame*), Rashi specifies which items in particular are susceptible to contamination.

ולא יטמא כל אשר בבית: שאם לא יפנהו ויבא הכהן ויראה הנגע,
נזקק להסגר, וכל מה שבתוכו יטמא. ועל מה חסה תורה, אם על
כלי שטף, יטבילם ויטהרו, ואם על אוכלין ומשקין, יאכלם בימי
טומאתו, הא לא חסה התורה אלא על כלי חרס, שאין להם טהרה
במקוה: (רש"י, שם)

so that nothing in the house may become unclean: For if [the owner] does not empty it, and the priest comes and sees the lesion, the house will have to be quarantined and everything inside it will become unclean. And regarding what [objects] was the Torah concerned [that they not become unclean]? . . . [E]arthenware vessels, which cannot be purified in a ritual bath [*mikveh*] [and would thus sustain permanent damage if they were to become unclean]. (Rashi, Lev. 14:36)

Rashi explains that to avoid the possible contamination of earthenware vessels, which cannot be purified in a ritual bath, a house that might be determined to have *tzara'at* must be emptied out before the priest inspects it.

Notably, the Torah specifies that even a slanderer, who is to be punished by having his house smitten by *tzara'at*, should be spared any avoidable loss. In other words, individuals who act improperly should bear the consequences of their actions, but do not deserve punishment beyond what is required. This perspective is also consistent with the Torah's prohibition against unnecessary destruction of property (*bal tashchit*), derived from a verse that forbids a besieging army from cutting down fruit trees (see Deut. 20:19).

Questions for Discussion

1. What is your general approach toward keeping or relinquishing items you currently do not need, such as furnishings, excess supplies, and clothing that no longer fits?

2. In the U.S. criminal justice system, after a convict has completed a prison sentence or otherwise fulfilled the sentencing terms, his or her conviction remains indefinitely in the public record, revealed by both background and credit checks. As a result, even a rehabilitated convict may face persistent obstacles to getting a job or renting an apartment. Do you think these ongoing burdens imposed by a prior conviction are justified? Why or why not?

3. Overall, do the people you know who've been found to act improperly face appropriate consequences for their actions? Do you believe their punishment has tended to be overly extensive, insufficient, or just right?

'AḤAREI MOT

❖ Family Business

Parashat 'Aḥarei Mot discusses the service that took place in the Temple on Yom Kippur. The High Priest (*Kohen Gadol*) was primarily responsible for performing this service, as described in a verse from the parashah.

וְכִפֶּר הַכֹּהֵן אֲשֶׁר יִמְשַׁח אֹתוֹ וַאֲשֶׁר יְמַלֵּא אֶת יָדוֹ לְכַהֵן תַּחַת אָבִיו וְלָבַשׁ אֶת בִּגְדֵי הַבָּד בִּגְדֵי הַקֹּדֶשׁ: (ויקרא טז, לב)

The priest who has been anointed and ordained to serve as priest in place of his father shall make expiation. He shall put on the linen vestments, the sacral vestments. (Lev. 16:32)

Rashi comments on the reference to the son of the High Priest serving in place of his father:

לכהן תחת אביו: ללמד שאם בנו ממלא את מקומו הוא קודם לכל אדם: (רש"י, שם)

to serve as priest in place of his father: This teaches us that if his son is capable of taking his father's place, he takes precedence over everyone else. (Rashi, Lev. 16:32)

Rashi explains that when the time comes to replace the High Priest, his son takes precedence over the other priests, provided he is qualified for the post. Thus Aaron, the first High Priest, was succeeded by his capable son Eleazar (see Deut. 10:6).

Is nepotism, or favoring one's own relatives when hiring, justified in our day? Bringing even the most competent relatives on staff may rub some the wrong way. And, occasionally, when personality differences arise, they can be more challenging to resolve because of complex loyalties.

That said, there are also good reasons for preferring relatives. First, they may have a long-term commitment to enrich the enterprise derived from their loyalty to and desire to help the family. Second, having grown up in the family, they may have extensive knowledge of the enterprise on day one. Third, due to the owner's familiarity with relatives—both their strengths and weaknesses—it may be less risky to hire them than candidates whose personalities and skills are known only from a resume and interview. Being "the boss's child" may be a legitimate qualification for a job.

Questions for Discussion

1. Have you ever worked with a family member? If so, how did your shared family background benefit and possibly upset the working relationship and your personal relationship?
2. Do you believe it is fair for an executive to hire his or her own children over other candidates whose qualifications are the same or even better? Does it make a difference whether the executive is self-employed or works for a private company or the government?
3. Would you want to be part of a family business? If so, what business and why? What strengths do you think your family would bring to the enterprise?

❖ Blood Libel

Widespread since the Middle Ages, the blood libel alleging that Jews murder non-Jews (especially Christian children) to use their blood for religious rituals (such as making matzah for Passover) has resulted in the murder of thousands of Jews and the persecution of countless Jewish communities. Its enduring nature is all the more shocking because its premise—that Jews consume blood—clearly contradicts a prohibition in the parashah:

עַל כֵּן אָמַרְתִּי לִבְנֵי יִשְׂרָאֵל כָּל נֶפֶשׁ מִכֶּם לֹא תֹאכַל דָּם וְהַגֵּר הַגָּר בְּתוֹכְכֶם לֹא יֹאכַל דָּם: (ויקרא יז, יב)

Therefore I say to the Israelite people: No person among you shall partake of blood, nor shall the stranger who resides among you partake of blood. (Lev. 17:12)

Rashi explains why the verse includes the word *kol* (כָּל), which means "every," as in "every person among you shall not partake of blood":

כל נפש מכם: להזהיר גדולים על הקטנים: (רש"י, שם)

Every person among you: [This phrase] comes to warn adults regarding minors [that they should not eat blood]. (Rashi, Lev. 17:12)

Rashi explains that even children who have not reached the age of majority (bar or bat mitzvah), and are thus not obligated to keep the mitzvot (commandments), should nevertheless be trained to avoid consuming blood.

The Torah's proscription against consuming blood is not fundamentally because some might find it distasteful—after all, animal organs that some people abstain from eating, such the brain and heart, are kosher. Rather, the Torah seems to regard blood as unsuitable to ingest because it is a fundamental element of life—inextricably linked to an animal's soul (see Lev. 17:11).

This is one of countless examples in the Torah in which Jewish children are to be educated so that they are prepared for the responsibilities of adulthood. As another example, the Torah teaches that very young Jewish children are to wear tzitzit, a four-cornered garment with fringes in the corners that symbolize the Torah's 613 mitzvot (commandments). The tzitzit are intended to cultivate a mitzvah consciousness that will grow with the child.

Questions for Discussion

1. The blood libel has often reared its ugly head when a non-Jewish child has been murdered and the killer has not been identified. What do you believe can be done to counter this fabricated incrimination?
2. Have you ever experienced being scapegoated as a Jew for a societal problem? If so, how did you respond at the time, and how would you react today?
3. When growing up, was Judaism presented to you as a way of life for which you needed to be prepared? If so, what type of preparation did you receive and how would you evaluate it? If not, does this paradigm make sense to you?

❖ Law and Order

While Judaism is referred to as a "religion," this term does not adequately capture its breadth. Like other religions, Judaism addresses

God, prayer, ritual, the origins of humankind, and the need for existential meaning. But Judaism also encompasses (among other things) a comprehensive legal system that has governed all facets of the Jewish nation in its homeland and in the Diaspora for thousands of years. As such, Judaism includes the entire range of civil and criminal laws typically found in most countries' legal codes. A verse in the parashah makes reference to this dimension of Judaism.

אֶת מִשְׁפָּטַי תַּעֲשׂוּ וְאֶת חֻקֹּתַי תִּשְׁמְרוּ לָלֶכֶת בָּהֶם אֲנִי יְהֹוָה אֱלֹהֵיכֶם: (ויקרא יח, ד)

My rules alone shall you observe, and faithfully follow My laws: I the Lord am your God. (Lev. 18:4)

Rashi clarifies what is meant by "My rules" (מִשְׁפָּטַי):

את משפטי תעשו: אלו דברים האמורים בתורה במשפט, שאלו לא נאמרו, היו כדאי לאמרן: (רש"י, שם)

My rules alone shall you observe: These are matters mentioned in the Torah as law, which if they were not mentioned, would have been proper to mention. (Rashi, Lev. 18:4)

As Rashi explains, "My rules" refers to laws (*mishpatim*) that the Jews would have enacted even if they had not been specified in the Torah, such as prohibitions against murder and robbery (see *Bavli Yoma* 67b). Rashi subsequently contrasts this category of laws with another called *chukim*—edicts that defy human understanding. *Chukim* such as the prohibitions against eating pork and against wearing a garment containing both wool and linen (*shatnez*) lack a readily understood rationale and thus would not have been enacted but for the Torah's command.

Ancient Israel had many of the hallmarks found in modern civil society, such as an extensive court system that governed all elements of civil and criminal life. Most cases were heard by a court of three judges (*beit din*), who interrogated witnesses, rendered verdicts, and imposed sentences without the use of juries (see *Mishnah Sanhedrin* 1:1).

Capital cases were heard by courts of twenty-three judges (lesser sanhedrin), many of which existed throughout the Land of Israel (see *Mishnah Sanhedrin* 1:4). The lesser sanhedrin conducted itself so as to maximize the likelihood of acquittal. For example, a majority of one (twelve of twenty-three) was sufficient to acquit, but a majority of two (thirteen of twenty-three) was necessary to convict; and an acquittal was allowed on the first day of deliberations, but a conviction was not allowed before the second day, so that the judges would have at least one night to possibly discover a basis for acquittal (see 4:1).

A court of seventy-one judges (Great Sanhedrin) sat on the Temple Mount in Jerusalem and had jurisdiction over certain capital cases, declarations of war, and establishing lesser sanhedrins (see *Mishnah Sanhedrin* 1:5). For testimony in a legal action to be admissible, two witnesses were generally required (see Deut. 19:15). Judicial punishments included monetary penalties, lashes, death penalty, and excommunication.

Questions for Discussion

1. Western society is largely based on the Judeo-Christian tradition. In what ways does your country reflect Jewish principles and values? In what ways do you believe your nation has benefited from these traditions?

2. As the discussion above indicates, Judaism is a religion that encompasses a comprehensive legal system. From your

perspective, what else does Judaism encompass? What part
or parts of Judaism are most important to you?

3. What institutions of your country's civil society do you believe function well, and why? What hallmarks do
you believe are in need of significant change, and why?
What changes would you like to see?

KEDOSHIM

❖ Do Something!

In 1964 a woman named Kitty Genovese was killed in Queens, New York. What made her murder memorable were the later reports that thirty-eight people had witnessed her attack, and yet no one did anything to protect her. Psychologists now call such situations where multiple onlookers fail to assist a victim the "bystander effect." While one might expect that the more people who witness an attack, the more likely the victim is to receive assistance, the bystander effect results in the opposite paradigm: multiple onlookers attenuate each bystander's sense of individual responsibility. Researchers have found that the greater the number of bystanders, the less likely it is that any one of them will help. These findings relate directly to a verse from Parashat Kedoshim.

לֹא תֵלֵךְ רָכִיל בְּעַמֶּיךָ לֹא תַעֲמֹד עַל דַּם
רֵעֶךָ אֲנִי יְהוָה: (ויקרא יט, טז)

Do not deal basely with your countrymen. Do not profit by the blood of your fellow: I am the Lord. (Lev. 19:16)

Rashi explains the meaning of the second part of this verse:

לא תעמד על דם רעך: לראות במיתתו ואתה יכול להצילו, כגון
טובע בנהר, וחיה או לסטים באים עליו: (רש"י, שם)

Do not profit by the blood of your fellow: to watch his death [when] you are able to save him, as, for example, if he is drowning in a river, or if a wild beast or robbers come upon him. (Rashi, Lev. 19:16)

Rashi explains that whenever it may be possible to help a person whose life is threatened, the bystander is obligated to come to his or her aid.

Bystanders, however, may be reluctant to intervene for reasons beyond the "bystander effect." First, people may be concerned about putting their own lives in jeopardy. Second, particularly in litigious societies such as ours, people may be concerned about exposing themselves to legal liability should they fail to save the victim. Many governments have therefore enacted Good Samaritan laws to protect rescuers from bearing legal liability for their good-faith efforts.

While the opportunity to prevent a murder may seem like a remote possibility, the exhortation to intercede can be understood to apply to everyday situations. For example, a bully in a school setting is often empowered through the silent acquiescence of bystanders, and the victim may experience his or her verbal assault as a psychological murder, a murder of the soul. There have been many reported instances of bullied young people committing suicide. Similarly, slander and *lashon ha-ra* can flourish only when people are willing to listen to the speaker.

Questions for Discussion

1. Do you know of someone whose life or safety was threatened? If so, did others intercede to assist? What happened?
2. If you witnessed someone in danger and many other people were present, do you believe you would be the first or

one of the first to act to save that person's life? Under what circumstances would you be more or less likely to do so?

3. Have you ever heard a friend or acquaintance make a comment you regarded as demeaning to a certain group of people (race, religion, etc.)? Did you protest? If not, why not?

❖ Making Excuses

Benjamin Franklin once wrote, "He that is good for making excuses is seldom good for anything else." While many people might agree that a person who overdoes excuses rubs them the wrong way, a verse from the parashah encourages us to view excusers—and everyone else—in a positive light.

לֹא תִקֹּם וְלֹא תִטֹּר אֶת בְּנֵי עַמֶּךָ וְאָהַבְתָּ לְרֵעֲךָ כָּמוֹךָ אֲנִי יְהוָֹה:
(ויקרא יט, יח)

You shall not take vengeance or bear a grudge against your countrymen. Love your fellow as yourself: I am the Lord. (Lev. 19:18)

Rashi comments on the mitzvah (commandment) to love your fellow as yourself:

וְאָהַבְתָּ לְרֵעֲךָ כָּמוֹךָ: אמר רבי עקיבא זה כלל גדול בתורה: (רש"י, שם)

Love your fellow as yourself: Rabbi Akiva said: "This is a fundamental principle of the Torah." (Rashi, Lev. 19:18)

Certain commandments in Judaism, such as keeping the Sabbath and observing kashrut (the dietary laws), are particular to Jews. Others, such as "love your fellow as yourself," have universal relevance. Note that Rashi stresses the imperative to observe this universal command to love others as we love ourselves by quoting Rabbi Akiva's comment: "This is a fundamental principle of the Torah."

Given the complexity of human relations, how can this ideal possibly be put into practice? Counterintuitively, understanding how people make excuses for themselves may help. After all, almost all of us have become experts at excusing ourselves. If we're late for an appointment, some of us launch into long stories describing all the events that led to our tardiness. Just as there may be legitimate excuses for our imperfect behavior, there may be equally legitimate excuses for other people's less than impeccable conduct. Giving other people the same slack we naturally give ourselves can be another way of expressing love of one's fellow as oneself.

Questions for Discussion

1. Describe a time when you were upset with someone, perhaps for being late. Can you recast that experience by making excuses for this person? Does that change your feelings about the incident in any way?

2. Who accepts you unconditionally? Did you do something to deserve this and, if so, what? If not, what is the source of this unconditional acceptance?

3. How do you understand the commandment to "Love your fellow as yourself"? How might you do this?

❖ Everyone's Business

The Talmud relates that when a person is escorted to the after-life, one of the six questions asked is whether you were honest in business (*Bavli Shabbat* 31a). A verse in the parashah delineates ethical business practices:

לֹא תַעֲשׂוּ עָוֶל בַּמִּשְׁפָּט בַּמִּדָּה בַּמִּשְׁקָל וּבַמְּשׂוּרָה: (ויקרא יט, לה)

You shall not falsify measures of length, weight, or capacity. (Lev. 19:35)

Rashi focuses on the meaning of the Hebrew word *mishpat* (מִשְׁפָּט), which usually means "justice" or "judgment":

לא תעשו עול במשפט: אם לדין, הרי כבר נאמר לא תעשו עול במשפט (פסוק טו), ומהו משפט השנוי כאן, הוא המדה והמשקל והמשורה. מלמד שהמודד נקרא דיין, שאם שיקר במדה הרי הוא כמקלקל את הדין וקרוי עול, שנאוי, ומשוקץ, חרם ותועבה. וגורם לחמשה דברים האמורים בדיין מטמא את הארץ, ומחלל את השם, ומסלק את השכינה, ומפיל את ישראל בחרב, ומגלה אותם מארצם: (רש"י, שם)

You shall not falsify measures: If we are dealing [here] with litigation, Scripture has already stated: "You shall not render an unfair decision [*mishpat*, מִשְׁפָּט]" (Lev. 19:15). So what is the meaning of the word *mishpat* [מִשְׁפָּט] that is taught here? It refers to [behavior in dealing with] measures, weights, or liquid measures. This teaches us that one who measures [some merchandise he is selling] is called a "judge," for if he falsifies the measure, he is considered to be as one who perverts justice. (Rashi, Lev. 19:35)

On a global scale, whether or not we are party to any questionable transactions, honesty in business affects every one of us—because a healthy economy is premised on integrity in commerce. If multiple businesses "pervert justice" by falsification of measures and other means, this erodes integrity, the volume of transactions declines, the cost of doing business increases, and eventually consumers pay the price. Given this reality, honesty in business is everyone's business.

Questions for Discussion

1. Retail sales are increasingly dominated by chain stores such as Walmart, Ikea, and cvs. In your opinion, are chains or mom-and-pop stores more likely to exhibit honesty in their business transactions, both with suppliers and with the public? Explain.

2. Why do you think honesty in business is considered so significant that the Talmud tells us it is one of six questions a person is asked about in the afterlife? Are the temptations toward dishonesty more alluring in business than in other areas?

3. Are you ever tempted to falsify or overlook a financial transaction in your favor at work or when shopping or dining out? Do you overcome these temptations? If so, how?

'EMOR

❖ Nobel Nobleman

When the Israeli writer Shmuel Yosef Agnon received the Nobel Prize in Literature in 1966, his acceptance speech was unique in the Nobel annals for its specifically Jewish content. In the presence of the Swedish king, Agnon recited the blessing the Talmud prescribes for a Jew who sees a non-Jewish monarch (see *Bavli Berakhot* 58a). Parashat 'Emor offers another example of Jewish law according special recognition to someone—in this instance, a priest (*kohen*)—because of his status in the community.

וְקִדַּשְׁתּוֹ כִּי אֶת לֶחֶם אֱלֹהֶיךָ הוּא מַקְרִיב קָדֹשׁ יִהְיֶה לָּךְ כִּי קָדוֹשׁ אֲנִי
יְהֹוָה מְקַדִּשְׁכֶם: (ויקרא כא, ח)

And you must treat them as holy, since they offer the food of your God; they shall be holy to you, for I the Lord who sanctify you am holy. (Lev. 21:8)

Rashi explains how the priest (*kohen*) is to be treated:

קדש יהיה לך: נהוג בו קדושה לפתוח ראשון בכל דבר ולברך ראשון
בסעודה: (רש"י, שם)

they shall be holy to you: Treat him with sanctity, to take precedence in all matters [of sanctity] and to bless first at a meal. (Rashi, Lev. 21:8)

In ancient times, *kohanim* were in charge of the Temple offerings. Rashi explains that now they are given precedence in all matters of sanctity. For example, when the Torah is read in synagogue, a *kohen* is to be given the honor of reciting the blessing over the first section of the Torah reading. Similarly, at a meal's conclusion a *kohen* is to lead the Grace after Meals (*Birkat ha-Mazon*). To this day, *kohanim* retain communal responsibilities, such as blessing those assembled in synagogues on the festivals.

Torah scholars are another group that receives special recognition under Jewish law, as reflected in the mitzvah (commandment) to stand in the presence of a Torah scholar (see *Bavli Kiddushin* 32b). Judaism thereby legislates public recognition of and respect for communal figures who embody Jewish values.

Questions for Discussion

1. Describe someone you know whose life embodies Jewish values. What character traits and accomplishments of his or hers do you admire? Does he or she receive public recognition and respect within the Jewish community?
2. If you were in a position of Jewish leadership, what would you consider to be its greatest challenges and rewards?
3. Describe a segment of society that you feel does not receive recognition commensurate with its contribution. What actions or policies would you propose to address this inequity?

❖ It's the Thought That Counts

Numerous studies have shown the significance of what's called the placebo effect—the perceived improvement in one's medical condition after taking a sugar pill or undergoing a sham procedure. This finding indicates that often our thoughts and beliefs can themselves affect how healthy we feel. More generally, research in fields such as medicine, sports, and relationships supports the notion that our thoughts can influence our reality. The importance of one's thoughts is a well-established principle in Judaism, as seen in the parashah concerning sacrifices.

וְכִי תִזְבְּחוּ זֶבַח תּוֹדָה לַיהֹוָה לִרְצֹנְכֶם תִּזְבָּחוּ: (ויקרא כב, כט)

When you sacrifice a thanksgiving offering to the Lord, sacrifice it so that it may be acceptable in your favor. (Lev. 22:29)

Rashi describes what is necessary for the sacrifice to be accepted:

לרצנכם תזבחו: תחלת זביחתכם הזהרו שתהא לרצון לכם. ומהו הרצון? ביום ההוא יאכל: לא בא להזהיר אלא שתהא שחיטה על מנת כן, אל תשחטוהו על מנת לאכלו למחר, שאם תחשבו בו מחשבת פסול לא יהא לכם לרצון: (רש"י, שם)

sacrifice it so that it may be acceptable in your favor: At the outset of its slaughtering, be careful that it should bring acceptance for you; and what is it that assures its acceptance? "It shall be eaten on the same day [that it is sacrificed]" [v. 30]. This comes to warn that the slaughtering should be for this purpose—do not slaughter it in order to eat it tomorrow, for if you have invalidating thoughts, it will not be acceptable for you. (Rashi, Lev. 22:29)

Rashi explains that for the sacrifice to be valid, the person offering it needs not only to eat the animal on the day of its slaughter, but to know in his mind at the time of slaughter that he will eat the animal that day. If he even thinks of eating the animal on the subsequent day, the sacrifice is unacceptable.

Here the Torah teaches that people have the ability to control their thoughts, and thus are held accountable for what they think. This recognition is at the base of cognitive behavioral therapy, a psychotherapeutic approach positing that replacing deluded and harmful thoughts with realistic and helpful thoughts can lead to positive self-development. For example, a person might despair of being able to complete a big assignment with the thought, "I'm a failure." But by recognizing, through an honest assessment of one's past, that one has had both successes and failures in life, a person may be helped to understand that it is not reasonable to believe this assignment will inevitably end in failure. Some people have achieved dramatic changes in their lives by changing their thoughts.

Questions for Discussion

1. Do you ever have self-defeating thoughts? Is it possible for you to scrutinize the accuracy of a negative thought and come to see a more nuanced truth?
2. Another thought-changing technique is visualization: generating a vivid mental image of oneself engaging successfully in a selected activity or situation, with the goal of achieving the same benefits when in the real situation. Can you think of an area in which you would like to improve? How might visualizations help?
3. Do you believe that people can control their thoughts? How do you account for the difficulty many individuals experience in turning off unpleasant thoughts?

❖ Parting Is Such Sweet Sorrow

In William Shakespeare's *Romeo and Juliet*, Juliet expresses her feelings about having to bid farewell to her beloved Romeo with the famous words, "Parting is such sweet sorrow." A verse from the parashah that discusses Shemini Atzeret, the holiday on the eighth day of Sukkot, expresses a similar sentiment.

שִׁבְעַת יָמִים תַּקְרִיבוּ אִשֶּׁה לַיהֹוָה בַּיּוֹם הַשְּׁמִינִי מִקְרָא קֹדֶשׁ יִהְיֶה לָכֶם וְהִקְרַבְתֶּם אִשֶּׁה לַיהֹוָה עֲצֶרֶת הִוא כָּל מְלֶאכֶת עֲבֹדָה לֹא תַעֲשׂוּ: (ויקרא כג, לו)

Seven days you shall bring offerings by fire to the Lord. On the eighth day you shall observe a sacred occasion and bring an offering by fire to the Lord; it is a solemn gathering: you shall not work at your occupations. (Lev. 23:36)

Rashi comments on the unusual use of the word *atzeret* (עֲצֶרֶת, gathering), which literally means "holding back," to describe the eighth day of the festival:

עצרת הוא: עצרתי אתכם אצלי כמלך שזימן את בניו לסעודה לכך וכך ימים, כיון שהגיע זמנן להפטר אמר בני בבקשה מכם, עכבו עמי עוד יום אחד, קשה עלי פרידתכם: (רש"י, שם)

it is a solemn gathering: I have held you back [*atzarti*, עָצַרְתִּי] with me, like a king who invited his children for a feast for a certain number of days, [and] when the time came for them to leave, he said: "My children, I beg of you, remain with me one more day; your leaving is difficult for me." (Rashi, Lev. 23:36)

In explaining why Shemini Atzeret is referred to by a word that means "holding back," Rashi vividly conveys God's love for the Jewish people.

Questions for Discussion

1. Recall a time when you had difficulty saying good-bye to someone. What feelings did you experience?
2. In the same situation, what thoughts underlay your feelings?
3. How can sorrow be described as "sweet"? Are there types of sorrow that cannot be described as "sweet"?

BE-HAR

❖ Universal Care

Parashat Be-har begins with a discussion of the sabbatical (*shemitah*) year—the final year of the seven-year agricultural cycle in Israel. The Torah teaches that during this year, one is not permitted to plant or tend one's crops, but rather must let one's land lie fallow. In addition, others are allowed equal access to any produce that happens to grow by itself on one's land, as specified in this verse:

וְהָיְתָה שַׁבַּת הָאָרֶץ לָכֶם לְאָכְלָה לְךָ וּלְעַבְדְּךָ וְלַאֲמָתֶךָ וְלִשְׂכִירְךָ וּלְתוֹשָׁבְךָ הַגָּרִים עִמָּךְ: (ויקרא כה, ו)

But you may eat whatever the land during its sabbath will produce—you, your male and female slaves, the hired and bound laborers who live with you. (Lev. 25:6)

Rashi clarifies who is referred to by the term "hired and bound laborers":

וְלִשְׂכִירְךָ וּלְתוֹשָׁבְךָ: אַף הַגּוֹיִם: (רַשִׁ"י, שם)

the hired and bound laborers: Even the non-Jews. (Rashi, Lev. 25:6)

Rashi explains that both Jewish and non-Jewish employees may partake of the land's produce during the sabbatical year—another example of the Torah's concern for all people's well-being.

As members of an extended family descended from the Patriarch Abraham, Jews have a special responsibility to help one another (see Rashi, Exod. 22:24). At the same time, consistent with their role as a "light unto the nations" (Isa. 42:6), they also bear responsibility to contribute to the welfare of humankind (see *Bavli Gittin* 61a). In our day, some Jewish institutions, such as synagogues and Jewish schools, focus on serving members of the Jewish community. Other organizations, such as Jewish hospitals and social service agencies, were often founded to address Jewish communal needs, but grew to serve the entire cross-section of society.

Questions for Discussion

1. Name a Jewish organization that you believe does important work. Who does it serve, and what has it accomplished?
2. Do you believe the Jews have fulfilled their biblical charge to be a "light unto the nations"? Have any other nations served in such a capacity?
3. When choosing to support an organization or cause, do you consider its connection (if any) to Jews or Judaism? If you principally support Jewish organizations, how would you respond to a charge that you are being too parochial? If you predominantly support non-Jewish organizations, how would you respond to a charge that you are abandoning your people?

❖ Early Intervention

In the United States, a network of government-run "early intervention" programs provides young children experiencing developmental delays with services to promote their healthy development. Such programs are premised on the belief that addressing developmental delays early in childhood will achieve better outcomes, at a lower cost, than intervening at a later time when the delays have become more severe. The parashah also advises a strategy of addressing problems at their inception.

וְכִי יָמוּךְ אָחִיךָ וּמָטָה יָדוֹ עִמָּךְ וְהֶחֱזַקְתָּ בּוֹ גֵּר וְתוֹשָׁב וָחַי עִמָּךְ:
(ויקרא כה, לה)

If your kinsman, being in straits, comes under your authority, and you hold him as though a resident alien, let him live by your side. (Lev. 25:35)

Rashi elaborates on the obligation to support one's kinsman in his time of need:

והחזקת בו: אל תניחהו שירד ויפול ויהיה קשה להקימו, אלא חזקהו משעת מוטת היד. למה זה דומה, למשאוי שעל החמור, עודהו על החמור אחד תופס בו ומעמידו, נפל לארץ, חמשה אין מעמידין אותו: (רש"י, שם)

and you hold him: Do not allow him to decline [financially] and collapse [altogether], in which case it would be difficult to raise him [from his dire poverty], rather strengthen him from the time his hand falters. To what can this be compared? To a load on a donkey. As long as it is still on the donkey, one person can grasp it and hold it up, [but if] it falls to the ground, [even] five people cannot pick it up. (Rashi, Lev. 25:35)

Rashi explains that the Torah's requirement to promptly assist a kinsman who experiences economic difficulty is necessary to prevent his financial collapse. If a person does not intercede in a timely fashion, the crisis is liable to worsen to such a degree that future interventions may fail.

In a similar fashion, early intervention operates under the principle that there are "critical periods" during which the nervous systems of young children are most receptive to developing certain skills. If children fail to develop the needed skills during each critical period, greater effort must be expended in hope of their subsequently developing those skills. Therefore, when children are delayed in meeting normal developmental milestones, early intervention provides remedial services in an effort to address these delays before the critical periods have passed.

Questions for Discussion

1. Describe a difficulty you encountered where, in retrospect, you might have benefited from taking corrective measures at an earlier time.

2. While it takes fewer resources to assist a person just beginning to experience economic distress than those required at a later stage of the process, and the likelihood of a successful outcome is greater in the former scenario, governmental interventions may be delayed for a number of reasons. Some assistance programs provide benefits only to the neediest people. Sometimes people who have recently experienced a setback are too embarrassed to accept charity. What can be done to address these and other shortcomings in the economic safety net?

3. If you could start an organization that would use a preventive approach to address a problem, what would it be and how would it work?

....

❖ Employee Relations

It is not unusual for a host or hostess to offer guests a cup of coffee following a meal and to graciously serve those who accept the offer. However, if the same host or hostess is asked to serve his or her boss a cup of coffee, that grace could well be replaced by resentment. A verse from the parashah addresses some of the issues involved in serving another human being:

וְכִי יָמוּךְ אָחִיךָ עִמָּךְ וְנִמְכַּר לָךְ לֹא תַעֲבֹד
בּוֹ עֲבֹדַת עָבֶד: (ויקרא כה, לט)

If your kinsman under you continues in straits and must give himself over to you, do not subject him to the treatment of a slave. (Lev. 25:39)

Rashi explains what is meant by "the treatment of a slave":

עבדת עבד: עבודה של גנאי, שיהא ניכר בה כעבד, שלא יוליך כליו
אחריו לבית המרחץ ולא ינעול לו מנעליו: (רש"י, שם)

the treatment of a slave: Degrading work, through which he is made to look like a slave—that he not carry his [the master's] clothes after him to the bathhouse, [or] that he not put on his shoes for him. (Rashi, Lev. 25:39)

Rashi explains that the verse prohibits a Jew from requiring his Hebrew slave to do work characteristic of a slave and provides examples of such work.

The Torah upholds the dignity of workers in multiple ways. They are not only to be treated justly; they cannot be required to perform work that would compromise their sense of self-respect.

Questions for Discussion

1. Describe a job or responsibility you were proud to have, and why you felt that way.
2. Have you ever been treated at work in a way that undermined your sense of dignity? If so, what happened and what insights did you gain from this experience?
3. Have you ever had a boss or supervisor who seemed to bring out the best in you? What personal qualities did he or she possess that helped create this dynamic?

....

BE-ḤUKKOTAI

❖ Worth the Effort

Parashat Be-ḥukkotai recounts the abundant blessings the Jewish people are to merit if they are faithful to the Torah. The opening verse specifies what is expected of them.

אִם בְּחֻקֹּתַי תֵּלֵכוּ וְאֶת מִצְוֹתַי תִּשְׁמְרוּ וַעֲשִׂיתֶם אֹתָם: (ויקרא כו, ג)

If you follow My laws and faithfully observe My commandments. (Lev. 26:3)

Rashi explains the opening words of this verse:

אם בחקתי תלכו: יכול זה קיום המצות, כשהוא אומר ואת מצותי תשמרו, הרי קיום המצות אמור, הא מה אני מקיים אם בחקתי תלכו, שתהיו עמלים בתורה: (רש"י, שם)

If you follow My laws: I might think that this [refers to] the fulfillment of the commandments. [However,] when [the verse] goes on to say, "and faithfully observe My commandments," the fulfillment of the commandments is [already] mentioned. So how do I interpret: "If you follow My laws"? [It means that] you should toil in [the study of] Torah. (Rashi, Lev. 26:3)

Rashi explains that this verse directs us not only to observe the Torah's commandments, but also to toil (שתהיו עמלים) in the study of Torah.

What else can we learn from Rashi's analysis?

While all Jews are instructed to toil in Torah study, how an individual Jew is to exert him or herself depends on the person. For someone with little formal Jewish education, reading a verse in the original Hebrew may be a significant achievement. For an experienced student of Torah, learning a Hebrew text with its commentaries may be a suitable goal.

Because a person is supposed to toil in the study of Torah, there is no reason to avoid difficult passages or to become discouraged when encountering obstacles in learning—after all, such challenges are to be expected.

And, given that Torah study is considered the preeminent mitzvah (commandment)—equivalent to many others combined—exerting oneself in the study of Torah is worth the effort (ותלמוד תורה כנגד כולם; *Bavli Shabbat* 127a). As it says concerning the Torah, "If you seek it as you do silver [a]nd search for it as for treasures, [t]hen you will . . . attain knowledge of God" (אִם תְּבַקְשֶׁנָּה כַכָּסֶף וְכַמַּטְמוֹנִים תַּחְפְּשֶׂנָּה. אָז תָּבִין יִרְאַת יְהוָֹה וְדַעַת אֱלֹהִים תִּמְצָא) (Prov. 2:4–5).

Questions for Discussion

1. Have you ever applied yourself to studying Torah or Judaism? If so, why, and what did you learn?
2. Is there a particular facet of the Torah or Judaism you would like to study? If so, why and what do you hope to learn?
3. What would it take for you to commit yourself to studying the Torah regularly? What would you seek to gain from your efforts?

❖ The Blessing of Peace

The United Nations was founded in the wake of World War II to "save succeeding generations from the scourge of war" and promote "international peace and security" (see the preamble to the Charter of the United Nations). There is perhaps no greater symbol of this mission than the iconic sculpture at UN headquarters featuring a man beating his sword into a plowshare, recalling the verse from Isaiah on which it is based ("And they shall beat their swords into plowshares . . . [t]hey shall never again know war," Isa. 2:4). Peace is also prominent among the myriad blessings God promises to bestow on the Jewish people if they are faithful to the Torah, as seen in this verse from the parashah.

וְנָתַתִּי שָׁלוֹם בָּאָרֶץ וּשְׁכַבְתֶּם וְאֵין מַחֲרִיד וְהִשְׁבַּתִּי חַיָּה רָעָה מִן הָאָרֶץ וְחֶרֶב לֹא תַעֲבֹר בְּאַרְצְכֶם: (ויקרא כו, ו)

I will grant peace in the land, and you shall lie down untroubled by anyone; I will give the land respite from vicious beasts, and no sword shall cross your land. (Lev. 26:6)

Rashi elaborates on the promise of peace:

ונתתי שלום: שמא תאמרו הרי מאכל והרי משתה, אם אין שלום אין כלום, תלמוד לומר אחר כל ז את ונתתי שלום בארץ, מכאן שהשלום שקול כנגד הכל. וכן הוא אומר עושה שלום ובורא את הכל: (רש"י, שם)

I will grant peace: Perhaps you will say, "Here is food, and here is drink [which are promised in the previous verse], but if there is no peace, there is nothing!" The verse [therefore] states after all this, "I will grant peace in the land." From here [we learn] that peace is equal to all [other blessings]. And thus it says [in the morning prayers], "He makes peace and creates everything." (Rashi, Lev. 26:6)

Rashi explains that even the blessings of prosperity promised in the previous verses may mean nothing in the absence of peace.

Today tens of millions of people around the world are living in war zones. Many are barely surviving, without adequate food, shelter, medical care, funds, or a safe environment for their families. Many of them face the constant threat of sudden death.

The blessing of peace is indeed equal to all other blessings.

Questions for Discussion

1. Do you think of peace as a blessing equal to all other blessings?
2. Do you believe it is possible to see more peace and less war in the future? What might it take to achieve this?
3. In his memoirs Winston Churchill, who led Great Britain to victory in World War II, wrote: "One day President Roosevelt told me that he was asking publicly for suggestions about what the war should be called. I said at once, 'The Unnecessary War.'" Why did Churchill call it "The Unnecessary War"? How might the lessons Churchill alluded to with that moniker be applied to potential flashpoints in the world today?

❖ Strength in Numbers

The parashah contains many blessings for the Jewish people, including one for victory over their enemies, described in the following verse:

וְרָדְפוּ מִכֶּם חֲמִשָּׁה מֵאָה וּמֵאָה מִכֶּם רְבָבָה יִרְדֹּפוּ וְנָפְלוּ אֹיְבֵיכֶם
לִפְנֵיכֶם לֶחָרֶב: (ויקרא כו, ח)

Five of you shall give chase to a hundred, and a hundred of you shall give chase to ten thousand; your enemies shall fall before you by the sword. (Lev. 26:8)

Rashi explains the inconsistency in the ratios of pursuer to pursued—5 pursuing 100 is 1:20, whereas 100 pursuing 10,000 is 1:100:

חמשה מאה ומאה מכם רבבה: וכי כך הוא החשבון, והלא לא
היה צריך לומר אלא מאה מכם שני אלפים ירדופו, אלא אינו דומה
מועטין העושין את התורה למרובין העושין את התורה: (רש"י, שם)

Five [of you shall give chase to a] hundred, and a hundred of you [shall give chase to] ten thousand: But is this calculation correct? Shouldn't it have stated: "and a hundred of you shall give chase to two thousand"? Rather, [this comes to tell us] there is no comparison between a few who fulfill the Torah and many who fulfill the Torah. (Rashi, Lev. 26:8)

Rashi explains that the inconsistent ratios in this verse teach us that when many fulfill the Torah's teachings, the consequences are multiplied beyond the expected proportionate impact.

In 2013 the chief rabbi of South Africa, Warren Goldstein, launched The Shabbos Project with the goal of having every South African Jew keep a single Sabbath in the company of others. Despite the fact that most South African Jews do not observe the Sabbath, that week the majority of the country's seventy-five thousand Jews kept the Sabbath—many for the first time. The impact was so powerful—both inside and outside South Africa—that The Shabbos Project has expanded into an annual event involving hundreds of Jewish communities worldwide. Exceeding his expectations, Rabbi Goldstein's initiative demonstrates what can be accomplished when Jews unite to fulfill the Torah.

Questions for Discussion

1. The largest undertaking of the Jewish community in the past two thousand years—and perhaps ever—was the establishment of the State of Israel in 1948. Israel had a Jewish population of six hundred thousand at its founding, and millions more Jews supported the Jewish people's return to their ancestral land during the pre-state years. What lessons do you take from the state's founding against seemingly insurmountable odds? How might these lessons be applied to address Israel's current challenges?

2. Are you part of or familiar with an organized Jewish community? If so, what do you regard as this community's crowning achievements? What else would you like to see this community achieve, and what role might you play in that process?

3. On the community level, The Shabbos Project typically includes a Thursday night challah bake, a Shabbat candle lighting, an interactive prayer service, a festive meal, a *Havdalah* service at Shabbat's conclusion, and a Saturday night

concert (although each participating community chooses its own programming). How would you feel about participating in The Shabbos Project if it were taking place in your community? What might you gain from participating, and what do you feel you have to give?

Numbers

BE-MIDBAR

❖ Love Languages

In *The Five Love Languages*, author Gary Chapman asserts that people express feelings of love or affection for one another in five primary ways: spending quality time together, giving gifts, speaking words of affirmation, performing acts of service, and sharing physical touch. Parashat Be-midbar, which opens with a census of the Jewish people, provides an example of a "love language" that God uses with the Jewish people.

וַיְדַבֵּר יְהֹוָה אֶל מֹשֶׁה בְּמִדְבַּר סִינַי בְּאֹהֶל מוֹעֵד בְּאֶחָד לַחֹדֶשׁ הַשֵּׁנִי בַּשָּׁנָה הַשֵּׁנִית לְצֵאתָם מֵאֶרֶץ מִצְרַיִם לֵאמֹר: (במדבר א, א)

On the first day of the second month, in the second year following the exodus from the land of Egypt, the Lord spoke to Moses in the wilderness of Sinai, in the Tent of Meeting, saying. (Num. 1:1)

God instructs Moses to take a census, whose details are described in subsequent verses. Rashi explains why God wanted to count the Jewish people at this time:

וידבר. במדבר סיני באחד לחדש: מתוך חיבתן לפניו מונה אותם כל שעה, כשיצאו ממצרים מנאן, וכשנפלו בעגל מנאן לידע מנין הנותרים. כשבא להשרות שכינתו עליהן מנאן. באחד בניסן הוקם המשכן, ובאחד באייר מנאם: (רש"י, שם)

On the first day . . . [the Lord] spoke [to Moses] in the wilderness of Sinai: Because they were dear to Him, He counted them often. (Rashi, Num. 1:1)

Rashi clarifies that God frequently counted the Jewish people as an expression of God's love for them.

Gary Chapman's notion of "love languages" is based on the premise that just as ineffective communication occurs when two people do not speak the same language, so too one's attempt to express caring for another can fail to have the desired impact when two people have different love languages. For example, a person who enjoys receiving gifts may naturally think that giving gifts is the best way to express affection. However, the gift recipient may think that spending quality time together is the ideal way to express affection and may not feel cherished when receiving gifts. By discussing what types of behaviors cause them to feel nurtured, people can be more fulfilled in their relationships.

Questions for Discussion

1. Which of the five primary ways to express love identified by Chapman would you most appreciate receiving from a family member? Does your choice change depending on the family member? Do your family members know your preference? If not, how would you feel about telling them?

2. Describe something memorable that a loved one did for you. Would you consider this as having been expressed in your "love language"?

3. Describe a time you gave a gift that reflected significant thought or effort on your part. What inspired you to give this gift to this person? How was it received?

❖ In Loco Parentis

The Latin term *in loco parentis* (in the place of a parent) refers to a relationship similar to that of a parent to a child, such as may occur in an educational setting. A verse in the parashah brings to mind such a relationship:

וְאֵלֶּה תּוֹלְדֹת אַהֲרֹן וּמֹשֶׁה בְּיוֹם דִּבֶּר יְהוָה
אֶת מֹשֶׁה בְּהַר סִינָי: (במדבר ג, א)

This is the line of Aaron and Moses at the time that the Lord spoke with Moses on Mount Sinai. (Num. 3:1)

Rashi explains why the verse refers to the descendants of "Aaron and Moses," given that the only descendants mentioned subsequently are those of Aaron, not Moses:

ואלה תולדת אהרן ומשה: ואינו מזכיר אלא בני אהרן. ונקראו תולדות משה, לפי שלמדן תורה. מלמד שכל המלמד את בן חבירו תורה, מעלה עליו הכתוב כאלו ילדו: (רש"י, שם)

This is the line of Aaron and Moses: It only mentions the sons of Aaron, yet they are called the descendants of Moses—because he [Moses] taught them Torah. This teaches us that whoever teaches another's son Torah is regarded as having begotten him. (Rashi, Num. 3:1)

Rashi explains that Aaron's children are considered to be Moses's children as well because Moses taught them Torah. This reflects the tremendous importance Judaism places on educating one's children.

Judaism considers it a mitzvah (commandment) for parents to teach their children Torah: "And teach them to your children—reciting them when you stay at home and when you are away, when you lie down and when you get up" וְלִמַּדְתֶּם אֹתָם אֶת בְּנֵיכֶם לְדַבֵּר בָּם בְּשִׁבְתְּךָ בְּבֵיתֶךָ וּבְלֶכְתְּךָ בַדֶּרֶךְ וּבְשָׁכְבְּךָ וּבְקוּמֶךָ (Deut. 11:19). The Talmud specifies five responsibilities a father has toward his son: circumcise him, redeem him (if he is a firstborn son), teach him Torah, marry him off, and teach him a trade (*Bavli Kiddushin* 29a).

While it may not be practical for most parents to educate their children themselves, they can arrange for their sons' and daughters' Jewish learning through a variety of means—perhaps more today than ever before in the history of the Jewish people.

Questions for Discussion

1. What was the primary source of your Jewish education? What role (if any) did your parents play?
2. Do you believe your knowledge of Judaism is sufficient to enable you to educate the next generation? If so, what would you like to teach? If not, would you like to become more knowledgeable?
3. Have you ever taught or been taught by someone in such a way that this person felt like family to you?

❖ Good Neighbors

Asking a neighbor to borrow a missing ingredient for a recipe may define the extent of our relationship with some neighbors, even though often there's much more to be gained from neighbors than a cup of flour or sugar. In the parashah, we find an example of the benefits that can be derived from a neighbor. During the years the Jews traveled through the desert after leaving Egypt, each of the twelve tribes camped in a specific place around the Tabernacle. A verse from the parashah describes how certain tribes were influenced by their neighbors.

וְהַחֹנִים לִפְנֵי הַמִּשְׁכָּן קֵדְמָה לִפְנֵי אֹהֶל מוֹעֵד | מִזְרָחָה מֹשֶׁה | וְאַהֲרֹן וּבָנָיו שֹׁמְרִים מִשְׁמֶרֶת הַמִּקְדָּשׁ לְמִשְׁמֶרֶת בְּנֵי יִשְׂרָאֵל וְהַזָּר הַקָּרֵב יוּמָת: (במדבר ג, לח)

Those who were to camp before the Tabernacle, in front—before the Tent of Meeting, on the east—were Moses and Aaron and his sons, attending to the duties of the sanctuary, as a duty on behalf of the Israelites; and any outsider who encroached was to be put to death. (Num. 3:38)

Rashi comments on Moses's influence on three neighboring tribes that also camped on the east side of the Tabernacle.

משה ואהרן ובניו: וסמוכין להם דגל מחנה יהודה, והחונים עליו יששכר וזבולן, טוב לצדיק טוב לשכנו, לפי שהיו שכניו של משה שהיה עוסק בתורה, נעשו גדולים בתורה, שנאמר (תהלים ס, ט) יהודה מחוקקי, ומבני יששכר יודעי בינה וגו' (דה"י א' יב, לג) מאתים ראשי סנהדראות, ומזבולן מושכים בשבט סופר (שופטים ה, יד): (רש"י, שם)

Moses and Aaron and his sons: Near them was the banner of the camp of Judah, next to whom camped Issachar and Zebulun. Good fortune to the righteous, good fortune to his neighbor! Because they were neighbors of Moses, who was engaged in Torah study, they became great Torah scholars. (Rashi, Num. 3:38)

Rashi explains that as a result of Moses's great diligence in Torah study, members of three neighboring tribes watched and learned from him, thereby becoming Torah scholars in their own right.

Because people can be greatly influenced by their neighbors, living in a community of people with shared values can help preserve, strengthen, and transmit those values to the next generation.

Questions for Discussion

1. Describe a neighbor from your childhood with whom you had a close relationship. Did that person have any impact on the person you've become?
2. Did you grow up with Jewish neighbors? If so, what did you learn from one such neighbor about Judaism or the Jewish people?
3. Do your relationships with your neighbors today extend beyond the bounds of borrowing a missing ingredient or the like? Are you satisfied with these relationships? If not, what would you like to be different?

NASO'

❖ Musical Accompaniment

Anyone who has attended a Jewish wedding has experienced the profound impact that music can have. While music is not the focus of a Jewish wedding, it often helps define the mood of various stages, with solemn music during the processional and lively music during the dancing. A verse in Parashat Naso' that defines who was included in the Levites' census also alludes to the role of music in the Tabernacle.

מִבֶּן שְׁלֹשִׁים שָׁנָה וָמַעְלָה וְעַד בֶּן חֲמִשִּׁים שָׁנָה כָּל הַבָּא לַעֲבֹד עֲבֹדַת עֲבֹדָה וַעֲבֹדַת מַשָּׂא בְּאֹהֶל מוֹעֵד: (במדבר ד, מז)

From the age of thirty years up to the age of fifty, all who were subject to duties of service and porterage relating to the Tent of Meeting. (Num. 4:47)

Rashi explains the term "duties of service":

עבדת עבדה: הוא השיר במצלתים וכנורות, שהיא עבודה לעבודה אחרת: (רש"י, שם)

duties of service: This refers to the music with cymbals and harps, which is service for another service [the offering of the sacrifices by the priests]. (Rashi, Num. 4:47)

Rashi explains that this verse refers to the Levites' role as musicians who played cymbal and harp music to accompany the sacrifices. The sacrificial service was indeed a feast for the senses—hearing the music of the Levites, seeing the costumed priests perform their duties, sniffing the burning of sacrifices and aromatic spices, and tasting the offerings.

The Levites' role serves as a model of how a person's creative talents can be used in the service of God and the Jewish people.

Questions for Discussion

1. Like all music, Jewish music has continued to evolve over the past century—from the Yiddish and cantorial music of the first decades of the last century, to the Zionist songs of Israel's early years, to Shlomo Carlebach's interactive songs of the 1960s and '70s, to contemporary Jewish hip-hop, rock, klezmer, and more today. What are your preferences in Jewish music? Who are your favorite artists?

2. Just as music was an important element of the Temple service, melodious songs have been incorporated into the synagogue services that substitute for the former Temple offerings (*Bavli Berakhot* 26b). Do you find that music or melodious songs enrich your experience of services? What musical styles speak most to you and why?

3. Describe any talents you have—musical or otherwise—that have been or might be of service to the Jewish community. How might they be put to good use?

❖ Keeping What You Have

One of our children's favorite parts of Sabbath dinner does not even involve food. It's the customary blessing that children receive from their parents before the meal. This blessing is modeled after the parashah's Priestly Blessing, with which Aaron and his sons blessed the Jewish people.

יְבָרֶכְךָ יְהֹוָה וְיִשְׁמְרֶךָ: (במדבר ו, כד)

The Lord bless you and protect you! (Num. 6:24)

Rashi explains the significance of this blessing's request for protection:

וישמרך: שלא יבואו עליך שודדים ליטול ממונך, שהנותן מתנה לעבדו אינו יכול לשמרו מכל אדם, וכיון שבאים לסטים עליו ונוטלין אותה ממנו, מה הנאה יש לו במתנה זו, אבל הקב"ה הוא הנותן הוא השומר: (רש"י, שם)

and protect you: that no thieves shall attack you and steal your money. For one who gives his servant a gift cannot protect him from all others, so if robbers descend on him and take it from him, what benefit does he have from the gift? But the Holy One, Blessed is He, is the One who [both] gives and protects. (Rashi, Num. 6:24)

Rashi uses a parable to illustrate that the benefits of a gift can be fleeting because the one who gives it is not able to assure that the recipient will retain it. This blessing therefore invokes divine assistance to secure the recipient's benefit from the gifts.

Many of us have a variety of blessings, both material and spiritual. Sometimes material blessings have resulted from personal effort or luck, and other times from the largesse of others. Regardless of the circumstances, maintaining these blessings can be very challenging.

Recognizing this, parents who bequeath significant assets to a child may stipulate that the child not be allowed any discretion over their management until he or she reaches a certain age of maturity.

Concern about someone's ability to properly care for what he or she receives extends to spiritual gifts. Despite having blessings that eluded earlier generations, such as societal acceptance, relief from poverty, and the State of Israel, the Jewish community—particularly in the Diaspora—faces great challenges in successfully transmitting its spiritual legacy to the next generation.

Questions for Discussion

1. Describe a cherished gift (material or spiritual) you received from someone else. Why is this blessing so important to you?
2. Warren Buffett, one of the world's richest people, is quoted as having said, "I want to give my kids just enough so that they would feel that they could do anything, but not so much that they would feel like doing nothing." What do you think of his approach? If you had a large fortune, how would you decide what to bequeath to your heirs, and why?
3. How central is Judaism to your identity? Is it important to you that your children have a Jewish identity? If so, what form would you like to see that identity take? What have you done (or do you intend to do) to help shape that identity?

❖ Holy Matrimony

According to Judaism, no relationship is more sacred than that of matrimony because a marriage results from choosing another to the exclusion of all others. In a verse about the Tabernacle, the parashah alludes to this understanding of marriage.

וַיְהִי בְּיוֹם כַּלּוֹת מֹשֶׁה לְהָקִים אֶת הַמִּשְׁכָּן וַיִּמְשַׁח אֹתוֹ וַיְקַדֵּשׁ אֹתוֹ וְאֶת כָּל כֵּלָיו וְאֶת הַמִּזְבֵּחַ וְאֶת כָּל כֵּלָיו וַיִּמְשָׁחֵם וַיְקַדֵּשׁ אֹתָם: (במדבר ז, א)

On the day that Moses finished setting up the Tabernacle, he anointed and consecrated it and all its furnishings, as well as the altar and its utensils. When he had anointed and consecrated them. (Num. 7:1)

Rashi comments on the word כַּלּוֹת (finished), which is written with the vowel *patach* under the first letter rather than the vowel *chirik* (כִּלּוֹת), as would have been expected:

ויהי ביום כלות משה: כלות כתיב, יום הקמת המשכן היו ישראל ככלה הנכנסת לחופה: (רש"י, שם)

On the day that Moses finished: The text reads כַּלּוֹת. On the day the Tabernacle was erected, the Israelites were like a bride [כַּלָּה] entering the wedding canopy [chuppah]. (Rashi, Num. 7:1)

Rashi explains that the Torah's use of a word reminiscent of the Hebrew word for bride (*kallah*) indicates that the Tabernacle served as a place where God and the Israelites joined in sacred union, like a bride and groom under the wedding canopy.

This allusion to a marriage between God and the Jewish people is particularly timely because Parashat Naso' is read in close proximity to Shavuot, the holiday celebrating the Jews' receiving the Torah. While there are many midrashim concerning the Jews receiving the Torah, one midrash relates that Mount Sinai, where the Jews received the Torah, was suspended over their heads like a wedding canopy with God being the groom and the Jewish

nation the bride (see *Mekhilta de-Rabbi Yishmael, Yitro, Bachodesh* 3). More than thirty-three hundred years later, this "marriage" at Mount Sinai continues as the foundation of the Jews' unique relationship with God.

Questions for Discussion

1. A midrash relates that God offered the Torah to other nations before the Jews, but each nation found something objectionable in it (*Sifrei Devarim* 343). When God offered it to the descendants of Esau, of whom it says "by your sword you shall live" (Gen. 27:40), they asked, "What's written in it?" to which God responded, "You shall not murder" (Exod. 20:13). When God offered it to the descendants of Ammon and Moab, nations conceived from Lot's union with his own daughters (see Gen. 19:36), they asked, "What's written in it?" to which God responded, "You shall not commit adultery" (Exod. 20:13). When God offered it to the descendants of Ishmael, described in Gen. 16:12 as having "his hand against everyone" (i.e., "a robber," see Rashi), they asked, "What's written in it?" to which God responded, "You shall not steal" (Exod. 20:13). By contrast, when God offered the Torah to the Jews, they responded, "We will do and we will hear" (נַעֲשֶׂה וְנִשְׁמָע) (Exod. 24:7), indicating their acceptance of the Torah even before they knew what it contained (see *Bavli Shabbat* 88a). What do you believe was significant about how the Jews responded to God's offering the Torah to them? What do you think this implies about the Jewish people's relationship to God?

2. How do you understand the teaching that God's relationship with the Jewish people is akin to a marriage?

3. Did you ever accept a major responsibility without fully knowing what it entailed? If so, why did you accept it? Did you fulfill it completely? What did you learn from the experience of just saying yes?

BE-HA‘ALOTEKHA

❖ Catching Flies

The old expression "You can catch more flies with honey than vinegar" reflects the fact that people are generally more cooperative when treated with kindness rather than harshness. Parashat Beha‘alotekha alludes to this idea in a verse directed toward Moses.

קַח אֶת הַלְוִיִּם מִתּוֹךְ בְּנֵי יִשְׂרָאֵל וְטִהַרְתָּ אֹתָם: (במדבר ח, ו)

Take the Levites from among the Israelites and cleanse them. (Num. 8:6)

Rashi explains how Moses is to "take" the Levites:

קח את הלוים: קחם בדברים, אשריכם שתזכו להיות שמשים למקום: (רש"י, שם)

Take the Levites: Take them with words: "You are fortunate that you have merited to become attendants to the Omnipresent." (Rashi, Num. 8:6)

Rashi explains that Moses has not been instructed to physically compel the Levites to undergo a purification process. Rather, Moses is told to persuade the Levites to partake in this process by praising the importance of their role.

In many relationships, particularly those involving an unequal balance of power, such as that of an employer with an employee, the person wielding the power may threaten the other with severe consequences (e.g., firing or suspending precious privileges) should she or he fail to do as requested. While such a threat may be effective in securing the desired short-term result, it simultaneously risks alienating and sapping the threatened person's good will and motivation. A better approach in an office setting may be to build employees' self-esteem and give them discretion in how to fulfill important responsibilities. While a supervisor may feel uncomfortable with the lost control engendered by such a strategy, it may nevertheless be the best way to retain the employee and to achieve the company's long-term goals.

Questions for Discussion

1. Describe a time you were responsible for getting others to do something. What did you find most challenging about this? Did you learn anything from the experience that you have applied (or plan to apply) in the future?
2. What do you think is the preferable approach to parenting—instilling fear or a "kinder, gentler" approach? What are the risks and benefits of both strategies? If you believe a "kinder, gentler" approach is warranted, how would you handle a child who insists on misbehaving?
3. What has been your most fulfilling experience as an employee, and what role did your supervisor play in that experience? What has been your least fulfilling experience as an employee and why?

❖ Retirement

If you believe the roadside billboards in Florida, retirement can be the "golden years" of life, filled with relaxing walks on the beach, scenic games of golf, and moonlit dances under the stars.

Some people aspire to a lifestyle of leisure in retirement; others try to continue working (professionally or as a volunteer) as long as possible; and still others seek some combination of the above. A verse from the parashah that describes the Levites' responsibilities also addresses the professional transition associated with aging.

וּמִבֶּן חֲמִשִּׁים שָׁנָה יָשׁוּב מִצְּבָא הָעֲבֹדָה
וְלֹא יַעֲבֹד עוֹד: (במדבר ח, כה)

But at the age of fifty they shall retire from the work force and shall serve no more. (Num. 8:25)

Rashi elaborates on the nature of this retirement:

ולא יעבוד עוד: עבודת משא בכתף, אבל חוזר הוא
לנעילת שערים ולשיר ולטעון עגלות, וזהו ושרת
את אחיו עם אחוהי, כתרגומו: (רש"י, שם)

and shall serve no more: at the task of carrying on the shoulder, but he returns to [the work of] locking the gates, singing, and loading the wagons. This is [the meaning of the next verse:] "They may assist their brother Levites." (Rashi, Num. 8:25)

Rashi explains that the Levites charged with carrying the Tabernacle's implements on their shoulders were to be relieved of their porterage responsibilities at age fifty (presumably because of the strenuous labor involved), but should continue to perform their other duties. And the Levites responsible for transporting items in wagons were to continue all their duties at age fifty without interruption.

Historically the loss of physical strength that accompanies aging was an important factor in determining the age of retirement. However, the shift in employment from blue-collar to white-collar jobs may have mitigated this impact and thereby prolonged people's careers.

Judaism holds the elderly in high regard, as indicated by the verse, "You shall rise before the aged and show deference to the old [*zaken*, זָקֵן]" (Lev. 19:32), which is the basis for the mitzvah to stand before an old person. The Talmud interprets the word *zaken* to be a sort of acronym for a wise person (זה שקנה חכמה), and thus mandates similar conduct toward both the elderly and the wise (see Rashi, *Bavli Kiddushin* 32b). While society may regard a person reaching his or her sixties as entering the era of retirement, *Pirkei Avot* 5:25 states, "A sixty-year-old attains *ziknah* [זקנה]"—and, according to the above interpretation, this may mean "wisdom."

By equating age with wisdom, Jewish tradition identifies what may be the greatest asset of an older employee—insightful judgment that often is acquired only through years of experience. Employers who do not appreciate the unique contributions of senior employees may cause those employees hardship and also harm the company's interests.

Questions for Discussion

1. At what age do you intend to retire and why? What have you gleaned from other people's retirement experiences that influences your thinking on this question?
2. How would you like to spend your retirement? Is there anything you can do now that may contribute to making your retirement a more fulfilling experience?
3. Traditionally elderly parents (or grandparents) lived with their children in multigenerational families. More recently elderly family members are more likely to live on their own

or with other seniors in a group setting. What do you think of this new model? Which model would you prefer if you were a senior or if you were the adult child of a senior? Why?

❖ Returning Lost Objects

The rhyme "finders keepers, losers weepers" does not accurately describe a found object's legal status. In both Jewish and Anglo-American law, the rights of the person who lost an object generally take precedence over those of the finder. While recording the order in which the encamped tribes traveled, the parashah explains how lost objects were handled.

וְנָסַע דֶּגֶל מַחֲנֵה בְנֵי דָן מְאַסֵּף לְכָל הַמַּחֲנֹת לְצִבְאֹתָם וְעַל צְבָאוֹ
אֲחִיעֶזֶר בֶּן עַמִּישַׁדָּי: (במדבר י, כה)

Then, as the rear guard of all the divisions, the standard of the division of Dan would set out, troop by troop. In command of its troop was Ahiezer son of Ammishaddai. (Num. 10:25)

Rashi clarifies why the tribe of Dan was the "rear guard of all the divisions":

מְאַסֵּף לְכָל הַמַּחֲנוֹת: תלמוד ירושלמי לפי שהיה שבטו של דן
מרובה באוכלוסין היה נוסע באחרונה וכל מי שהיה מאבד דבר היה
מחזירו לו: (רש"י, שם)

the rear guard of all the divisions: The Jerusalem Talmud [states]: Because the tribe of Dan was large in population,

they traveled last; and if anyone lost anything, they would [find it and] return it to him. (Rashi, Num. 10:25)

Rashi explains that in traveling last the tribe of Dan was charged with finding lost property and returning it to its rightful owner. In this way Jewish law goes one step further than its secular counterpart. Under Anglo-American law a person who sees a lost object may ignore it, thereby avoiding any responsibility to return it. Jewish law imposes an affirmative obligation to take custody of a lost object in order to restore it to its rightful owner, warning, "You must not remain indifferent" (לֹא תוּכַל לְהִתְעַלֵּם) (Deut. 22:3).

Questions for Discussion

1. Describe a time you lost something of value to you. Did you get it back? If so, how did that occur? Did you take away any insights from the experience?
2. Describe a time you found something of value. What did you do with it and why?
3. In 2013 a Connecticut rabbi bought a used desk on Craigslist for $150. As he took it apart so that it would fit through a narrow doorway in his house, he discovered a bag containing $98,000 cash behind one of its drawers. He promptly returned the money to the seller, who had no idea she had left it in the desk. Do you think he had a moral or legal obligation to return it? Was the fact that the buyer was a rabbi relevant to the decision? Would you have returned the money had you been in his shoes?

SHELAH-LEKHA

❖ The Blessing of a Skinned Knee

In *The Blessing of a Skinned Knee*, child psychologist and author Wendy Mogel warns against "helicopter parenting," parents who watch their children's every step, coddle them, and swoop in to rescue them from any possible failure. To raise happy, healthy children, she says, one of the best things parents can do is to let them make their own choices—and bear the consequences. By giving children opportunities to learn from their mistakes, parents will help them develop the tools they need to successfully transition to independence.

As Parashat Shelah-Lekha begins, the Jews are poised to enter the Land of Israel after the momentous Exodus from Egypt the previous year. However, in choosing to first investigate the Land of Israel, as indicated in the following verse, the Jews will make a fateful mistake.

שְׁלַח לְךָ אֲנָשִׁים וְיָתֻרוּ אֶת אֶרֶץ כְּנַעַן אֲשֶׁר אֲנִי נֹתֵן לִבְנֵי יִשְׂרָאֵל אִישׁ אֶחָד אִישׁ אֶחָד לְמַטֵּה אֲבֹתָיו תִּשְׁלָחוּ כֹּל נָשִׂיא בָהֶם: (במדבר יג, ב)

Send men to scout the land of Canaan, which I am giving to the Israelite people; send one man from each of their ancestral tribes, each one a chieftain among them. (Num. 13:2)

This verse recounting God's command to Moses begins with the words *shelach-lekha* (שְׁלַח לְךָ), which literally mean "send for yourself." Rashi explains that the additional term "for yourself"

(*lekha*, לְךָ) indicates that the Jewish people proposed sending the scouts.

שלח לך: לדעתך, אני איני מצוה לך, אם תרצה שלח, לפי שבאו ישראל ואמרו (דברים א, כב) נשלחה אנשים לפנינו, כמה שנאמר (שם) ותקרבון אלי כלכם וגו', ומשה נמלך בשכינה. אמר אני אמרתי להם שהיא טובה, שנאמר (שמות ג, יז) אעלה אתכם מעני מצרים וגו', חייהם שאני נותן להם מקום לטעות בדברי המרגלים למען לא יירשוה: (רש"י, שם)

Send for yourself: According to your opinion. I [God] am not commanding you, but if you wish, you may send [them], since the Israelites came and said, "Let us send men ahead" (Deut. 1:22). . . . [God] said, "I told them that it [the Land of Israel] is good, as it says, 'I will take you out of the misery of Egypt . . . [to a land flowing with milk and honey]' (Exod. 3:17). By their lives! I will give them the opportunity to err through the words of the scouts, so that they will not inherit it [the land]." (Rashi, Num. 13:2)

Even though God had told the Jews the land was good, they nevertheless wanted to send scouts, and God granted their request.

But when the scouts returned with an ominous report that emphasized the land's fearsome inhabitants, the Jews concluded they would rather die in the wilderness or return to Egypt than proceed to the Land of Israel. As a result, the Jews wandered in the wilderness for forty years, until the men of that generation had died. It would take a wholly new generation to emerge before the Jewish people could enter and settle in the Promised Land.

People are held accountable for their choices—good and bad.

Questions for Discussion

1. Describe an undertaking you initiated that could be characterized as a "failure." What did you learn from it? Have you applied those lessons to subsequent decisions?

2. Do you believe your parents oversheltered you or otherwise took actions that may have impaired your personal development? If so, how do you understand your parents' concerns? Could these concerns have been addressed in another way that would not have impeded your development?

3. A 1970s public service announcement on television showed children spilling a glass of milk, falling off a bicycle, and having their ice cream fall off their cones, followed by the refrain "Ooops, I made a mistake, that's all, and mistakes can happen to anyone." As you grew up, did you receive this message or a contrary one about your mistakes? Do you believe parents who generally accept their children's mistakes end up supporting or undermining their drive toward achievement?

❖ A Separate Piece

Candles, wine, and challah traditionally grace the Sabbath table. While in common parlance challah refers to the loaf of bread eaten at the Sabbath or holiday meal, the term also denotes a mitzvah (commandment) associated with baking bread, the subject of a verse in the parashah.

רֵאשִׁית עֲרִסֹתֵכֶם חַלָּה תָּרִימוּ תְרוּמָה כִּתְרוּמַת גֹּרֶן כֵּן תָּרִימוּ אֹתָהּ:
(במדבר טו, כ)

As the first yield of your baking, you shall set aside a loaf as a gift; you shall set it aside as a gift like the gift from the threshing floor. (Num. 15:20)

For the mitzvah of challah, the bread baker was obligated to set aside a portion of the dough as a gift for the priests (*kohanim*)—but only when he or she had made the minimum requisite quantity of dough, here defined by Rashi:

רֵאשִׁית עֲרִסֹתֵכֶם: כשתלושו כדי עיסתכם שאתם רגילין ללוש במבה. וכמה היא, (שמות טז, יח) וימודו בעומר (שם טז) עומר לגלגלת, תרימו מראשיתה, כלומר קודם שתאכלו ממנה ראשית חלקה חלה אחת תרימו תרומה לשם ה': (רש"י, שם)

As the first yield of your baking: [The obligation to separate a portion of the dough applies] [w]hen you knead the amount of dough you [were] accustomed to kneading in the desert. And how much is that? "They measured it by the omer" (Exod. 16:18), "an omer to a person" (v. 16). You shall separate from its first portion, that is to say, before you eat the first portion from it, you shall separate one loaf as a gift for the sake of the Lord. (Rashi, Num. 15:20)

As Rashi explains, a Jew's obligation to separate a portion of the dough applies only when making at least an omer's worth of dough, in keeping with each Jew's daily practice of collecting an omer of manna during the Jews' desert sojourn.

An omer is equivalent in volume to 43.2 eggs (about 3.8 quarts). Today, to end up with the required amount of dough to perform the mitzvah, the baker uses at least five pounds of flour. Then he or she separates an olive-sized portion of dough and recites the blessing on the mitzvah of challah. Whereas in previous times the separated portion was given to a priest, these days (because of uncertainty about priestly lineage) it is destroyed by burning it until it becomes inedible.

Questions for Discussion

1. Did or does your family routinely make challah for the Sabbath? If yes, can you describe your family's challah (the shape of the loaf, the number of strands of dough if braided, and special features of the recipe)? What preferences do you have for challah?

2. As indicated above, the mitzvah of challah requires tremendous precision, from the amount of dough that must be made (volume of 43.2 eggs) to the amount to be separated (volume of one olive). In Judaism many mitzvot require detailed measurement of one kind or another: quantity, time, or distance. Why do you think mitzvot tend to be defined so precisely? What problems might arise in the absence of such definitions?

3. Most Jewish occasions are celebrated with customary foods, such as *cholent* and kugel for the Sabbath, matzah and *haroset* for Passover, cheesecake for Shavuot, latkes for Hanukkah, hamantashen for Purim, and apples with honey for Rosh Hashanah. What is your favorite Jewish food? Can you share a food-related memory?

❖ Strings Attached

The expression "tie a string around your finger" refers to a technique to remind yourself to do something. The parashah discusses a different type of memory device that also involves string.

וְהָיָה לָכֶם לְצִיצִת וּרְאִיתֶם אֹתוֹ וּזְכַרְתֶּם אֶת כָּל מִצְוֹת יְהֹוָה וַעֲשִׂיתֶם אֹתָם וְלֹא תָתוּרוּ אַחֲרֵי לְבַבְכֶם וְאַחֲרֵי עֵינֵיכֶם אֲשֶׁר אַתֶּם זֹנִים אַחֲרֵיהֶם: (במדבר טו, לט)

That shall be your fringe; look at it and recall all the commandments of the Lord and observe them, so that you do not follow your heart and eyes in your lustful urge. (Num. 15:39)

Rashi explains the significance of the word tzitzit (צִיצִית), the fringes one is required to place on the corners of a four-cornered garment (see v. 38):

וזכרתם את כל מצות ה': שמנין גימטריא של ציצית שש מאות, ושמונה חוטים וחמשה קשרים הרי תרי"ג: (רש"י, שם)

and recall all the commandments of the Lord: because the numerical value of the word צִיצִית [tzitzit] is 600 [צ = 90, י = 10, צ = 90, י = 10, ת = 400]; [add to this the] eight threads and five knots, and we have [a total of] 613 [the number of commandments in the Torah]. (Rashi, Num. 15:39)

Rashi explains that since the word tzitzit has a numerical value of 613, equivalent to the number of mitzvot (commandments) in the Torah, seeing the tzitzit will remind a person to observe the mitzvot. Another ritual object that serves such a function is the mezuzah, which is affixed to the doorposts of a house, to be seen when entering and leaving. It contains verses from the Torah, including the fundamental declaration of faith, the *Shema*—"Hear, O Israel! The Lord is our God, the Lord alone" (Deut. 6:4).

Questions for Discussion

1. Name something you frequently forget or misplace. What reminders might you institute to prevent this from happening?

2. The book *Mesillat Yesharim* (Path of the Righteous), written by the eighteenth-century Italian rabbi Moshe Chaim Luzzatto, states in its introduction: "I did not write this book to tell you that which you do not know. Rather, I am only putting it down in book form to remind you of that which you already know." What moral principle do you value but sometimes not express consistently? Why does it matter to you? What might you do to keep it at the top of your mind?

3. Do you have any Jewish ritual objects in your home? If yes, when and how do they affect you? Do they serve the purpose of reminding you to observe Jewish teachings?

KORAH

❖ Bad Neighbors

Parashat Koraḥ opens with Korah's brazen rebellion against Moses. Moses and Korah were both grandsons of Levi's son Kohath, but Moses was from Kohath's firstborn son, Amram, and Korah was from Kohath's second-born son, Izhar. Since Amram's two sons have already served as national leaders, Korah believes that he, as the next-most-senior grandson of Kohath, should have been appointed the family's leader. He resents that Moses has assigned this role instead to Elizaphan, a son of Kohath's youngest son, Uzziel. Others join Korah in his rebellion.

וַיִּקַּח קֹרַח בֶּן יִצְהָר בֶּן קְהָת בֶּן לֵוִי וְדָתָן וַאֲבִירָם בְּנֵי אֱלִיאָב וְאוֹן בֶּן פֶּלֶת בְּנֵי רְאוּבֵן: (במדבר טז, א)

Now Korah, son of Izhar son of Kohath son of Levi, betook himself, along with Dathan and Abiram sons of Eliab, and On son of Peleth—descendants of Reuben. (Num. 16:1)

Rashi explains why the tribe of Reuben joined in Korah's rebellion.

ודתן ואבירם: בשביל שהיה שבט ראובן שרוי בחנייתם תימנה, שכן לקהת ובניו החונים תימנה, נשתתפו עם קרח במחלוקתו, אוי לרשע אוי לשכנו: (רש"י, שם)

Dathan and Abiram: Since the tribe of Reuben made its camp in the south, neighboring Kohath and his sons, who [also] camped in the south, they joined with Korah in his dispute. Woe to the wicked, [and] woe to his neighbor! (Rashi, Num. 16:1)

Rashi notes that the tribe of Reuben's physical proximity to Korah influenced the tribe's members to join Korah's rebellion. Consequently, it is important to exercise vigilance regarding neighbors who might exert a negative influence.

Questions for Discussion

1. When deciding to move to your current neighborhood, did you consider who your neighbors would be? Did you find out anything about them in advance? Are your neighbors different than what you had expected?
2. Have you ever joined in an action of consequence because of your proximity to someone who initiated it? What happened?
3. Describe the Jewish community in your neighborhood. If Jews are numerous, does this tend to promote a sense of Jewish peoplehood or provoke rebellion (or both)? Do you believe Jews should make the effort to live among other Jews in order to foster Jewish community?

❖ Cooling-Off Period

While the Second Amendment of the U.S. Constitution guarantees the right to bear arms, concern about increasing gun-related violence has prompted legislation imposing restrictions on acquiring firearms. For example, some states require mandatory waiting periods between the time of a firearm's purchase and its time of delivery—a cooling-off phase designed to help prevent impulsive acts of violence. In similar fashion, when answering Korah's rebellion Moses provides for a cooling-off period, hoping lives can be saved.

וַיְדַבֵּר אֶל קֹרַח וְאֶל כָּל עֲדָתוֹ לֵאמֹר בֹּקֶר וְיֹדַע יְהוָה אֶת אֲשֶׁר לוֹ וְאֶת הַקָּדוֹשׁ וְהִקְרִיב אֵלָיו וְאֵת אֲשֶׁר יִבְחַר בּוֹ יַקְרִיב אֵלָיו: (במדבר טז, ה)

Then he [Moses] spoke to Korah and all his company, saying, "Come morning, the Lord will make known who is His and who is holy, and will grant him access to Himself; He will grant access to the one He has chosen." (Num. 16:5)

Rashi explains why Moses proposed that everyone wait until the next day for God to decide on the merit of Korah's challenge:

בקר ויודע וגו': עתה עת שכרות הוא לנו ולא נכון להראות לפניו והוא היה מתכוין לדחותם שמא יחזרו בהם: (רש"י, שם)

Come morning, the Lord will make known: Now is a time of drunkenness for us, and it is not proper to appear before Him. His [Moses's] intention was to delay, with the hope that they might retract [their challenge]. (Rashi, Num. 16:5)

It is not clear from Rashi's comment whether the rebellious parties are actually intoxicated or have simply lost their rationality in the heat of the dispute. In either case, however, Rashi explains that Moses seeks to delay the resolution until the following day to give Korah and his followers the opportunity to come to their senses and back down.

Nowadays, taking a cooling-off period is a recognized tool for anger management. Before a person says something in anger, it is recommended that he or she take five deep breaths, count to ten, or wait to respond until later when he or she is calmer.

As the parashah goes on to relate, Korah refuses to back down before the confrontation with Moses scheduled for the following day and meets his demise as a result. Not availing oneself of a cooling-off period can have disastrous consequences.

Questions for Discussion

1. The Second Amendment, ratified in 1791, states: "A well regulated Militia being necessary to the security of a free State, the right of the people to keep and bear Arms, shall not be infringed." What realities and concerns of the time led the framers of the Constitution to include the right to bear arms? Do you believe the scope of this constitutional right should be rethought in our time? Why or why not?

2. Anger has often been described as "temporary insanity" in the sense that it compels someone to do something that would be unthinkable under normal circumstances. Have you ever acted while in the throes of "temporary insanity" in a way you later regretted? What happened?

3. When you were growing up, how did people in your family express themselves when they became angry? What did you learn from this? Do you handle anger in a similar or different way? What do you or might you do to avoid acting under the press of anger?

❖ Pursuing Peace

Had there been a Nobel Peace Prize thirty-three hundred years ago, Moses would have likely received it. A verse from the parashah illustrates the lengths to which Moses went to seek peace with his antagonists.

וַיִּשְׁלַח מֹשֶׁה לִקְרֹא לְדָתָן וְלַאֲבִירָם בְּנֵי אֱלִיאָב וַיֹּאמְרוּ לֹא נַעֲלֶה:
(במדבר טז, יב)

Moses sent for Dathan and Abiram, sons of Eliab; but they said, "We will not come!" (Num. 16:12)

Rashi explains why Moses sent for Dathan and Abiram, Korah's accomplices:

וישלח משה וגו': מכאן שאין מחזיקין במחלוקת, שהיה משה מחזר אחריהם להשלימם בדברי שלום: (רש"י, שם)

Moses sent: From here [we derive] that one should not maintain a dispute, for Moses sought them out to conciliate them with peaceful words. (Rashi, Num. 16:12)

As Rashi explains, Moses summoned Dathan and Abiram in an overture of peace.

In Western society, where the legal system is primarily based on rights rather than responsibilities, adversarial parties are typically driven to make pragmatic concessions that will result in the most gain for themselves. If a litigant genuinely believes that he is "right" and the other party "wrong," that the evidence is strongly in his favor, and that pursuing litigation promises a big payoff, he is unlikely to consider settling the case.

Judaism, however, is based primarily on responsibilities—one of which is pursuing peace. Rashi indicates that a person should exert himself to end a dispute. Judaism may therefore impose an obligation to seek reconciliation even when the other party is "wrong." After all, Moses literally acted in accordance with God's instructions in appointing Elizaphan rather than Korah as tribal leader (see Rashi, Num. 16:1), and then did his best to end the dispute by initiating reconciliation with his adversaries.

Questions for Discussion

1. If you could award a peace prize to someone, who would it be and why?
2. In recent years, many U.S. courts have required that parties to a lawsuit first meet for nonbinding mediation (settlement discussions) before being allowed to pursue their case in court. What do you think led to such a requirement? Do you believe it is a wise protocol?
3. Have you ever initiated reconciliation with someone when you believed you were still largely in the right? If yes, why did you do it and what happened? In your view, are some things more important than being right, and, if so, what are they?

ḤUKKAT

❖ Outsider-Insider Relations

While hospitality to guests is an important element of Jewish life, this topic is usually considered from the host's perspective. An episode from Parashat Ḥukkat, however, presents an opportunity to consider hospitality from the guest's point of view. In the Jews' final year of desert travels, as they prepare to enter the Land of Israel, they request permission to pass through territory held by the king of Edom, a descendant of Jacob's brother, Esau.

נַעְבְּרָה נָּא בְאַרְצֶךָ לֹא נַעֲבֹר בְּשָׂדֶה וּבְכֶרֶם
וְלֹא נִשְׁתֶּה מֵי בְאֵר דֶּרֶךְ הַמֶּלֶךְ נֵלֵךְ לֹא נִטֶּה יָמִין
וּשְׂמֹאול עַד אֲשֶׁר נַעֲבֹר גְּבֻלֶךָ: (במדבר כ, יז)

Allow us, then, to cross your country. We will not pass through fields or vineyards, and we will not drink water from wells. We will follow the king's highway, turning off neither to the right nor to the left until we have crossed your territory. (Num. 20:17)

Rashi clarifies the nature of this request:

ולא נשתה מי באר: מי בורות היה צריך לומר אלא כך אמר משה
אף על פי שיש בידינו מן לאכול ובאר לשתות, לא נשתה ממנו
אלא נקנה מכם אוכל ומים להנאתכם, מכאן לאכסנאי שאף על
פי שיש בידו לאכול, יקנה מן החנוני כדי להנות את אושפיזו:
(רש"י, שם)

and we will not drink water from wells: It should have [instead] said "cistern water" [since that was the water that would have been available along the route]. Rather, this is what Moses said: "Although we have in our possession manna to eat and well [water] to drink, we will not drink from it; rather, we will buy food and drink from you, for your benefit." From here [we learn] that even though a guest may have provisions in his possession, he should buy from the shopkeeper [in alternative texts, "homeowner"] in order to benefit his host. (Rashi, Num. 20:17)

Rashi says that even though the Jews possessed ample food and water, they nevertheless offered to purchase these provisions from the nation of Edom in order to benefit their hosts.

Typically, when someone has invited a guest to his or her home, it is appropriate for the invitee to offer a small gift or otherwise acknowledge the host's generosity. The circumstances of this parashah present an even more compelling case for the "guest" to exhibit sensitivity: the king of Edom does not invite the Jews to pass through his territory; the Jews request the privilege. They are turned down, despite their offer to buy their provisions from their hosts and their promise not to veer off the road. Even offering benefits, as suggested by Rashi, may not be sufficient incentive when the host is hostile to a would-be guest's request.

More generally, Rashi touches on the dynamic between outsiders and locals. In our day this issue commonly arises when towns near big cities start to attract well-heeled urbanites who seek a home in a more pastoral setting, or chain stores threaten to replace mom-and-pop retailers. The residents may feel that "foreigners" with opposing agendas are threatening their way of life. By showing sensitivity to the existing residents, the newcomers may be able to reach accommodations acceptable to all involved.

Questions for Discussion

1. What advice would you offer someone on how to be a good guest? Have you learned anything from hosting others that figures into your answer?
2. Describe a time when you felt awkward, either because you invited yourself to another's house or another person requested hospitality from you under inconvenient circumstances. What did you do to try to mitigate the discomfort of this situation? What advice would you offer to prevent such awkwardness from recurring?
3. If Walmart plans to open a store in a small town that has only local retailers, do you think the company has any obligation to mitigate its negative impact on existing stores? If so, how might this be done? If not, why not?

❖ Strong Suit

Many a parent whose child exhibits atypical behavior will bring the child for a psychological assessment to determine what is "wrong" with the child. Such knowledge may be important, but by itself it usually provides limited insight since it is also critical to know a person's strengths—an inherent point in this verse, in which the king of Edom responds to the Jews' request to pass through his land.

וַיֹּאמֶר אֵלָיו אֱדוֹם לֹא תַעֲבֹר בִּי פֶּן בַּחֶרֶב אֵצֵא לִקְרָאתֶךָ: (במדבר כ, יח)

But Edom answered him, "You shall not pass through us, else we will go out against you with the sword." (Num. 20:18)

Rashi explains what prompts the king of Edom to refer specifically to "the sword":

פֶּן בחרב אצא לקראתך: אתם מתגאים בקול שהורישכם אביכם, אמרתם ונצעק אל ה' וישמע קולנו, ואני אצא עליכם במה שהורישני אבי (בראשית כז, מ) ועל חרבך תחיה: (רש"י, שם)

else we will go out against you with the sword: You [the descendants of Jacob] pride yourselves on the "voice" you inherited from your forefather [Jacob], saying [v. 16], "We cried to the Lord [in Egypt] and He heard our plea [literally, "voice"]." Well, I [the descendant of Jacob's brother, Esau] will go out against you with my forefather's legacy (Gen. 27:40): "Yet by your sword you shall live." (Rashi, Num. 20:18)

Rashi explains that the Jews' reference to their "voice" in verse 16 recalled the blessing for effective prayer that Isaac conferred on his son Jacob: "The voice is the voice of Jacob" (Gen. 27:22). Hearing this reference to the Jews' legacy from their forefather Jacob prompted the king of Edom to refer to his legacy from his forefather Esau—that he would live by his sword. Both the Jews and the Edomites thus recognized their individual strengths, effective prayer for the former and the sword for the latter, and expressed their intention to employ strategies that drew on them.

Similarly, when looking at children, better psychological assessments can provide a fuller picture of both their strengths and weaknesses. Drawing on a child's strengths then becomes just as important (if not more important) than working on any weaknesses.

The same can be true of adults. Psychologist Martin Seligman, a pioneer in the emerging field of positive psychology—which focuses on achieving a fulfilled life rather than treating mental illness—calls for "using your signature strengths every day to produce authentic happiness and abundant gratification." Some adults never have asked themselves "what are my signature strengths?" outside the context of preparing for a job interview, after which the answers are usually soon forgotten. Other adults may have asked themselves this question earlier in their lives, but it would elicit a very different response today.

Even people who are well established in their personal and professional lives may benefit by understanding and acting on what they do well and what brings them fulfillment.

Questions for Discussion

1. Have you ever taken any type of psychological, personality, or career assessment? If so, what were the results? Did they influence any decisions you have made?
2. What do you believe are your strengths, and in what ways does your job (or other activity) capitalize on them?
3. If you compare your strengths and the most important qualities needed for your job (or other activity), is your job is well suited for you? If yes, why? If not, what other type of work might be a better match? What actions might you take to try to spend more of your life in your zones of strength?

❖ Forgive and Forget

When the Jews criticize God and Moses, complaining that they have no food or water but only rotten bread, God punishes them with a deadly plague of fiery serpents. In the parashah Moses hears the people's lament and intercedes to end the plague.

וַיָּבֹא הָעָם אֶל מֹשֶׁה וַיֹּאמְרוּ חָטָאנוּ כִּי דִבַּרְנוּ בַיהֹוָה וָבָךְ הִתְפַּלֵּל אֶל יְהֹוָה וְיָסֵר מֵעָלֵינוּ אֶת הַנָּחָשׁ וַיִּתְפַּלֵּל מֹשֶׁה בְּעַד הָעָם: (במדבר כא, ז)

The people came to Moses and said, "We sinned by speaking against the Lord and against you. Intercede with the Lord to take away the serpents from us!" And Moses interceded for the people. (Num. 21:7)

Rashi relates a lesson we learn from Moses's conduct:

ויתפלל משה: מכאן למי שמבקשים ממנו מחילה שלא יהא אכזרי מלמחול: (רש"י, שם)

And Moses interceded: From here [we derive] that someone from whom forgiveness is asked should not be cruel in withholding forgiveness. (Rashi, Num. 21:7)

Rashi explains that, despite the people's verbal assault against Moses, he forgave them and proceeded to pray on their behalf.

Inevitably people will do and say things that offend others—sometimes quite severely. If a perpetrator asks the offended party for forgiveness, Rashi indicates that it behooves the hurt person to grant it. Forgiveness can benefit both the wrongdoer and the one who forgives. Together they may be able to restore a damaged relationship to health.

Questions for Discussion

1. Why is it that different people respond very differently when subjected to the same conditions? How do you tend to respond when encountering harsh physical challenges?

2. What would you like to hear in the apology of someone who has wronged you that would move you toward reconciliation?

3. Have you ever experienced a period of estrangement from a relative or a close friend? If it was resolved, how did that happen and how do you feel about it? If it remains unresolved, what do you think it would take to reconcile, and what role might you play in it?

BALAK

❖ Common Enemies

At the end of last week's parashah, the Israelites have won an impressive military victory against the Amorite kingdom. Parashat Balak opens with the fearful reaction of Balak, king of Moab, to a seemingly invincible Jewish nation. Balak shares his concern with the neighboring Midianites.

וַיֹּאמֶר מוֹאָב אֶל זִקְנֵי מִדְיָן עַתָּה יְלַחֲכוּ הַקָּהָל אֶת כָּל סְ־
בִיבֹתֵינוּ כִּלְחֹךְ הַשּׁוֹר אֵת יֶרֶק הַשָּׂדֶה וּבָלָק בֶּן צִפּוֹר
מֶלֶךְ לְמוֹאָב בָּעֵת הַהִוא: (במדבר כב, ד)

And Moab said to the elders of Midian, "Now this horde will lick clean all that is about us as an ox licks up the grass of the field." Balak son of Zippor, who was king of Moab at the time. (Num. 22:4)

Rashi explains why Balak consulted with the Midianites:

אל זקני מדין: והלא מעולם היו שונאים זה את זה, שנאמר
(בראשית לו, לה) המכה את מדין בשדה מואב, שבאו מדין על
מואב למלחמה. אלא מיראתן של ישראל עשו שלום ביניהם.
ומה ראה מואב ליטול עצה ממדין, כיון שראו את ישראל נוצחים
שלא כמנהג העולם, אמרו מנהיגם של אלו במדין נתגדל, נשאל
מהם מה מדתו. אמרו להם אין כחו אלא בפיו. אמרו אף אנו נבא
עליהם באדם שכחו בפיו: (רש"י, שם)

to the elders of Midian: But did they not always hate each other, as it says, "who defeated the Midianites in the country of Moab" (Gen. 36:35), when Midian came against Moab in battle? However, because of their mutual fear of Israel they made peace with each other. And what did Moab see [that caused him] to take counsel with Midian? Since they saw the supernatural victories of Israel, they said, "The leader of these people [Moses] was raised in Midian. Let us ask them what his character is." They [the Midianites] said to them, "He has no power except in his mouth." They [the Moabites] said, "We will come against them [the Israelites] with a person whose power is in his mouth." (Rashi, Num. 22:4)

Rashi explains that the Moabites and Midianites put aside their historical animosity to unite in opposing the Israelites. This pattern of adversaries putting differences aside to join forces against the Jews has repeated itself many times in Jewish history. Through such bodies as the Organisation of Islamic Cooperation and the Arab League, Israel's neighbors have unified around the issue of hostility toward the Jewish state, even though military conflicts between and within neighboring Muslim countries have claimed over a million lives since Israel's founding—one million in the Iran-Iraq War, four hundred thousand in the Syrian Civil War, one hundred thousand in the Lebanese Civil War, and thirty thousand in the Gulf War.

The Israeli-Arab conflict also unites the Jewish people. When confronted with an external threat, Ashkenazim and Sephardim, religious and secular, left wing and right wing readily appreciate that their commonalities as Jews are more significant than their differences. More generally, wars and disasters—both natural and manmade—have a way of forging shared experiences among a population and, in the process, uniting people from different walks of life.

Questions for Discussion

1. Israel signed peace treaties with two of its four neighbors: Egypt in 1979 and Jordan in 1994. The two neighbors who remain in official states of hostility toward Israel—Syria and Lebanon—have both had bloody civil wars in recent decades and remain deeply divided internally. Do you think it is possible for Israel to reach peace accords with Lebanon or Syria? If so, how do the peace accords with Egypt and Jordan inform possible paths for achieving this peace?

2. Describe a relationship you have had with someone whose religious, ethnic, or political group is considered to be hostile to your own. Did getting to know this person challenge any stereotypes you held?

3. Describe a relationship you have had with someone who belongs to a different segment of the Jewish community. Did getting to know this person challenge any stereotypes you held?

❖ Free to Choose

After consulting with the Midianites, Balak learns that the power of the Israelites' leader, Moses, stems from his mouth—the power of prayer. Therefore, Balak decides to engage the services of Balaam, the greatest gentile prophet, who wields a different power stemming from his mouth—the power to curse (see Rashi, Num. 22:4). Balak then sends emissaries to recruit Balaam, whom God addresses during this visit.

וַיָּבֹא אֱלֹהִים אֶל בִּלְעָם וַיֹּאמֶר מִי הָאֲנָשִׁים הָאֵלֶּה עִמָּךְ: (במדבר כב, ט)

God came to Balaam and said, "What do these people want of you?" (Num. 22:9)

After Adam ate from the Tree of Knowledge in the Garden of Eden, God asked him, "Where are you?" (Gen. 3:9). Rashi understands this question not to mean that God didn't know where Adam was, but rather to demonstrate God's intention to engage Adam in conversation about his actions. Here too God questions Balaam to engage him in conversation (see Rashi, Gen. 3:9). As Rashi explains, Balaam is free to either understand the question as intended or interpret it another way:

מִי הָאנשים האלה עמך: להטעותו בא. אמר פעמים שאין הכל גלוי לפניו, אין דעתו שוה עליו, אף אני אראה עת שאוכל לקלל ולא יבין: (רש"י, שם)

What do these people want of you: [By asking a question that could be misunderstood to imply that God did not know what Balaam's visitors wanted, God] gave him the opportunity to err. [Balaam] said, "Sometimes, not everything is revealed to Him. He is not omniscient, so I will find a time when I am able to curse, and He will not realize it." (Rashi, Num. 22:9)

Rashi explains that God asked Balaam the question to open a dialogue with him. God also recognized the possibility that Balaam might interpret the question to mean there were things God did not know and therefore Balaam could get away with cursing the Israelites. Balaam chose the latter interpretation, thereby distancing himself from God.

God's asking Adam and Balaam direct, but open-ended questions that prompted their choices might serve as a model for how we relate to others. Although at times we might like to tell employees, spouses, friends, or children what to do, such an approach may cause them to feel as if their autonomy is not being respected and they are being controlled. We might instead broach the conversation more generally, opening the door to hear their perspectives. Then, perhaps, we might provide them with different options and encourage their consideration of the individual pros and cons, thereby giving them a more empowered stake in the outcome.

Questions for Discussion

1. Relationships of substance generally result from a succession of experiences in which the parties have had considerably more interactions that solidify the relationship than undermine it. Usually in such relationships people feel free to be themselves. Sometimes they have taken the risk to make themselves vulnerable and decided the risk was justified. Describe someone with whom you have a relationship of substance. What has made it so strong?

2. Have you ever wanted to direct a family member or friend to act in a certain way, but held back from saying this because you believed it would backfire? Have there been other times in which you were direct and it seemed to work? When you have strong opinions about other people's actions, how do you generally decide what approach to take with them?

3. Have you ever been responsible for managing others? What have you learned about how much space and direction is best when trying to be an effective manager?

❖ Rise and Shine

Despite Balaam's best efforts he fails to curse the Israelites. More so, each attempt to curse has the opposite effect, resulting in a blessing for the Jewish people. The following verse relays one such example:

הֶן עָם כְּלָבִיא יָקוּם וְכַאֲרִי יִתְנַשָּׂא לֹא יִשְׁכַּב עַד יֹאכַל טֶרֶף וְדַם חֲלָלִים יִשְׁתֶּה: (במדבר כג, כד)

Lo, a people [the Israelites] that rises like a lion, [l]eaps up like the king of beasts, [r]ests not till it has feasted on prey [a]nd drunk the blood of the slain. (Num. 23:24)

Rashi explains the analogy of the Israelites to a lion:

הן עם כלביא יקום וגו': כשהן עומדים משנתם שחרית, הן מתגברין כלביא וכארי לחטוף את המצות, ללבוש טלית לקרוא את שמע ולהניח תפילין: (רש"י, שם)

Lo, a people [the Israelites] that rises like a lion: When they awaken from their sleep in the morning, they are as vigorous as a lion and the king of beasts in grasping the commandments [mitzvot]—wearing a prayer shawl [tallit], reading the declaration of God's unity [*Shema*, Deut. 6:4], and putting on phylacteries [tefillin]. (Rashi, Num. 23:24)

Rashi explains that Balaam's comparing the Israelites to an awakening lion is a reference to the zeal with which they perform the commandments each morning. The inference is that a Jew should bound out of bed in the morning with a sense of purpose—to live fully, as God intended—and a vigorous desire to fulfill that purpose.

Questions for Discussion

1. Would you say you bound out of bed in the morning? What is your typical morning routine, and how does that affect the rest of your day?

2. According to Jewish law, one should immediately recite an expression of gratitude (*Modeh Ani*) upon awakening in the morning (see, e.g., *Mishnah Berurah* 1:8). Is this tradition part of your morning ritual? Whether it is or not, what do you find yourself thankful for every day?

3. Have you ever experienced being "vigorous as a lion and the king of beasts" in grasping a mitzvah? If so, what particular mitzvah most brings this forth from you, and why?

PINḤAS

❖ Order

Order is important in Judaism. For example, the word *seder* literally means "order," and the Passover seder begins with reciting, in order, the fifteen steps that constitute the evening's festive meal. When making *Kiddush* (sanctifying the Sabbath over a cup of wine), one first recites the blessing and then drinks the wine, but when one lights Sabbath candles, one first lights the candles and then recites the blessing. Parashat Pinḥas raises the importance of order in a different context: an appeal by the daughters of Zelophehad concerning their inheritance in the Land of Israel.

וַתִּקְרַבְנָה בְּנוֹת צְלָפְחָד בֶּן־חֵפֶר בֶּן־גִּלְעָד בֶּן־מָכִיר בֶּן־מְנַשֶּׁה לְמִשְׁפְּחֹת מְנַשֶּׁה בֶן־יוֹסֵף וְאֵלֶּה שְׁמוֹת בְּנֹתָיו מַחְלָה נֹעָה וְחָגְלָה וּמִלְכָּה וְתִרְצָה: (במדבר כז, א)

The daughters of Zelophehad, of Manassite family—son of Hepher son of Gilead son of Machir son of Manasseh son of Joseph—came forward. The names of the daughters were Mahlah, Noah, Hoglah, Milcah, and Tirzah. (Num. 27:1)

Rashi comments on the order of their names:

מחלה נעה וגו': ולהלן הוא אומר (במדבר לו, יא) ותהיינה מחלה תרצה, מגיד שכולן שקולות זו כזו, לפיכך שנה את סדרן: (רש"י, שם)

Mahlah, Noah, etc.: Later it says [in a different order], "Mahlah, Tirza . . . were" (Num. 36:11). This teaches us that they were all equal to one another, therefore the order was changed. (Rashi, Num. 27:1)

Rashi explains that the inconsistent order of the daughters' names indicates that they were all equal (since a consistent order would signify that the first was the most distinguished). (See *Bavli Bava Batra* 120a and Rashi on Num. 36:11).

Order can be significant in everyday life. When an article appears in a journal, the lead author is listed first. When food is packaged, the ingredients are listed in descending order of quantity. When work experience appears on a resume, it is arranged in reverse chronological order.

Rashi signals us to be attentive to why things are presented in a particular order—and examine whether or not that order is meaningful.

Questions for Discussion

1. If you have siblings, where are you in the birth order (if you don't, answer for one of your parents)? What impact do you believe your birth order had on your upbringing? Do you wish you had been born in a different order? If so, why?

2. Share something you habitually do in a particular order even though others do it differently. How did you decide on this order?

3. If you were to compose a "thank you" speech acknowledging the people who have made the greatest difference in your life, who would you include and in what order?

❖ Leading by Example

After God informs Moses that he will not enter the Land of Israel (because he struck a rock rather than speaking to it as instructed), Moses requests that God appoint a new leader to guide the people in the land. The following verse points to the qualities Moses believes this leader should possess.

אֲשֶׁר יֵצֵא לִפְנֵיהֶם וַאֲשֶׁר יָבֹא לִפְנֵיהֶם וַאֲשֶׁר יוֹצִיאֵם וַאֲשֶׁר יְבִיאֵם וְלֹא תִהְיֶה עֲדַת יְהוָה כַּצֹּאן אֲשֶׁר אֵין לָהֶם רֹעֶה: (במדבר כז, יז)

Who shall go out before them and come in before them, and who shall take them out and bring them in, so that the Lord's community may not be like sheep that have no shepherd. (Num. 27:17)

Rashi describes the type of leader Moses is requesting:

אשר יצא לפניהם: לא כדרך מלכי האומות שיושבים בבתיהם ומשלחין את חיילותיהם למלחמה, אלא כמו שעשיתי אני שנלחמתי בסיחון ועוג, שנאמר (במדבר כא, לד) אל תירא אותו. וכדרך שעשה יהושע, שנאמר (יהושע ה, יג) וילך יהושע אליו ויאמר לו הלנו אתה וגו'. וכן בדוד הוא אומר (ש"א יח, טז) כי הוא יוצא ובא לפניהם, יוצא בראש ונכנס בראש: (רש"י, שם)

Who shall go out before them: unlike the approach of the gentile kings, who sit at home and send their armies to war. Rather, as I did, for I fought against Sihon and Og, as [God] said [to me before I smote Og], "Do not fear him" (Num. 21:34); and as Joshua [Moses's successor] did, as it says, "Joshua went up to him and asked him, 'Are you one of us [or our enemies]?'" (Josh. 5:13). Similarly, concerning [King] David it says, "For he marched at their head" (1 Sam. 18:16). He goes forth at their head, and enters at their head. (Rashi, Num. 27:17)

As Rashi explains, Moses requests a leader who, like himself, will lead the Jews into battle rather than remain a safe distance from the battlefield. This approach remains part of the ethos of the Israel Defense Forces (IDF), where officers are expected to lead their soldiers into battle. In fact, the IDF paratroopers' motto is *Acharai!* (Follow me!).

Moses's leadership style brings to mind a concept in psychology called modeling, in which a person engages in a behavior with the intention that others are likely to imitate it. For example, a parent who wants to teach a child how to resolve conflicts amicably could demonstrate this in how he or she resolves personal disagreements with family members. Modeling may help us exert a positive influence on others while also helping ourselves become the people we aspire to be.

Questions for Discussion

1. Even though Moses was not permitted to enter Israel, he nevertheless helped assure that the best person for the job (Joshua) would succeed him to lead the Jews into the Promised Land. From your experiences with and observations concerning leadership succession, what factors support—and which harm—an effective transition and why? How important is the outgoing leader's involvement in the process?

2. As commander in chief of the armed forces, the president of the United States has the authority to order U.S. forces to war even though the president remains at a safe distance from the battlefield and may never have even served in the military. How do you feel about this system? Might others

view this situation differently? Could potential problems with this system be addressed and, if so, how?

3. Discuss an effort you made to model behavior. Did it have the desired outcome? Why or why not?

....

❖ Going the Extra Mile

In accordance with God's instructions, Moses passes the mantle of leadership to Joshua in full view of the entire nation, as described in the following verse:

וַיִּסְמֹךְ אֶת יָדָיו עָלָיו וַיְצַוֵּהוּ כַּאֲשֶׁר דִּבֶּר
יְהוָה בְּיַד מֹשֶׁה: (במדבר כז, כג)

He [Moses] laid his hands upon him [Joshua] and commissioned him—as the Lord had spoken through Moses. (Num. 27:23)

Rashi notes a discrepancy between what Moses has been commanded to do and what he actually does:

ויסמך את ידיו: בעין יפה יותר ויותר ממה שנצטווה. שהקב"ה אמר
לו וסמכת את ידך, והוא עשה בשתי ידיו, ועשאו ככלי מלא וגדוש
ומלאו חכמתו בעין יפה: (רש"י, שם)

He laid his hands: Generously, over and above what he had been commanded. For the Holy One, Blessed is He, said to him [v. 18], "lay your hand," but he did [it] with both his hands. He [Moses] fashioned him like a vessel filled to overflowing, filling him generously with his wisdom. (Rashi, Num. 27:23)

Rashi explains that although Moses is commanded to lay only one hand on Joshua, Moses lays both hands on him. This act reflects Moses's desire to prepare Joshua for his new leadership role to the maximum extent possible.

Moses's dedication to Joshua's success is all the more impressive given that God rejected Moses's request to have his own sons succeed him as leader (see Rashi, v. 16).

Questions for Discussion

1. As Rashi describes, Moses exerted himself to assure that Joshua would be optimally prepared to lead the Jewish nation. Can you describe an instance where a leader wholly groomed a successor to successfully assume the mantle of leadership? What characteristics and actions of leadership helped make this possible?

2. Describe a time you invested yourself in helping someone else and exceeded that person's expectations. What was your motivation?

3. The dairy supermarket Stew Leonard's has the following etched on a huge granite slab at the store's entrance: "Rule #1: The Customer is Always Right! Rule #2: If the Customer is Ever Wrong, Re-Read Rule #1." Have you ever dealt with a store or employee that operated according to this principle? If so, what impact did it have on your patronizing this business?

....

MATTOT

❖ The Sound of Silence

Imagine that while you are in the kitchen, your young child enters and, without a word, starts making cookies. Half an hour later, after the dough is ready, your child asks you to turn on the oven. Would you now be justified in objecting because your child did not first ask permission to make cookies? Your silence during the previous half hour would likely constitute acquiescence to your child's baking adventure. A verse from Parashat Mattot addresses the issue of silence indicating approval when a wife accepts a vow and her husband does not object to it.

וְשָׁמַע אִישָׁהּ בְּיוֹם שָׁמְעוֹ וְהֶחֱרִישׁ לָהּ וְקָמוּ נְדָרֶיהָ וֶאֱסָרֶהָ אֲשֶׁר אָסְרָה עַל נַפְשָׁהּ יָקֻמוּ: (במדבר ל, ח)

And her husband learns of it and offers no objection on the day he finds out, her vows shall stand and her self-imposed obligations shall stand. (Num. 30:8)

Rashi comments:

ושמע אישה וגו': הרי לך שאם קיים הבעל שהוא קיים: (רש"י, שם)

And her husband heard: Here you have [the ruling] that if the husband endorses it, it stands. (Rashi, Num. 30:8)

Rashi informs us that the husband's silence constitutes tacit endorsement of the wife's vows.

In many instances, people convey their approval by simply remaining silent. For example, if a typically opinionated participant in a meeting does not raise any objections when a proposal is discussed, people may assume the silence indicates approval.

In other circumstances, however, individuals may remain silent reluctantly and despite their opposition to other people's actions. In such cases, silence may be the practical and moral equivalent of consent—sometimes with dire consequences. For example, the failure of both leaders and citizens to speak up against the Nazi regime may have greatly exacerbated the Holocaust.

Rashi instructs us that one can be accountable both for what one says and for what one refrains from saying.

Questions for Discussion

1. Describe a time you chose to keep silent rather than voice your perspective. What motivated you then? Would you act similarly if you were in the same situation today?
2. Describe a time you chose to speak your mind and later questioned whether it might have been better for you to stay silent. Under what circumstances (if any) do you think choosing silence is wisdom?
3. Describe someone you know (or know of) who consistently speaks out against wrongdoing when he or she could easily choose to remain silent. Would you want to be more like this person? Why or why not?

❖ Anger Costs

Mark Twain is quoted as having said, "Anger is an acid that can do more harm to the vessel in which it is stored than to anything on which it is poured." In other words, the primary victim of one's anger may be oneself. Today, medical experts acknowledge that the stress of anger can be detrimental to one's health. In addition, an angry person tends to be susceptible to misjudgments. While discussing the procedure for kashering the metal utensils that the Jews captured from the Midianites in battle, the parashah also shows the impact of anger.

וַיֹּאמֶר אֶלְעָזָר הַכֹּהֵן אֶל אַנְשֵׁי הַצָּבָא הַבָּאִים לַמִּלְחָמָה זֹאת חֻקַּת הַתּוֹרָה אֲשֶׁר צִוָּה יְהֹוָה אֶת מֹשֶׁה: (במדבר לא, כא)

Eleazar the priest said to the troops who had taken part in the fighting, "This is the ritual law that the Lord has enjoined upon Moses." (Num. 31:21)

Rashi explains why Eleazar, rather than Moses, promulgated a law that was originally given to Moses:

ויאמר אלעזר הכהן וגו': לפי שבא משה לכלל כעס בא לכלל טעות, שנתעלמו ממנו הלכות גיעולי נכרים. וכן אתה מוצא בשמיני למלואים, שנאמר (ויקרא י, טז) ויקצוף על אלעזר ועל איתמר, בא לכלל כעס, בא לכלל טעות, וכן (במדבר כ, י–יא) שמעו נא המורים ויך את הסלע, ע"י הכעס טעה: (רש"י, שם)

Eleazar the priest said: Because Moses came to a state of anger, he came to err, for the laws of purging gentile vessels eluded him. . . . Similarly, [when Moses said]

(Num. 20:10–11), "Listen, you rebels . . . and [Moses] struck the rock"—because of anger, he erred. (Rashi, Num. 31:21)

Moses becomes angry when he sees a Jewish youth seizing some of the spoils of war, and as a result, Rashi explains, he forgets the laws of purging a non-Jew's vessels. Eleazar therefore relates this law that has been taught to Moses.

Similarly, Moses faces grave consequences after he angrily strikes a rock instead of speaking to it, as God instructed: he is not allowed to enter the Land of Israel.

Questions for Discussion

1. Do you tend to get angry easily? What tends to fuel your anger? Do you face consequences because of it?

2. Describe a situation where someone you know expressed anger, with negative results for himself or others. How might this situation have been handled differently?

3. According to Maimonides, "One should teach oneself to not get angry, even over a matter where anger is justified. If one wants to instill fear in one's children or family members, or in the community if one is its leader, and wants to be angry at them so they will return to the correct path, then one should show them one's anger in order to chastise them, but inwardly should remain calm. One should present oneself like an angry person in the time of one's wrath, but not really be angry" (*Mishneh Torah, Hilkhot De'ot* 2:3). He teaches that even when anger is justified, it should still be avoided. Do you agree? Do you think it is possible to derive the perceived benefits of exhibiting anger without actually being angry, as Maimonides suggests? Why or why not?

❖ Children First

As the parashah concludes, the tribes of Reuben and Gad request to be settled on the Jordan River's east side, where the Israelites currently find themselves, rather than on its west side, where the other tribes will reside after conquering the Land of Israel. These two tribes are attracted to the river's east side because it is well suited for grazing their large herds of cattle. The tribes of Reuben and Gad agree, nevertheless, to cross the Jordan with the other tribes in the impending war of conquest; and they explain how they will safeguard their families and the possessions left behind during the military campaign.

וַיִּגְּשׁוּ אֵלָיו וַיֹּאמְרוּ גִּדְרֹת צֹאן נִבְנֶה לְמִקְנֵנוּ
פֹּה וְעָרִים לְטַפֵּנוּ: (במדבר לב, טז)

Then they [the tribes of Reuben and Gad] stepped up to him [Moses] and said, "We will build here [on the east bank of the Jordan] sheepfolds for our flocks and towns for our children" [before joining the other tribes to conquer the Land of Israel]. (Num. 32:16)

Rashi comments on the order of the words in this verse:

נבנה למקננו פה: חסים היו על ממונם יותר מבניהם ובנותיהם,
שהקדימו מקניהם לטפם. אמר להם משה לא כן עשו, העיקר עיקר
והטפל טפל, בנו לכם תחלה ערים לטפכם ואחר כך גדרות לצאנכם:
(רש"י, שם)

We will build here [sheepfolds] for our flocks: They were more concerned about their possessions than about their sons and daughters, since they gave precedence to their flocks over their children. Moses said to them, "Not so! Treat what is fundamental as fundamental, and what is secondary as secondary. First build yourselves cities for your children, and afterward pens for your flocks." (Rashi, Num. 32:16)

As Rashi explains, by talking about their animals at the outset, the tribes of Reuben and Gad demonstrate misplaced priorities: their flocks first, their children second. Moses corrects them accordingly.

In our modern era, economic blessings have sometimes come at the cost of rising materialism. People tend to regard as necessities many things that were once considered luxuries. Pressures to work to provide "the best" for the family have contributed to parents and children spending less time together. The challenge to prioritize children is as relevant today as ever.

Questions for Discussion

1. In 1960, according to the Pew Research Center, 25 percent of American married couples with children under eighteen had two incomes; in 2012 the figure had escalated to 60 percent. What do you think are the driving forces behind the rise in two-earner families? Do you think parents and children are better off for this change?

2. Can you name a possession that was considered a luxury when you were growing up, but now has come to be regarded as a necessity? Is this shift in priorities an inevitable by-product of economic and technological progress? Is it beneficial, problematic, or both?

3. Have you had the experience of treating something fundamental as secondary, and something secondary as fundamental? What happened?

MASE'EI

❖ A Matter of Perspective

A common charitable appeal states: "For less than the daily cost of a cup of coffee, you can make a difference in the life of a needy child." This fundraising approach is effective in part because it takes a large sum that people may be reluctant to give and breaks it down into several small amounts that people regard as insignificant. Such reframing—seeing something from a different perspective—calls to mind the opening verse of Parashat Mase'ei, which lists all the places the Jews encamped during their forty years in the wilderness.

אֵלֶּה מַסְעֵי בְנֵי יִשְׂרָאֵל אֲשֶׁר יָצְאוּ מֵאֶרֶץ מִצְרַיִם לְצִבְאֹתָם בְּיַד מֹשֶׁה וְאַהֲרֹן: (במדבר לג, א)

These were the marches of the Israelites who started out from the land of Egypt, troop by troop, in the charge of Moses and Aaron. (Num. 33:1)

Rashi addresses why the Torah recounts all the Jews' travels:

אלה מסעי: למה נכתבו המסעות הללו, להודיע חסדיו של מקום, שאעפ״י שגזר עליהם לטלטלם ולהניעם במדבר, לא תאמר שהיו נעים ומטולטלים ממסע למסע כל ארבעים שנה ולא היתה להם מנוחה, שהרי אין כאן אלא ארבעים ושתים מסעות. צא מהם י״ד, שכולם היו בשנה ראשונה, קודם גזירה, משנסעו מרעמסס עד שבאו לרתמה. שמשם נשתלחו המרגלים, שנאמר (במדבר יב, טז) ואחר נסעו העם מחצרות וגו׳ (שם יג, ב) שלח לך אנשים וגו׳. וכאן

הוא אומר ויסעו מחצרות ויחנו ברתמה, למדת שהיא במדבר פארן. ועוד הוצא משם שמונה מסעות שהיו לאחר מיתת אהרן מהר ההר עד ערבות מואב בשנת הארבעים, נמצא שכל שמנה ושלשים שנה לא נסעו אלא עשרים מסעות: (רש״י, שם)

These were the marches: Why were these journeys recorded? To make known the kindness of the Omnipresent, for although He decreed to move them around and make them wander in the desert, do not say that they were moving about and wandering from journey to journey for all forty years and they had no rest, because there are only forty-two journeys here. Deduct fourteen of them, which all took place in the first year before the decree [of wandering]. . . . Subtract a further eight journeys, which took place after Aaron's death . . . during the fortieth year, and you will find that throughout the thirty-eight years they made only twenty journeys. (Rashi, Num. 33:1)

Rashi reframes God's decree of wandering, intended as divine punishment, as an expression of divine mercy; because the majority of the Israelites' travels occurred in the first and last years, God was exhibiting kindness by letting the people remain at rest for much of their desert sojourn.

Rashi reminds us that each of us is equipped with a powerful tool to reassess a situation by changing our perspective.

Questions for Discussion

1. Describe a situation that has been challenging for you to accept or handle. How might you reframe it?
2. Is there a challenge facing the Jewish people that you could view more positively by reframing it? If yes, how could you see it in a different light?

3. Have you ever overcome a major challenge by breaking it down into more manageable chunks? If so, describe how you accomplished it. What did you learn from the process?

❖ Name That Town

Even if we have never been to Hershey, Pennsylvania, we know something about the city based on its iconic name. Another example of a place's name reflecting its history appears in the parashah's accounting of the Israelites' wilderness travels.

וַיִּסְעוּ מֵחֲצֵרֹת וַיַּחֲנוּ בְּרִתְמָה: (במדבר לג, יח)

They set out from Hazeroth and encamped at Rithmah. (Num. 33:18)

Rashi comments on the name Rithmah (literally, "smoldering [coals]"):

ויחנו ברתמה: על שם לשון הרע של מרגלים, שנאמר (תהלים קכ, ג–ד) מה יתן לך ומה יוסיף לך לשון רמיה חצי גבור שנונים עם גחלי רתמים: (רש"י, שם)

and encamped at Rithmah: So named because of the slander of the scouts [who slandered the Land of Israel], as it says (Ps. 120:3–4), "What can you profit, what can you gain, O deceitful tongue? A warrior's sharp arrows, with hot coals of broom-wood [*gachalei rithamim,* גַּחֲלֵי רְתָמִים]." (Rashi, Num. 33:18)

Rashi explains that Rithmah was so named to recall the place of the scouts' incendiary slander, and he cites a passage from Psalms to support the connection between defamatory speech and fire.

Throughout the Torah, place-names recall both dark chapters for the Jewish nation as well as the people's glorious history. For example, the name Hebron (literally, "attachment") recalls how Abraham attached himself to God by building an altar there (see Rashi, Gen. 13:18). Hebron is also called Kiriath-arba (literally, "City of the Four"), a reference to the four couples buried there: Adam and Eve, Abraham and Sarah, Isaac and Rebekah, and Jacob and Leah (see Rashi, Gen. 23:2).

Questions for Discussion

1. Have you lived in a place whose name is indicative of its history? If so, what is the background of the name?

2. The names of many Israeli towns and cities have historical or religious significance, among them Beit El (House of God, where Jacob had his dream of a ladder connecting heaven and earth), Maccabim (named for the Maccabees who battled the Greeks at the time of the Hanukkah miracle), and Yavneh (the seat of the Sanhedrin, or Jewish High Court, after the Roman destruction of Jerusalem). Other locales were named to express the zeitgeist of the Zionist movement and its personalities, such as Petah Tikva (Opening of Hope), Ness Ziona (Banner to Zion), and Herzliya, named for modern Zionism founder, Theodor Herzl. If you could name a new Israeli town, what Jewish event, figure, concept, or hope do you think would serve well as the basis for a fitting name?

3. While Hershey may be the most famous company town in the United States, there are many others rooted in American history, such as Endicott, New York (Endicott

Johnson—shoes); Kohler, Wisconsin (Kohler—plumbing); and Alcoa, Tennessee (Alcoa—aluminum). Do you think new company towns are likely to be founded in the future, or is this tradition an American relic? What does this say about America today and tomorrow?

❖ Urban Planning

The Talmud states: "Ten measures of beauty descended to the world—nine were taken by Jerusalem and one by the rest of the world" (*Bavli Kiddushin* 49b). Even in ancient times, a city prided itself on its beauty—and this concern for beauty extended to other cities throughout the Land of Israel, as the parashah indicates.

צַו אֶת בְּנֵי יִשְׂרָאֵל וְנָתְנוּ לַלְוִיִּם מִנַּחֲלַת אֲחֻזָּתָם עָרִים לָשָׁבֶת וּמִגְרָשׁ לֶעָרִים סְבִיבֹתֵיהֶם תִּתְּנוּ לַלְוִיִּם: (במדבר לה, ב)

Instruct the Israelite people to assign, out of the holdings apportioned to them, towns for the Levites to dwell in; you shall also assign to the Levites pasture land around their towns. (Num. 35:2)

Rashi explains the reason for the pastureland around the cities:

ומגרש: ריוח מקום חלק חוץ לעיר סביב להיות לנוי לעיר, ואין רשאין לבנות שם בית ולא לנטוע כרם ולא לזרוע זריעה: (רש"י, שם)

pasture land: An open space set aside surrounding the city, to beautify it. One is not permitted to build a house there, or plant a vineyard, or sow seeds. (Rashi, Num. 35:2)

Instead of receiving a contiguous territory like the other tribes, the Levites are granted forty-eight cities throughout the Land of Israel. As Rashi explains, each city is ringed by an open area intended to beautify it.

Aesthetic concerns remain a vital consideration in urban planning. Beautiful cities often feature wide-open spaces that integrate into bustling areas of commercial, residential, and cultural life. In Manhattan, for example, Central Park serves as the city's unofficial playground, supporting activities as varied as ice-skating, running, horseback riding, and boating. The park's greenery also provides a welcome visual contrast to a dense cityscape.

Questions for Discussion

1. What city do you think is especially beautiful and why? Would you like to live there?
2. What aspect of the city in which you live most enhances your experience of living there? Could other cities benefit by including this feature?
3. What do you believe could be done to beautify the city in which you live? What could your city learn from others?

Deuteronomy

DEVARIM

❖ Veiled Criticism

Kent State, Watergate, Tiananmen Square—the mere mention of these places calls to mind national calamity and questions of personal conduct. Moses makes references to such places in his address to the Israelites before they enter the Land of Israel.

אֵלֶּה הַדְּבָרִים אֲשֶׁר דִּבֶּר מֹשֶׁה אֶל כָּל יִשְׂרָאֵל בְּעֵבֶר הַיַּרְדֵּן בַּמִּדְבָּר בָּעֲרָבָה מוֹל סוּף בֵּין פָּארָן וּבֵין תֹּפֶל וְלָבָן וַחֲצֵרֹת וְדִי זָהָב: (דברים א, א)

These are the words that Moses addressed to all Israel on the other side of the Jordan.—Through the wilderness, in the Arabah near Suph, between Paran and Tophel, Laban, Hazeroth, and Di-zahab. (Deut. 1:1)

Rashi explains the relevance of the place-names, whose significance is otherwise not clear:

אלה הדברים: לפי שהן דברי תוכחות ומנה כאן כל המקומות שהכעיסו לפני המקום בהן, לפיכך סתם את הדברים והזכירם ברמז מפני כבודן של ישראל: (רש"י, שם)

These are the words: Because these are words of rebuke and he [Moses] enumerates here all the places where they [the Israelites] angered the Omnipresent, he therefore makes no explicit mention of the incidents [in which they transgressed], but rather merely alludes to them [by mentioning the names of the places], out of respect for Israel. (Rashi, Deut. 1:1)

As Rashi explains, Moses wishes to rebuke the Jewish nation and simultaneously to preserve the Israelites' honor. Therefore, he does not mention the people's transgressions, but cites the places where the incidents occurred.

Offering constructive criticism effectively is one of the most difficult things to do. Unless the person offering criticism exercises great discretion, the listener is liable to perceive it as an attack, become defensive, justify his or her conduct, and avenge hurt feelings. To avoid this destructive cycle, researchers in the field recommend that the person offering the criticism (1) describe the problematic conduct as specifically as possible and (2) direct the criticism toward the behavior rather than the person. Additionally, as the Torah's example emphasizes, preserving the other person's dignity should be a foremost concern.

Questions for Discussion

1. "Kent State" refers to the Ohio National Guard's fatal shooting of four students protesting the Vietnam War at Kent State University in 1970. "Watergate" refers to the bungled 1972 break-in at the Democratic National Committee headquarters located within the Watergate office complex, which led to an investigation that ultimately implicated President Richard Nixon and led to his 1974 resignation. "Tiananmen Square" refers to China's violent killing of hundreds of antigovernment protestors in Beijing's Tiananmen Square in 1989. Are there any government scandals you would add to this list? If so, what was

disconcerting about the event? Have the underlying issues been resolved?

2. The Torah highlights the failings of the Jewish nation—including those of its great prophet, Moses, who is denied the privilege of leading the Jews into the Promised Land (see Deut. 34:4–6). What is the legacy of a Jewish tradition that recognizes the fallibility of its leaders? How do you believe this has shaped the development of the Jewish nation and its ethos?

3. Even when constructive criticism is delivered using the above best practices, sometimes the receiver may still become defensive. What do you think can be done then to help the person open up enough to accept the feedback? Alternatively, can you think of other best practices for communicating criticism that might avert this situation? What experiences of giving or receiving criticism inform your answer?

....

❖ George Washington Slept Here

When visiting sites from the Revolutionary War period (1775–83), one often hears the claim "George Washington slept here." George Washington, as the American military commander, would have lodged in a variety of places, but it seems unlikely that all these claims of association with greatness are reliable. As the parashah details the Israelites' approach to the Land of Israel, a verse highlights another association conferring status and prestige.

פְּנוּ | וּסְעוּ לָכֶם וּבֹאוּ הַר הָאֱמֹרִי וְאֶל כָּל שְׁכֵנָיו בָּעֲרָבָה בָהָר וּבַשְּׁפֵלָה וּבַנֶּגֶב וּבְחוֹף הַיָּם אֶרֶץ הַכְּנַעֲנִי וְהַלְּבָנוֹן עַד הַנָּהָר הַגָּדֹל נְהַר פְּרָת:
(דברים א, ז)

Start out and make your way to the hill country of the Amorites and to all their neighbors in the Arabah, the hill country, the Shephelah, the Negeb, the seacoast, the land of the Canaanites, and the Lebanon, as far as the Great River, the river Euphrates. (Deut. 1:7)

Rashi comments on the description of the Euphrates as the "Great River":

עד הנהר הגדול: מפני שנזכר עם ארץ ישראל, קראו גדול. משל הדיוט אומר עבד מלך מלך, הדבק לשחוור וישתחוו לך, קרב לגבי דהינא ואידהן: (רש"י, שם)

as far as the Great River: Because it [the Euphrates] is mentioned [in association] with the Land of Israel, it is referred to as "great." [This is consistent with the] proverbs that state: "A king's servant is a king"; "Attach yourself to the chief and [people] will bow down to you"; "Become close to one who is anointed [distinguished] and you become anointed." (Rashi, Deut. 1:7)

Rashi explains that the designation of the Euphrates as the "Great River" derives from its connection with the Land of Israel. He also cites proverbs teaching that people's associates influence both how they are perceived and how they see themselves. Rashi advises us to choose with care the company we keep.

Questions for Discussion

1. The Jewish world has traditionally attached great importance to one's *yichus* (lineage)—so much so that in earlier generations it was common to create a family tree highlighting any famous ancestors to improve children's

marriage prospects. How far back can you trace your family line? Have there been any famous (or infamous) relatives in your family? If so, what is your relationship to them, and how, if it all, has this association affected your life?

2. Have you ever had a relationship with someone you consider to be "great" in some way? If so, describe this relationship and any influence it has had on you. Also, how might your relationship with this person have enriched his or her life?

3. If you could add the designation "great" to an area of land, sea, or sky, what area would you choose and why?

❖ Mirror Image

While recalling the events since the Exodus from Egypt, Moses recounts that thirty-nine years earlier the Israelites had stood poised to enter the Land of Israel—until they heard the scouts' ominous report about the land. Then they became despondent, lost their resolve to proceed, and began to level outrageous accusations against God.

וַתֵּרָגְנוּ בְאָהֳלֵיכֶם וַתֹּאמְרוּ בְּשִׂנְאַת יְהוָה אֹתָנוּ הוֹצִיאָנוּ מֵאֶרֶץ מִצְרָיִם לָתֵת אֹתָנוּ בְּיַד הָאֱמֹרִי לְהַשְׁמִידֵנוּ: (דברים א, כז)

You sulked in your tents and said, "It is because the Lord hates us that He brought us out of the land of Egypt, to hand us over to the Amorites to wipe us out." (Deut. 1:27)

Rashi explains how the Israelites could make such an accusation against God:

בְּשִׂנְאַת ה' אֹתָנוּ: וְהוּא הָיָה אוֹהֵב אֶתְכֶם, אֲבָל אַתֶּם שׂוֹנְאִים אוֹתוֹ. מָשָׁל הֶדְיוֹט אוֹמֵר, מַה דְּבִלְבָּךְ עַל רַחְמָךְ מַה דְּבִלְבֵּיהּ עֲלָךְ: (רש"י, שם)

It is because the Lord hates us: In reality, He loved you, but you hated Him. There is a proverb that says: "What is in your own heart regarding your friend, [you imagine] is in his heart regarding you." (Rashi, Deut. 1:27)

Rashi explains that the Israelites believed that God hated them because they in fact hated God. A common proverb expresses the fundamental psychological insight that our beliefs about how others perceive us can be strongly informed by how we perceive them.

If our assessments of other people's speech or behavior are colored by our own conceptions and feelings, how can we really know what another person feels about us? A start may be to bear in mind that our perceptions are not objectively accurate, but rather highly subjective.

Questions for Discussion

1. Is there someone or a group of people who you believe judges you harshly? If so, what does this person or group say or do that leads you to this conclusion? Might your own impression of this person or group be playing a role in your assessment?

2. Is there an individual or a group toward whom you harbor hostile feelings? If so, what actions have provoked your feelings? Might your own impression of this person or group be playing a role in your assessment?

3. Have you ever believed someone disliked you, only to later discover this was not at all true? If yes, what influenced your original impressions, and what (if anything) did you take away from the experience?

VA-ETḤANNAN

❖ It's All a Gift

Getting to Israel was not always as easy for Jews as it is today. Prior to the state's founding in 1948, Jews who embarked on a voyage to the Holy Land were at risk of being turned back while still at sea by the British blockade that restricted Jewish immigration. Even those who managed to avoid the blockade could be denied entry by British authorities upon their arrival.

Moses too was denied permission to enter the Land of Israel. In the opening verse of Parashat Va-etḥannan, Moses tries to convince God to change this decree barring his entry.

וָאֶתְחַנַּן אֶל יְהֹוָה בָּעֵת הַהִוא לֵאמֹר: (דברים ג, כג)

I pleaded with the Lord at that time, saying. (Deut. 3:23)

Rashi comments on Moses's use of the word *va'etchannan* (וָאֶתְחַנַּן, I pleaded):

ואתחנן: אין חנון בכל מקום אלא לשון מתנת חנם. אף על פי שיש
להם לצדיקים לתלות במעשיהם הטובים, אין מבקשים מאת המקום
אלא מתנת חנם. לפי שאמר לו (שמות לג, יט) וחנותי את אשר
אחון, אמר לו בלשון ואתחנן: (רש"י, שם)

I pleaded: [The word] *chinun* [חִנּוּן] in all cases is an expression [requesting] an undeserved gift. Even though the righteous may [be justified in] basing a request on the merit of their good deeds, they [nevertheless] ask the Lord only for an undeserved gift. (Rashi, Deut. 3:23)

Rashi explains that out of many possible expressions of request, Moses chose to use the word *va'etchannan* (וָאֶתְחַנַּן, I pleaded) because it denotes requesting the privilege of an undeserved gift.

How, some might ask, could Moses not have deserved to enter the Land of Israel? After all, he confronted Pharaoh, the world's most powerful leader, led the Jewish slaves from bondage to freedom, endured forty days without food or water as he received the Torah on Mount Sinai, taught the Torah to the Israelites, led them for forty years to the Promised Land, and assiduously advocated on their behalf despite their many transgressions.

Even after all Moses had achieved, he eschewed an attitude of entitlement. Rashi reminds us that whatever we have—even our hard-earned attainments—ultimately constitutes a gift.

Questions for Discussion

1. In 1947 the ss *Exodus*, carrying forty-five hundred Jewish passengers, most of them Holocaust survivors, left France bound for the Holy Land. As the ship approached the future State of Israel, the British boarded it—killing a crew member and two passengers in the process—and commandeered it into the Port of Haifa. British officials then transferred the passengers to three British ships and deported them to France. Upon arrival, when the Jews refused to disembark in France, the British rerouted them to Hamburg, Germany (then in the British occupation zone), and forcibly ejected them onto German soil. What parallels and differences do you see between Jewish immigration under the

Palestine Mandate as exemplified here and the millions of migrants from the Middle East and Africa seeking asylum today in Europe?

2. While Moses may seem to have been more deserving to enter the Land of Israel than anyone else, it was, perhaps paradoxically, his special relationship with God that may have militated against such a result. The Talmud states: "God is exacting with those who surround him [the righteous] even to the extent of a hairbreadth" (*Bavli Bava Kamma* 50a). Why do you believe the Jewish ethos is to apply the highest standards to the most righteous human beings? Do you agree that such standards should be upheld in our generation?

3. Do you agree that even our hard-earned attainments constitute a gift? Why or why not?

❖ The Challenges of Leadership

People often focus on the power and prestige that accompany a leadership position and do not consider the sizeable day-to-day challenges that a leader confronts. In this verse from the parashah, God instructs Moses to prepare his successor, Joshua, for impending challenges.

וְצַו אֶת יְהוֹשֻׁעַ וְחַזְּקֵהוּ וְאַמְּצֵהוּ כִּי הוּא יַעֲבֹר לִפְנֵי הָעָם הַזֶּה וְהוּא יַנְחִיל אוֹתָם אֶת הָאָרֶץ אֲשֶׁר תִּרְאֶה: (דברים ג, כח)

Give Joshua his instructions, and imbue him with strength and courage, for he shall go across at the head of this people, and he shall allot to them the land that you may only see. (Deut. 3:28)

Rashi describes the particulars that Moses was commanded to impart to Joshua:

וצו את יהושע: על הטרחות ועל המשאות ועל הריבות: (רש"י, שם)

Give Joshua his instructions: regarding the troubles, the burdens, and the quarrels [inherent in leadership]. (Rashi, Deut. 3:28)

Rashi explains that Moses was instructed to counsel Joshua about the difficulties endemic to leadership. During the forty years Moses led the Jewish people, he endured their complaints about the quality of the food, the lack of water, and the dangers awaiting them in Israel. He also faced a brazen rebellion against his leadership. Moses therefore sought to prepare Joshua for potential internal challenges his successor might not have envisioned.

The insight to fully ground a successor in a position's challenges, internal or otherwise, would likely resonate with any contemporary leader.

Questions for Discussion

1. In 1952 Israel, under Prime Minister David Ben-Gurion, reached an agreement with Germany to accept payment of three billion marks (equivalent to $6.5 billion in 2017) as reparations for Jewish slave labor and theft of Jewish property during the Holocaust. Menachem Begin, the opposition leader in the Knesset, Israel's legislature, bitterly opposed the agreement. Years later Bennie Begin, Menachem Begin's son, said to Daniel Gordis, author of a book about Menachem Begin: "You were too hard on Ben-Gurion. Of course, I think my father's points were correct. But Ben-Gurion had a country to feed. He had

hundreds of thousands of immigrants who needed roofs over their heads. This country was out of money, and the Germans were offering Israel an opportunity to get on its economic feet. My father was in the opposition—Ben-Gurion's responsibilities weren't his. What was Ben-Gurion supposed to do?" What do you think of Ben-Gurion's decision? Does understanding the difficulties Israel was experiencing when Ben-Gurion led the country affect your assessment?

2. When you served in a leadership capacity, what unrecognized or unappreciated challenges did you encounter?

3. If you were tasked with mentoring a protégé to assume a position of leadership, how would you go about it? What lessons have you learned that you would like to impart to this person?

....

❖ Modesty

In 1956 a Jewish butcher sued the London Beth Din (LBD, the rabbinic court charged with kosher supervision) in an English court of law for having revoked his kosher certification. During the trial the butcher's attorney asked Dayan Yechezkel Abramsky, the rabbinic judge heading the LBD, a question focusing on his credentials: "Dayan Abramsky, it is said that you are the greatest halakhic [Jewish legal] authority in the United Kingdom and His Majesty's dominion overseas. Do you agree with this view?" This question seemed designed to make the witness look bad—arrogant if answered in the affirmative or unauthoritative if answered in the negative. After a pause the witness responded, "Yes." The judge then addressed the witness, "Dayan Abramsky, have you not heard of humility even

amongst great scholars?" The witness responded, "I have, my lord, but I am on oath and have to tell the truth." A verse in the parashah raises a similar issue.

לֹא מֵרֻבְּכֶם מִכָּל הָעַמִּים חָשַׁק יְהוָה בָּכֶם וַיִּבְחַר בָּכֶם כִּי אַתֶּם הַמְעַט מִכָּל הָעַמִּים: (דברים ז, ז)

It is not because you are the most numerous of peoples that the Lord set His heart on you and chose you—indeed, you are the smallest of peoples. (Deut. 7:7)

Rashi offers a midrashic interpretation of this verse:

לֹא מרבכם: כפשוטו. ומדרשו לפי שאין אתם מגדילים עצמכם כשאני משפיע לכם טובה לפיכך חשקתי בכם: (רש"י, שם)

It is not because you are the most numerous: [This is to be understood] according to its simple meaning. But its midrashic interpretation [understanding לֹא מֵרֻבְּכֶם as "not because of your greatness"] is: Because you do not boast about yourselves when I shower you with goodness, therefore I [God] delighted in you. (Rashi, Deut. 7:7)

Contemporary society seems to endorse a "look at me" mentality. On social media, people reveal the details of their lives in part to gain others' esteem and admiration. Smartphone users take "selfies" (self-portraits) for instant sharing. Some individuals who have mastered the art of self-promotion via online publishing and social networks have become media stars.

Rashi, in contrast, encourages us to view modesty as an appealing quality. He observes that greatness encompasses being humble about one's honorable actions.

Questions for Discussion

1. In a scene from the 1987 movie *Baby Boomer*, two mothers are with their toddlers at a Manhattan playground when a third mother arrives with her toddler (named Cosby) and confesses to her friends, "We heard from Dalton [an elite private school]; Cosby didn't get in." They respond aghast, "Oh no!" Cosby's mother continues, "I'm so upset. If she doesn't get into the right preschool, she's not going to get into the right kindergarten. If she doesn't get into the right kindergarten, I can forget about a good prep school and any hope of an Ivy League college. . . . I just don't understand it. Her resume was perfect, her references were impeccable." However exaggerated, this scene illustrates many families' tremendous drive to ensure that their children get ahead in life. Concerns about one's "resume" may begin years before entering the job market, and one's youth may be filled with activities chosen specifically to make a good impression on others. Within this culture, is it possible for young people to act humbly and still remain competitive?

2. Have you struggled to decide whether to post certain information online? How do you determine what is and is not appropriate to share? Did you ever share something you later regretted?

3. Would you say that you tend to be modest or immodest or both or neither? Do you find the trait of modesty and the actions associated with it to be appealing and desirable in your life? Why or why not?

'EKEV

❖ Don't Tread on Me

The Gadsden flag, designed in 1775 by American general and statesman Christopher Gadsden, features a coiled rattlesnake with the words "Don't Tread on Me." Like the bald eagle, the rattlesnake was found throughout the thirteen colonies and thus became a symbol of America. The flag's motto calls to mind the opening verse from Parashat 'Ekev.

וְהָיָה | עֵקֶב תִּשְׁמְעוּן אֵת הַמִּשְׁפָּטִים הָאֵלֶּה וּשְׁמַרְתֶּם וַעֲשִׂיתֶם אֹתָם וְשָׁמַר יְהוָה אֱלֹהֶיךָ לְךָ אֶת הַבְּרִית וְאֶת הַחֶסֶד אֲשֶׁר נִשְׁבַּע לַאֲבֹתֶיךָ: (דברים ז, יב)

And if you do obey these rules and observe them carefully, the Lord your God will maintain faithfully for you the covenant that He made on oath with your fathers. (Deut. 7:12)

Rashi comments on the unusual usage of the word *ekev* (עֵקֶב, literally, "heel," but here meaning "if"):

והיה עקב תשמעון: אם המצות הקלות שאדם דש בעקביו תשמעון: (רש"י, שם)

And if you do obey: If even the lesser commandments [mitzvot] that a person [sometimes] tramples with his heels you will obey. (Rashi, Deut. 7:12)

While it may be true—borrowing a phrase from the Declaration of Independence—that all mitzvot are created equal, it does not follow, as Rashi points out, that they are all treated with the same regard. The rationale for following some of the Torah's 613 mitzvot, such as honoring one's parents, is easier to understand than others, such as not wearing garments that contain both wool and linen (*shatnez*). Some mitzvot, such as discussing the Exodus from Egypt on the first night of Passover, are easy to fulfill, while others, such as writing a Torah scroll, may be considerably more difficult. Rashi teaches us to strive to perform all the mitzvot to the best of our abilities.

Questions for Discussion

1. Is there a mitzvah you particularly enjoy performing? If so, what do you find appealing about it?
2. Is there a mitzvah you find either difficult to understand or challenging to perform? If so, would you be open to learning more about it in an effort to become more receptive to its performance?
3. Is there a mitzvah you believe could have a positive impact on society if many more people observed it? If so, how would you propose engaging more people to perform it?

❖ Follow-Through

In 1961 President John F. Kennedy expressed his intention "of landing a man on the moon and returning him safely to the earth" before the decade was over. While thousands of people played a role in enabling the United States to achieve this goal, the person most associated with the accomplishment is Neil Armstrong, who in 1969 became the first person to walk on the moon. A verse in the parashah touches on the issue of an achievement being associated with the person who brought it to fruition.

כָּל הַמִּצְוָה אֲשֶׁר אָנֹכִי מְצַוְּךָ הַיּוֹם תִּשְׁמְרוּן לַעֲשׂוֹת לְמַעַן תִּחְיוּן וּרְבִיתֶם וּבָאתֶם וִירִשְׁתֶּם אֶת הָאָרֶץ אֲשֶׁר נִשְׁבַּע יְהוָֹה לַאֲבֹתֵיכֶם: (דברים ח, א)

You shall faithfully observe all the Instruction that I enjoin upon you today, that you may thrive and increase and be able to possess the land that the Lord promised on oath to your fathers. (Deut. 8:1)

Rashi comments on the Hebrew verse's opening words, *kol ha-mitzvah* (כָּל הַמִּצְוָה), which can be translated as "the entire commandment":

כל המצוה: כפשוטו. ומדרש אגדה אם התחלת במצוה גמור אותה, שאינה נקראת המצוה אלא על שם הגומרה, שנאמר (יהושע כד, לב) ואת עצמות יוסף אשר העלו בני ישראל ממצרים קברו בשכם, והלא משה לבדו נתעסק בהם להעלותם, אלא לפי שלא הספיק לגומרה וגמרוה ישראל, נקראת על שמם: (רש"י, שם)

all the Instruction: This may be understood in its plain sense. There is also a midrashic explanation: If you have started a commandment [mitzvah], complete it, because it is attributed only to the one who completes it, as it says, "The bones of Joseph, which the Israelites had brought up from Egypt, were buried at Shechem [in the Land of Israel]" (Josh. 24:32). But didn't Moses alone attend to them [the bones] to bring them up [from Egypt]? [See Exod. 13:19.] However, since he had no opportunity to complete it [since he did not enter the Land of Israel] and the Israelites completed it, it is credited to their name. (Rashi, Deut. 8:1)

Rashi emphasizes that a person is to complete any mitzvah he or she has begun—a reminder of the importance of follow-through in everything we undertake.

Questions for Discussion

1. Neil Armstrong's moon walk marked the successful conclusion of an ambitious national undertaking launched years earlier. Describe an achievement that required you to follow through over an extended period. How did you maintain the discipline to conclude the initiative? Did you encounter any setbacks, and, if so, how did you overcome them?

2. Name something you would like to do but have refrained from starting because of a concern that you may not be able to complete it. Is there something you can do to help assure that you can finish it?

3. In 1897 Theodor Herzl organized the First Zionist Congress in Basel, Switzerland, which gave birth to the modern Zionist movement. After the Congress ended, Herzl wrote in his diary: "At Basel I founded the Jewish State. If I said this out loud today l would be greeted by universal laughter. In five years perhaps, and certainly in fifty years, everyone will perceive it." Fifty years later, in 1947, the United Nations adopted the UN Partition Plan for Palestine, which created the State of Israel. Herzl died seven years after the First Zionist Congress, at the age of forty-four, and therefore never lived to see the Jewish state he "founded" come to fruition. Reflecting on this aspect of Herzl's life brings

to mind the sages' statement: "You are not obligated to complete the task, but you are not free to withdraw from it either" (*Pirkei Avot* 2:21). What task do you believe is important to undertake even though no single individual can complete it? Why is this enterprise important to you? What contribution have you made or might you make to it?

⸺⸺⸺⸺⸺⸺⸺⸺⸺⸺⸺⸺⸺

❖ *Mameloshen*

The story is told of a newlywed Jewish couple in czarist Russia that lived in poverty but aspired to a life of affluence. Their mother tongue (*mameloshen*) was Yiddish. However, as the husband established himself in business, he increasingly dealt with other upwardly mobile Jews who had abandoned speaking their native Yiddish in favor of the voguish Russian. The husband followed their example, and after a period of time he no longer conversed in Yiddish—not even with his wife, who had also switched to speaking Russian. His wife became pregnant. One day she went into labor with their first child. Seeing her seemingly in great pain, he called the town's Jewish doctor, who came quickly but did nothing, saying the time had not arrived for him to get involved. Though she screamed in Russian, the doctor remained passive. "Why are you making my wife go through this agony?" the husband implored the doctor. "Do something to ease the pain." "It is not yet time," the doctor reiterated, adding, "Do not worry—when the time comes, I will do what is necessary." This persisted for another hour. Finally, the woman screamed in Yiddish— "Momma, help mir!" (Mother, help me!). "Now," exclaimed the doctor, "she is ready."

A verse in the parashah touches on a different *mameloshen*, from a much earlier period in Jewish history.

וְלִמַּדְתֶּם אֹתָם אֶת בְּנֵיכֶם לְדַבֵּר בָּם בְּשִׁבְתְּךָ בְּבֵיתֶךָ וּבְלֶכְתְּךָ בַדֶּרֶךְ וּבְשָׁכְבְּךָ וּבְקוּמֶךָ: (דברים יא, יט)

And teach them to your children—reciting them when you stay at home and when you are away, when you lie down and when you get up. (Deut. 11:19)

Rashi comments on this verse:

לדבר בם: משעה שהבן יודע לדבר, למדהו תורה צוה לנו משה (דברים לג, ד), שיהא זה למוד דבורו. מכאן אמרו, כשהתינוק מתחיל לדבר אביו מדבר עמו בלשון הקדש ומלמדו תורה: (רש״י, שם)

reciting them: From the moment your son knows how to speak, teach him [the verse], "When Moses charged us with the Teaching" (Deut. 33:4), so that this develops his speech. From here [the sages] said that when an infant begins to speak, his father should converse with him in the Holy Tongue [Hebrew] and teach him Torah. (Rashi, Deut. 11:19)

Rashi explains that the first thing a father should teach his son is Torah, spoken in Hebrew. While through the generations Jews have taught their children Torah from infancy, now millions of Jews living in the State of Israel are also making the Holy Tongue their children's *mameloshen*.

Questions for Discussion

1. What is your mother tongue, and for how many generations has that been your family's native language? What
   languages did your family speak previously, and has any
   knowledge of them been transmitted to you?

2. A century ago, large segments of the Jewish community
   were unified through shared Jewish languages: Yiddish
   among the Jews of Eastern Europe, and Ladino (Judeo-
   Spanish) among the Jews of the former Ottoman Empire
   (the Balkans, Turkey, the Middle East, and North Africa). In
   recent generations Hebrew has replaced these languages as
   the lingua franca of the Jewish people. What is your knowledge of Hebrew, and how did you gain it? Would you like
   to improve your Hebrew? If so, how might you do that?

3. Rashi instructs parents that the first words a Jewish child
   should be taught to say describe the Torah that Moses
   transmitted as "the heritage of the congregation of Jacob
   [the Jewish people]" (תּוֹרָה צִוָּה לָנוּ מֹשֶׁה מוֹרָשָׁה קְהִלַּת יַעֲקֹב)
   (Deut. 33:4). Do you believe that internalizing this message
   early in life can change a person's relationship with Judaism? Why or why not?

RE'EH

❖ Personal Best

The Torah states, "[And] Enoch walked with God" (Gen. 5:22), on which the sages say, "Enoch was a cobbler, and with every single stitch that he made, he achieved mystical unions [מייחד יחודים] with his Creator" (*Midrash Talpiot*). Citing Rabbi Yisrael Salanter (1810–83), Rabbi Eliyahu Dessler (1892–1953) writes that this midrash cannot possibly mean that while Enoch was stitching shoes for his customers, he was engaged in mystical thoughts, because this would constitute an impermissible distraction from the work for which he was being paid. Rather, this means that Enoch lavished attention on every stitch to assure that it would result in a sturdy and comfortable pair of shoes for its owner. In the process Enoch achieved "mystical unions" with his Creator, who also lavishes beneficence on others. Enoch's focus on giving his best to others touches on a theme raised in a verse from Parashat Re'eh that describes the offerings to be brought to the Temple in Jerusalem.

וְהָיָה הַמָּקוֹם אֲשֶׁר יִבְחַר יְהֹוָה אֱלֹהֵיכֶם בּוֹ לְשַׁכֵּן שְׁמוֹ שָׁם שָׁמָּה תָבִיאוּ אֵת כָּל אֲשֶׁר אָנֹכִי מְצַוֶּה אֶתְכֶם עוֹלֹתֵיכֶם וְזִבְחֵיכֶם מַעְשְׂרֹתֵיכֶם וּתְרֻמַת יֶדְכֶם וְכֹל מִבְחַר נִדְרֵיכֶם אֲשֶׁר תִּדְּרוּ לַיהֹוָה: (דברים יב, יא)

Then you must bring everything that I command you to the site where the Lord your God will choose to establish His name: your burnt offerings and other sacrifices, your tithes and contributions, and all the choice votive offerings that you vow to the Lord. (Deut. 12:11)

Rashi comments on one of these offerings:

מבחר נדריכם: מלמד שיביאו מן המובחר: (רש"י, שם)

the choice votive offerings: This teaches that one should bring [offerings] from the choicest. (Rashi, Deut. 12:11)

Rashi explains that this verse instructed Jews to bring their very best offerings to the Temple. The inherent message—to put forth one's best efforts—is just as relevant to our social relationships, work, and community involvements today. Not only are we more likely to achieve better results in our endeavors, but, like Enoch, by attending to rich detail, we may realize a purity of process that draws us closer to our Creator and to God's creation.

Questions for Discussion

1. The story of Enoch the cobbler illustrates how a beautifully done job can itself be an act of religious devotion. Have you undertaken any task or responsibility with a similar level of devotion? If so, how do you understand why you acted this way? Would you consider your deed an act of religious devotion? Did a matter of principle underlie your resolve?
2. What person do you know or know of who best resembles Enoch the cobbler in elevating a seemingly ordinary responsibility into something akin to a mystical union?
3. Do you believe you consistently give your best efforts to your social relationships? Is there anything more you might do?

❖ According to His Needs

Karl Marx, the founder of communism, captured the promise of this sociopolitical movement with his famous slogan, "From each according to his ability, to each according to his needs." The utopian vision Marx articulated included certain biblical themes. In fact, the latter part of this slogan echoes a verse from the parashah that discusses the obligation to care for the poor.

כִּי פָתֹחַ תִּפְתַּח אֶת יָדְךָ לוֹ וְהַעֲבֵט תַּעֲבִיטֶנּוּ דֵּי מַחְסֹרוֹ אֲשֶׁר יֶחְסַר לוֹ: (דברים טו, ח)

Rather, you must open your hand and lend him sufficient for whatever he needs. (Deut. 15:8)

Rashi comments:

אשר יחסר לו: אפילו סוס לרכוב עליו ועבד לרוץ לפניו: (רש"י, שם)

whatever he needs: Even a horse on which to ride, and a servant to run before him [to announce his arrival, if this was his custom]. (Rashi, Deut. 15:8)

As Rashi explains, when assisting a poor person, one must endeavor to return him to his accustomed standard of living, even if it seems extravagant.

In broader terms, when helping someone who is struggling financially, it is not enough to only take into account that person's basic physical requirements. We are also to attend to the individual's social, emotional, and psychological needs.

This approach can extend to all interactions with others. When attempting to genuinely help someone, rather than simply giving what we want to offer, Rashi advises us to be sensitive to the unique needs of this recipient.

Questions for Discussion

1. Describe a time you helped a person in need. In what ways, if any, was your assistance tailored to this individual?
2. What purpose do you believe is served by sustaining a poor person in his or her accustomed lifestyle? If you were responsible for disbursing funds to people who needed them, would you allocate them in this way?
3. Describe a time someone helped you more than you had asked, because he or she understood your social, emotional, or psychological needs.

❖ Spring Break

For most people the term "spring break" conjures up images of college students congregating at a beach resort for fun in the sun. However, long before this term had any such connotations, the springtime marked a break for the Jewish people from their normal routine to celebrate the Passover holiday. A verse from the parashah describes this observance.

שָׁמוֹר אֶת חֹדֶשׁ הָאָבִיב וְעָשִׂיתָ פֶּסַח לַיהוָה אֱלֹהֶיךָ כִּי בְּחֹדֶשׁ הָאָבִיב הוֹצִיאֲךָ יְהוָה אֱלֹהֶיךָ מִמִּצְרַיִם לָיְלָה: (דברים טז, א)

Observe the month of Abib and offer a passover sacrifice to the Lord your God, for it was in the month of Abib, at night, that the Lord your God freed you from Egypt. (Deut. 16:1)

Rashi comments on the requirement that Passover fall in the month of Abib (springtime):

שמור את חדש האביב: מקודם בואו שמור שיהא ראוי לאביב להקריב בו את מנחת העומר, ואם לאו, עבר את השנה: (רש"י, שם)

Observe the month of Abib: Before [the Hebrew month of Nisan (in which Passover falls)] arrives, take heed that [Passover] fall in the springtime, so that you may bring [in the springtime] an offering [of freshly harvested barley] measuring an omer. And if [it would] not [yet be spring at the time Passover was scheduled to fall], proclaim a leap year [by adding a thirteenth month to the previous year, thereby delaying Passover until the springtime]. (Rashi, Deut. 16:1)

Rashi explains that the omer offering of freshly harvested barley, which took place on the second day of Passover, had to occur in the spring. This requirement could only be met through an elaborate Hebrew calendar that combined elements of both the solar and lunar calendars.

Most of the world uses the Gregorian calendar, a solar calendar based on the 365-day year that corresponds to a full cycle of the seasons. Islam, however, uses a 354-day lunar calendar consisting of twelve months, each of which has 29 or 30 days, corresponding to the 29.5-day period from one new moon to the next. The lunar year is 11 days shorter than the solar year and has no connection to the cyle of seasons; a date on the lunar calendar is not linked to any particular season. As a result, the Islamic month of Ramadan, for example, progresses (in reverse chronological order) through each season over the course of thirty-two years—so if Ramadan now falls at the start of the winter, it will shift successively over the course of thirty-two years through the fall, summer, and spring before it falls again at the start of winter.

The Jewish calendar, by contrast, combines elements of both calendars. It has a nineteen-year cycle consisting of twelve years with twelve months and seven years with thirteen months. Each month has either 29 or 30 days, and, consistent with other lunar calendars, begins with the new moon.

The thirteenth month (Adar II) always falls immediately before Nisan, the month in which Passover is celebrated. Through the periodic insertion of this additional month into the Hebrew calendar, Passover is assured of always falling in the spring, as required.

Questions for Discussion

1. In Western countries, celebrating holidays in a particular season is an entrenched practice, and holiday activities often call attention to the seasonal nature of the festival, for example, outdoor fireworks on the Fourth of July, cozy family feasts on Thanksgiving. How do you think your experience of Jewish or secular holidays would be different if they were based solely on a lunar calendar and thus were stripped of all seasonal symbols and activities?

2. In your life do you connect more with the Gregorian solar calendar, the Hebrew solar-lunar calendar, equally to both, or something else?

3. How do you relate the springtime to the themes of the Exodus and Passover?

SHOFETIM

❖ Honorable Discharge

Israel is renowned worldwide for its military prowess, which derives in part from weapons it has developed, such as the Uzi submachine gun, unmanned aerial vehicles (drones), and the Iron Dome missile defense system. Long before these innovations, however, a protocol established in the Torah helped prepare the Jewish nation for success on the battlefield. Parashat Shofetim describes how officers are to treat their soldiers. Soldiers are to be given the opportunity to return home before the battle begins if they have (1) built a new house but did not inaugurate it, (2) planted a vineyard but did not harvest it, or (3) betrothed a woman but did not marry her. The next verse continues:

וְיָסְפוּ הַשֹּׁטְרִים לְדַבֵּר אֶל הָעָם וְאָמְרוּ מִי הָאִישׁ הַיָּרֵא וְרַךְ הַלֵּבָב יֵלֵךְ וְיָשֹׁב לְבֵיתוֹ וְלֹא יִמַּס אֶת לְבַב אֶחָיו כִּלְבָבוֹ: (דברים כ, ח)

The officials shall go on addressing the troops and say, "Is there anyone afraid and disheartened? Let him go back to his home, lest the courage of his comrades flag like his." (Deut. 20:8)

Rashi discusses this verse in light of the verses that precede it:

הירא ורך הלבב: רבי עקיבא אומר כמשמעו, שאינו יכול לעמוד בקשרי המלחמה ולראות חרב שלופה. רבי יוסי הגלילי אומר הירא מעבירות שבידו, ולכך תלתה לו תורה לחזור על בית וכרם ואשה

לכסות על החוזרים בשביל עבירות שבידם, שלא יבינו שהם בעלי עבירה, והרואהו חוזר אומר שמא בנה בית או נטע כרם או ארש אשה: (רש"י, שם)

afraid and disheartened: Rabbi Yossi HaGalili says [it refers to] one who is afraid of his transgressions [that they will cause him to fall in war, as he is unworthy of divine protection], and therefore the Torah provides the pretext of returning because of one's house, or vineyard, or wife, to cover up for those who return because of their transgressions, so that nobody realizes that they are transgressors. One who sees him return will say, "Perhaps he built a house, or planted a vineyard, or betrothed a woman." (Rashi, Deut. 20:8)

Rashi cites the talmudic opinion that if a soldier fears he is vulnerable on the battlefield because of his transgressions, his officer should let him return home before the battle—and let him cover up the true reason for his departure. The preceding verses provide a pretext for him to return home honorably. The Torah exhibits great sensitivity in hiding the true reason the soldier is abandoning his comrades in arms, lest it lower his esteem in their eyes. Once again, the Torah emphasizes the importance of preserving other people's dignity.

Questions for Discussion

1. Who do you know who has served in the military? What were that person's most significant takeaways from this experience?
2. Israel has had mandatory conscription since its founding. The United States has had mandatory conscription during times of war, but ended its most recent draft in 1973. The

163

prospect of risking one's life on the battlefield fills many people with trepidation. How do you feel about mandatory conscription for military service? If you were drafted by your country's military, would you feel "afraid and disheartened" and try to find a way out of serving? How would you justify your decision?

3. Describe something people regularly do that they likely regard as shameful or embarrassing. What could be done to enable them to preserve their dignity as they accomplish their objective?

❖ Protecting the Environment

In Israel, planting trees is a national obsession. In fact, Israel is the only country in the world that began the twenty-first century with more trees than it had at the start of the previous century. Perhaps the high regard Jews have for trees can be traced back to this verse from the parashah.

כִּי תָצוּר אֶל עִיר יָמִים רַבִּים לְהִלָּחֵם עָלֶיהָ לְתָפְשָׂהּ לֹא תַשְׁחִית אֶת עֵצָהּ לִנְדֹּחַ עָלָיו גַּרְזֶן כִּי מִמֶּנּוּ תֹאכֵל וְאֹתוֹ לֹא תִכְרֹת כִּי הָאָדָם עֵץ הַשָּׂדֶה לָבֹא מִפָּנֶיךָ בַּמָּצוֹר: (דברים כ, יט)

When in your war against a city you have to besiege it a long time in order to capture it, you must not destroy its trees, wielding the ax against them. You may eat of them, but you must not cut them down. Are trees of the field human to withdraw before you into the besieged city? (Deut. 20:19)

Rashi clarifies how to interpret the word *ki* (כִּי), which introduces the verse's concluding question and has several possible meanings:

כי האדם עץ השדה: הרי כי משמש בלשון דלמא. שמא האדם עץ השדה להכנס בתוך המצור מפניך להתייסר ביסורי רעב וצמא כאנשי העיר למה תשחיתנו: (רש"י, שם)

Are trees of the field human: The word *ki* [כִּי] here means "perhaps." Are trees of the field perhaps human to be included in your siege, and suffer famine and thirst along with the city's inhabitants? Why should you destroy them? (Rashi, Deut. 20:19)

As Rashi explains, human beings are not to destroy trees, even during a war. Trees are a source of sustenance. They are not disposable. And since trees cannot defend themselves, it is incumbent on human beings to afford them protection.

Here the Torah exhorts consideration for the environment in appreciation of its essential contribution to the well-being of humanity.

Questions for Discussion

1. In his classic book *I and Thou*, the philosopher Martin Buber wrote: "I contemplate a tree. I can accept it as a picture: a rigid pillar in a flood of light, or splashes of green traversed by the gentleness of blue silver ground. I can feel it as movement: the flowing veins around the sturdy, thriving core, the sucking of the roots, the breathing of the leaves, the infinite commerce with earth and air—and the growing itself in the darkness. I can assign it to a species and observe it as an instance, with an eye to its construction and its way of life. . . . Throughout all of this the tree remains my object and has its place and its time span, its kind and condition. But it can also happen, if will and grace are joined, then as I contemplate the tree I am drawn into

a relation, and the tree ceases to be an It." Have you ever spent time contemplating a tree? If so, what observations did you draw from the tree?

2. While environmental damage has always been a consequence of war, it occurred on an unprecedented scale during the Vietnam War when the United States sprayed the defoliant Agent Orange over millions of acres in South Vietnam to destroy crops and deny the enemy cover. President John F. Kennedy authorized the use of defoliants on the advice of Secretary of State Dean Rusk, who stated, "[t]he use of defoliant does not violate any rule of international law concerning the conduct of chemical warfare and is an accepted tactic of war." Do you agree that defoliant use is appropriate when it furthers a military objective? Why or why not?

3. Environmentalism has gone from being a marginal movement in the early 1970s to a widely embraced value today. Do you agree that protecting the environment is imperative in our times? Why or why not? If yes, what aspects of the environment do you believe most need human protection?

❖ Kindness to Strangers

In most countries, discovering a corpse in the countryside would lead to an investigation to determine the cause of death. However, the discovery of a corpse in the Land of Israel triggers an elaborate procedure, described in the parashah, which requires (1) determining which city is closest to the corpse, (2) assembling the elders of the city to slaughter a calf, and (3) washing the elders' hands over the calf while making the declaration contained in the following verse:

וְעָנוּ וְאָמְרוּ יָדֵינוּ לֹא שָׁפְכוּ אֶת הַדָּם הַזֶּה וְעֵינֵינוּ לֹא רָאוּ: (דברים כא, ז)

And they shall make this declaration: "Our hands did not shed this blood, nor did our eyes see it done." (Deut. 21:7)

Rashi explains their declaration:

יָדֵינוּ לֹא שָׁפְכוּ: וכי עלתה על לב שזקני בית דין שופכי דמים הם, אלא לא ראינוהו ופטרנוהו בלא מזונות ובלא לויה. והכהנים אומרים כפר לעמך ישראל: (רש"י, שם)

Our hands did not shed [this blood]: Is it possible to imagine that the elders of the court are murderers? Rather, [they declare:] "We did not see him and let him depart without food or escort." (Rashi, Deut. 21:7)

Rashi explains that the city elders' declaration is not intended to establish their innocence in the murder—they would never be suspected of such a crime—but to ascertain whether they had taken responsibility for this person who had presumably passed through their city prior to the trip that led to his death. Did they provide him with food for his journey? Did they escort him as he left the city? If not, their neglect could have contributed to the traveler's demise.

The Torah stresses the importance of being hospitable to visitors, even when those individuals have not been invited and are just passing through. This is in keeping with the talmudic dictum: "All Jews are responsible for one another" כל ישראל ערבים זה בזה) (*Bavli Shevuot* 39a).

Questions for Discussion

1. A few centuries ago, a trip we make quickly today would have taken days if not weeks, involved days and nights on

isolated rural paths, and required obtaining food and water for oneself and one's animal (if accompanied by one) along the route. A journey to another city took considerable preparation and perhaps elicited some apprehension too. Are there any experiences today that evoke the same types of concerns that accompanied travel in earlier times?

2. The elders described in the above verse, who disavow having let the unfortunate traveler depart "without food or escort," were expected to model exemplary treatment of strangers. Have you or someone you know ever given or received this degree of hospitality? What happened?

3. Prior to the urbanization that began in the nineteenth century, most people lived in rural and small-town settings where they knew their neighbors and recognized when people were visiting from out of town. By contrast, the urban environments in which most people live today are characterized by a sense of anonymity in which a person can be surrounded by thousands of others yet feel alone. What can be done to create a greater sense of community and belonging in urban areas?

KI TETSE'

❖ Lending a Hand

Imagine that you see two cars parked on the side of the road, one with a flat tire. Since you observe two able-bodied men changing the tire, you assume a passerby has stopped to assist the hapless driver of the disabled car. Now imagine the same scene, except that one of the men is busily changing the tire, while the other is reclining on a lounge chair sipping a piña colada. A verse from Parashat Ki Tetse' alludes to both scenarios.

לֹא תִרְאֶה אֶת חֲמוֹר אָחִיךָ אוֹ שׁוֹרוֹ נֹפְלִים בַּדֶּרֶךְ וְהִתְעַלַּמְתָּ מֵהֶם הָקֵם תָּקִים עִמּוֹ: (דברים כב, ד)

If you see your fellow's ass or ox fallen on the road, do not ignore it; you must help him raise it. (Deut. 22:4)

Rashi comments on the requirement to assist the owner of the fallen animal:

עמו: עם בעליו, אבל אם הלך וישב לו, ואמר לו הואיל ועליך מצוה אם רצית לטעון טעון, פטור: (רש"י, שם)

with him: [You must lift the animal] with its owner. But if he walked off and sat down, and said to him [the one providing assistance], "Since you were commanded, if you want to load, [go ahead and] load," he [the one providing assistance] is exempt. (Rashi, Deut. 22:4)

Rashi explains that a person is required to assist another whose animal has fallen, but only when the animal's owner is also attending to his animal. If the owner shirks his responsibility and seeks to shift the burden of raising up his animal onto the other person, then the other person is absolved of any further obligation to assist.

Rashi highlights that people in need of assistance must act to help themselves to the extent they can. Otherwise they forego the moral claim to other people's assistance. Assisting others entails a partnership in which each party upholds its obligations.

Questions for Discussion

1. Have you ever provided assistance to a driver with a disabled car? If not, why not? If yes, what happened?
2. Have you ever received assistance from a stranger when you had a disabled car? If yes, what happened?
3. How would you characterize the humanitarian principle Rashi is describing? Can you give examples of where this principle is followed in providing assistance to others, as well as examples of when people are helped even when they do not work in tandem to help themselves? What are the relative merits of these two approaches?

❖ Acknowledging the Good

The name Benedict Arnold has become synonymous with being a traitor—and for good reason. In 1780 Arnold, a general in the U.S. Army, made a secret agreement with the British to surrender to them the fortifications under his command at West Point, New York. When this plot was discovered, Arnold fled to Great Britain. Previously, however, Arnold fought valiantly for the United States. He was injured in the Battles of Saratoga (1777); today, a monument there describes his military exploits but omits his name. A verse in the parashah addresses the same issue of acknowledging the good, even when it is overshadowed by the bad.

לֹא תְתַעֵב אֲדֹמִי כִּי אָחִיךָ הוּא לֹא תְתַעֵב מִצְרִי כִּי גֵר הָיִיתָ בְאַרְצוֹ:
(דברים כג, ח)

You shall not abhor an Edomite, for he is your kinsman. You shall not abhor an Egyptian, for you were a stranger in his land. (Deut. 23:8)

Rashi comments on the verse's directive regarding Egyptians:

לא תתעב מצרי: מכל וכל אף על פי שזרקו זכוריכם ליאור. מה טעם, שהיו לכם אכסניא בשעת הדחק. לפיכך: (רש"י, שם)

You shall not abhor an Egyptian: totally, even though they cast your male [infants] into the Nile. What is the reason [that you may not totally despise them]? Because they hosted you in a time of dire need. (Rashi, Deut. 23:8)

As Rashi explains, even though the Israelites suffered persecution at the hands of the Egyptians (and today Jews recount those details annually at the Passover seder), Jews are not permitted to wholly hate Egyptians because they did offer our ancestors refuge during the famine in the days of our forefather Jacob, prior to enslaving the Israelites.

The Torah imparts two broader messages here. First, people (or groups, countries, political parties, movements, etc.) are not wholly good or wholly bad, but rather reflect the range of their choices, which may vary greatly. Second, we are to acknowledge peoples' good acts, even when they stand in stark contrast to their other deeds.

Questions for Discussion

1. Describe a positive aspect of a person or group of people regarded as being hostile to the Jews or Israel.
2. Describe a positive aspect of a person whose views are otherwise very different from yours. Does acknowledging this good quality have any impact on the way you feel about the person?
3. The Talmud relates the following story: "Rabbi Yehuda, Rabbi Yossi, and Rabbi Shimon ben Yochai were sitting together, and Rabbi Yehuda ben Gerim was seated with them. Rabbi Yehuda opened by praising the deeds of the Romans [who ruled the Land of Israel at the time], stating that they established marketplaces, built bridges, and constructed bathhouses. Rabbi Yossi was silent. Rabbi Shimon ben Yochai exclaimed that anything they established was only for their own needs—marketplaces to accommodate harlots, bathhouses to indulge themselves, and bridges to collect taxes. Rabbi Yehuda ben Gerim proceeded to recount this conversation, which ended up being heard by the Roman governors. They said that Rabbi Yehuda, who elevated the Romans, would himself be elevated; Rabbi Yossi, who was silent, would be exiled to Tzippori; and Rabbi Shimon ben Yochai, who denigrated the Romans, would be killed" (*Bavli Shabbat* 33b). Like the Romans in their era, the European imperial powers left an enduring physical legacy in their erstwhile colonies and spheres of influence that contributed significantly to building national infrastuctures. For example, imperial Britian built India's railways for British

military and freight transport; today the trains are among the world's leaders in passenger volume. Similarly, the French Universal Company of the Maritime Suez Canal built the Suez Canal with forced Egyptian labor; today the canal constitutes one of Egypt's leading sources of vital foreign reserves. Do you believe these European imperialists should therefore be viewed in a more positive light? Why or why not?

....

❖ Newlyweds

In Western countries, a wedding is customarily followed by a honeymoon, typically a trip by the newlyweds to a resort destination. In a traditional Jewish community, the week after the wedding is typically spent close to family, celebrating *Sheva Brachot* (seven blessings), a weeklong series of meals, each concluding with the recitation of the seven marriage blessings. The Jewish tradition also accords special status to the first year of marriage (*shana rishona*), based on a verse from the parashah.

כִּי יִקַּח אִישׁ אִשָּׁה חֲדָשָׁה לֹא יֵצֵא בַּצָּבָא וְלֹא יַעֲבֹר
עָלָיו לְכָל דָּבָר נָקִי יִהְיֶה לְבֵיתוֹ שָׁנָה אֶחָת וְשִׂמַּח
אֶת אִשְׁתּוֹ אֲשֶׁר לָקָח: (דברים כג, ה)

When a man has taken a bride, he shall not go out with the army or be assigned to it for any purpose; he shall be exempt one year for the sake of his household, to give happiness to the woman he has married. (Deut. 24:5)

Rashi explains the exemption from army service:

לכל דבר: שהוא צורך הצבא, לא לספק מים ומזון ולא לתקן דרכים,
אבל החוזרים מעורכי המלחמה על פי כהן, כגון בנה בית ולא חנכו
או ארס אשה ולא לקחה, מספיקין מים ומזון ומתקנין את הדרכים:
(רש"י, שם)

for any purpose: that is required by the army: [for instance,] he must not supply water and food or repair the roads. (Rashi, Deut. 24:5)

Rashi explains that the groom is exempt from any type of army service, even noncombat roles. Therefore, the concern is not the prospect of the groom being injured in combat, but the husband's availability to spend time with his wife and bring her joy during their first year of marriage. In getting married, two individuals who have led separate lives embark on a unique undertaking—to create a shared destiny. The Torah recognizes the importance of building this sacred relationship on a firm foundation by assuring that the new couple spends the first year together.

Questions for Discussion

1. Describe your (or your parents') first week as newlyweds. What would you prefer: spending the first week of marriage with family, or with your spouse in an exotic locale (or something else)?

2. As indicated above, for a newly married couple the first year of marriage is a critical time to create a solid foundation. What do you think can be done (or what have you done) during the first year to benefit the marriage?

3. After conducting extensive studies on marital stability, psychologist John Gottman developed models that enabled him to predict with 90 percent accuracy which newlywed

couples would remain married after four to six years. Key to marriage stability, he discovered, is a couple's ability to successfully reconcile after an argument. Since disagreements are inevitable in relationships, and they may be more intense and frequent in marital relationships, what do you believe the individuals need to do separately and collectively to seek reconciliation? How can strong differences in perspectives be handled in ways that do not damage—and perhaps even strengthen—the relationship?

KI TAVO'

❖ Keeping It Fresh

Do you remember the exhilaration you felt the first time you drove a car (or rode a bicycle)? An exciting new experience makes an enduring impression—but when we repeat the experience over time, we typically lose the excitement we felt at its inception. A verse from Parashat Ki Tavo' touches on this tendency for the passage of time to transform the novel into the routine.

הַיּוֹם הַזֶּה יְהֹוָה אֱלֹהֶיךָ מְצַוְּךָ לַעֲשׂוֹת אֶת הַחֻקִּים הָאֵלֶּה וְאֶת הַמִּשְׁפָּטִים וְשָׁמַרְתָּ וְעָשִׂיתָ אוֹתָם בְּכָל לְבָבְךָ וּבְכָל נַפְשֶׁךָ: (דברים כו, טז)

The Lord your God commands you this day to observe these laws and rules; observe them faithfully with all your heart and soul. (Deut. 26:16)

Rashi comments on the verse's opening words:

היום הזה ה' אלקיך מצוך: בכל יום יהיו בעיניך חדשים, כאלו בו ביום נצטוית עליהם: (רש"י, שם)

The Lord your God commands you this day: Every day you shall regard the commandments as if they are brand new, as if, on that very day, you had been commanded concerning them. (Rashi, Deut. 26:16)

Rashi explains that this verse instructs the Jews to regard the commandments as if they had been given this very day.

In fact, many people listening to this exhortation had already heard the commandments, having been present during the revelation at Mount Sinai thirty-nine years earlier. Furthermore, the Jews were still experiencing miracles, such as daily manna from heaven. Nevertheless, they were urged to regard the commandments as if they were being given anew every day.

We who live thirty-three hundred years later and did not experience any of the Exodus miracles have an even greater challenge in maintaining vitality in our relationship with the Torah. Holidays we have observed annually since we were children and mitzvot (commandments) we perform regularly have the potential to become routine in our eyes.

One way to reinvigorate Judaism is to build on our knowledge of the things we are already doing. As we study what interests us, glean new understandings, acknowledge the insights, and make our own discoveries, we may well experience some of those "aha!" moments once again.

Questions for Discussion

1. Describe something you do that is not as fulfilling today as it once was. What feelings did you experience when you first engaged in this activity, and how and why have they changed? Is it possible to regain some of the excitement you experienced initially? If so, how?

2. Describe something you do now that you find to be as fulfilling as—or even more fulfilling than—when you initially did it. To what do you attribute this progression? What lesson can you derive from this that might be applied to other areas of endeavor?

3. If you suddenly felt deeply inspired to regard the commandments as being brand new, every day of your life, do

you imagine your life would change? If so, what would it look like?

....

❖ Counting Your Blessings

The story is told of two strangers sitting on a park bench. One of them is dressed plainly and sits idly with a smile stretching from ear to ear. The other is wearing a suit and eats his lunch with a cheerless countenance. The one in the suit asks the other, "What are you so happy about?" The other answers, "I have five dollars in my pocket and can sit on this bench all day and watch the people pass by." Not satisfied with this answer, the man in the suit probes further and learns that his new acquaintance was just released from prison that morning. In a verse that explains why the Jews will later be subjected to devastating curses, the parashah addresses the perspectives we bring to the experiences of our lives.

תַּחַת אֲשֶׁר לֹא עָבַדְתָּ אֶת יְהוָה אֱלֹהֶיךָ בְּשִׂמְחָה וּבְטוּב לֵבָב מֵרֹב כֹּל:
(דברים כח, מז)

Because you would not serve the Lord your God in joy and gladness over the abundance of everything. (Deut. 28:47)

Rashi explains the verse's concluding words:

מֵרֹב כֹּל: בְּעוֹד שֶׁהָיָה לְךָ כָּל טוּב: (רש"י, שם)

over the abundance of everything: when you still had all good things. (Rashi, Deut. 28:47)

Rashi explains that the future curses resulted from the Jewish people's failure to serve God with joy while they still experienced great abundance. Had the Jews appreciated the goodness in their lives and expressed this recognition in their service of God, they would have avoided the suffering described in the parashah.

Unfortunately, one often comes to appreciate what one had only after it has been lost. Instead of waiting for the harsh reality of changed circumstances to realize our now-vanished blessings, the Torah advises us to develop the mindset to recognize and value the blessings we have every day.

Questions for Discussion

1. What blessing in your life do you tend to take for granted? What can you do to both develop and express appreciation for this blessing?

2 In what ways do you consider your life to be characterized by abundance and in what ways by dearth? Do you tend to focus more on one than the other? If so, please elaborate.

3. It has been suggested that people would become more mindful of the blessings society confers on them if they spent a few days alone foraging for their own food and shelter in a wilderness setting. Do you think this idea would achieve its stated objective? Why or why not? What do you believe could help people develop a greater sense of appreciation for what they have?

....

❖ Taking Ownership

People sometimes caution against buying a pre-owned car that was owned by a rental company, since its many drivers may have treated the rented car with less care than their personal cars. A verse from the parashah alludes to this phenomenon of people treating something (be it an object, a problem, or a heritage) differently when they regard it as their own.

וְלֹא־נָתַן יְהֹוָה לָכֶם לֵב לָדַעַת וְעֵינַיִם לִרְאוֹת וְאָזְנַיִם לִשְׁמֹעַ עַד הַיּוֹם הַזֶּה: (דברים כט, ג)

Yet to this day the Lord has not given you a mind to understand or eyes to see or ears to hear. (Deut. 29:3)

Rashi explains what was significant about "this day":

עַד הַיּוֹם הַזֶּה: שמעתי שאותו היום שנתן משה ספר התורה לבני לוי, כמו שכתוב (לקמן לא, ט) ויתנה אל הכהנים בני לוי, באו כל ישראל לפני משה ואמרו לו משה רבינו אף אנו עמדנו בסיני וקבלנו את התורה ונתנה לנו, ומה אתה משליט את בני שבטך עליה, ויאמרו לנו יום מחר לא לכם נתנה, לנו נתנה. ושמח משה על הדבר, ועל זאת אמר להם היום הזה נהיית לעם וגו' (לעיל כז, ט), היום הזה הבנתי שאתם דבקים וחפצים במקום: (רש"י, שם)

to this day: [O]n the very day when Moses gave the Torah scroll to the sons of Levi [his tribe], as the verse says (Deut. 31:9), "and gave it to the priests, sons of Levi," all Israel came before Moses and said to him: "Our master Moses, we also stood at [Mount] Sinai and accepted the Torah and it was [also] given to us. Why then are you giving the members of your tribe control over it, so that they may tell us some day in the future, 'It was not given to you; it was given [only] to us!'?" Moses rejoiced over this matter, and it was on account of this that he said to them (Deut. 27:9), "Today you have become the people [of the Lord your God]," [meaning]

today I understand that you cleave to and desire the Omnipresent. (Rashi, Deut. 29:3).

Rashi explains that Moses rejoiced when the Israelites challenged his giving the Torah scroll to his own tribesmen, because it indicated that the Israelites regarded the Torah as their own. As it was in the days of Moses, the Torah remains today the legacy of both the Jewish nation and each individual Jew.

Questions for Discussion

1. Describe a possession of yours that you are particular about preserving in pristine condition. Why does this mean so much to you?

2. Do you tend to treat items on loan to you (rental cars, library books, a friend's article of clothing, etc.) with less care, the same care, or more care than you would if you owned the item (or does the care vary depending on the circumstances)? What accounts for your chosen level of care?

3. The Jewish community is greatly concerned that this generation of Jews does not own and prize its Jewish heritage. Do you agree with this perspective? If not, why? If so, what do you think has caused this, and what might be done to counteract it?

NITSAVIM/VA-YELEKH

❖ Empathy

The adage "misery loves company" expresses the truism that people prefer to experience a difficult situation in the company of others rather than alone. Among the most enduring challenges faced by the Jewish people has been their two thousand-year exile from the Land of Israel. A verse from Parashat Nitsavim promises them that they will not be alone during all the vicissitudes of exile.

וְשָׁב יְהֹוָה אֱלֹהֶיךָ אֶת שְׁבוּתְךָ וְרַחֲמֶךָ וְשָׁב וְקִבֶּצְךָ מִכָּל הָעַמִּים אֲשֶׁר הֱפִיצְךָ יְהֹוָה אֱלֹהֶיךָ שָׁמָּה: (דברים ל, ג)

Then Lord your God will restore your fortunes and take you back in love. He will bring you together again from all the peoples where the Lord your God has scattered you. (Deut. 30:3)

The first phrase of this verse, which can be translated as "The Lord, your God, will return your exiles," starts with a form of the verb לשוב (return) that does not seem appropriate in this context. Rashi comments on this:

ושב ה' אלקיך את שבותך: היה לו לכתוב והשיב את שבותך, רבותינו למדו מכאן שהשכינה כביכול שרויה עם ישראל בצרת גלותם, וכשנגאלין הכתיב גאולה לעצמו, שהוא ישוב עמהם: (רש"י, שם)

The Lord, your God, will return your exiles: [The literal meaning of the verse is "The Lord, your God, will Himself return (וְשָׁב) with your exiles."] It should have been written [consistent with how the verse is understood], "will return [וְהֵשִׁיב] your exiles." Our Rabbis derived from here that the Divine Presence resides with Israel, so to speak, in the suffering of their exile, so that when they are redeemed He ascribes redemption to Himself, so that He will return with them. (Rashi, Deut. 30:3)

As Rashi explains, the verse's use of the word וְשָׁב (will return) rather than וְהֵשִׁיב (will cause to return) indicates that the Divine Presence accompanied the Jews into exile. This "accompanying" took the form of divine empathy—identifying with the Jewish people's thoughts, feelings, and experiences in exile. The Jews could therefore take comfort. They were not alone; God resided with them.

One of the most far-reaching mitzvot (commandments) is the imperative to emulate the ways of God (וְהָלַכְתָּ בִּדְרָכָיו, "and walk in God's ways" [Deut. 28:9]). The parashah points to empathy as a pathway. When one person exhibits compassionate understanding of someone else's thoughts, feelings, and experiences, it can have a transformative impact on both people, individually and in relationship with one another.

Questions for Discussion

1. Describe a time you experienced adversity with one or more people. What impact, if any, did the fact that you were not alone have on your experience?
2. How do you believe the Jews were able to maintain their distinctive indentity during two thousand years of exile—all the while nurturing their longing to return to their ancestral land? Are there any lessons from the period of exile that could be applied to our day?

3. Can you recall a time that you were comforted by another person's empathy? If so, what aspect of the other person's empathy had the intended impact?

❖ Not in Heaven

Jews are referred to as the "People of the Book"—for good reason. If you walk into any Jewish home, you are likely to find books in abundance. In the 1400s, when the printing press was invented, Jews used the new technology to print sacred texts for the home and synagogue, furthering the dissemination of Torah. A verse from the parashah alludes to the imperative of Torah study.

לֹא בַשָּׁמַיִם הִוא לֵאמֹר מִי יַעֲלֶה לָּנוּ הַשָּׁמַיְמָה וְיִקָּחֶהָ לָּנוּ וְיַשְׁמִעֵנוּ אֹתָהּ וְנַעֲשֶׂנָּה: (דברים ל, יב)

It [the Torah] is not in the heavens, that you should say, "Who among us can go up to the heavens and get it for us and impart it to us, that we may observe it?" (Deut. 30:12)

Rashi comments on the verse's opening words:

לֹא בַשָּׁמַיִם הִיא: שֶׁאִלּוּ הָיְתָה בַּשָּׁמַיִם הָיִיתָ צָרִיךְ לַעֲלוֹת אַחֲרֶיהָ וְלִלְמֹדָהּ: (רש"י, שם)

It is not in the heavens: For if it were in the heavens, you would have to ascend after it [in order] to learn it. (Rashi, Deut. 30:12)

Drawing on the Rabbinic tradition, Rashi makes an unexpected inference. The fact that the Torah "is not in the heavens" does not imply that if it were, we would be excused from learning it. Rather, Rashi explains that even if the Torah were in the heavens, we would still be required to pursue it.

Today we are fortunate to have copious ways to learn Torah. Books on almost every conceivable facet of Judaism are widely available in Hebrew, English, and other languages. In addition, just like Jews of the fifteenth century employed the then newly invented printing press, modern Jews are harnessing today's technology—the Internet, apps, videos, social media, and so forth—to impart the Torah to us.

Questions for Discussion

1. Were you an avid reader growing up? What was your favorite book or author, and why?
2. Is there a Jewish book that made a strong impression on you? If so, describe the book and its impact on you.
3. Have you have used today's technology to enhance your knowledge of Judaism? If so, what resources have you found to be particularly valuable?

❖ Choose Life

"To be, or not to be, that is the question," from Shakespeare's *Hamlet*, is perhaps the best-known line in all of English literature. With these words Prince Hamlet asks himself whether it is better to live or to die. In the parashah, the Torah provides an unequivocal answer to this question.

הַעִדֹתִי בָכֶם הַיּוֹם אֶת הַשָּׁמַיִם וְאֶת הָאָרֶץ הַחַיִּים וְהַמָּוֶת נָתַתִּי לְפָנֶיךָ הַבְּרָכָה וְהַקְּלָלָה וּבָחַרְתָּ בַּחַיִּים לְמַעַן תִּחְיֶה אַתָּה וְזַרְעֶךָ: (דברים ל, יט)

I call heaven and earth to witness against you this day: I have put before you life and death, blessing and curse. Choose life—if you and your offspring would live. (Deut. 30:19)

Rashi elaborates on the Torah's directive to "Choose life":

ובחרת בחיים: אני מורה לכם שתבחרו בחלק החיים, כאדם האומר לבנו בחר לך חלק יפה בנחלתי ומעמידו על חלק היפה ואומר לו את זה ברור לך: (רש"י, שם)

Choose life: [God says: "Even though you have free choice, nevertheless] I instruct you to choose the portion of life." It is like a man who says to his son, "Choose for yourself a fine portion of my estate," and then directs him to the best portion, saying to him, "This [is the portion that] you should choose for yourself." (Rashi, Deut. 30:19).

Rashi's parable imparts that just as a father loves his son and wants what is best for him, so too God loves us and seeks our welfare. Judaism believes that life is sacred, and for our own welfare we are to choose life.

The Torah's imperative to "choose life" also applies when we are hurting or angry or feeling otherwise cut off from the world. For example, after the death of a close relative (spouse, parent, child, or sibling), Jewish law provides for a seven-day period of intense mourning (shivah) during which the family gathers and receives visitors, together sharing memories and appreciating the life of the deceased. Shivah can help those who are most affected by the loss to feel a measure of comfort in the community's outpouring at typically the most intense time of grieving.

Shivah is followed by a period of attenuated mourning, extending for up to one year, during which the mourners recite a prayer for the deceased (*Kaddish*) in the presence of a required prayer quorum (minyan). The Jewish community thereby continues to comfort the mourner by publicly acknowledging the loss, recognizing that the departed lives on through the mitzvot (commandments) and acts of kindness he or she performed, and consistently reminding the surviving family members that they are not alone in their loss.

Questions for Discussion

1. Describe a choice you made that significantly enhanced your life. At the time you made this decision, did you foresee the impact it would have?
2. Have you ever struggled to "choose life"? If so, how did you handle this? If you sought out counsel and someone helped you address important issues you faced, can you share an example of the advice you received?
3. Is there anything you feel is as important as life itself or for which you would be willing to give up your own life?

HA'AZINU

❖ Jewish Exceptionalism

In *Democracy in America* (1840), French historian and political scientist Alexis de Tocqueville described America as "exceptional." While many people still believe this is true, the notion of "exceptionalism"—that any country or culture is extraordinary—has come under attack in recent years. Long before de Tocqueville visited America, however, a different nation was the subject of a claim of exceptionalism, as seen in a verse from a poetic song in Parashat Ha'azinu.

הַ‌לְיהֹוָה תִּגְמְלוּ זֹאת עַם נָבָל וְלֹא חָכָם הֲלוֹא הוּא אָבִיךָ קָנֶךָ הוּא עָשְׂךָ וַיְכֹנְנֶךָ: (דברים לב, ו)

Do you thus requite the Lord, O dull and witless people?
Is not He the Father who created you, [f]ashioned you and made you endure! (Deut. 32:6)

Rashi comments on the verse:

הוא עשך: אומה באומות: (רש"י, שם)

[He] fashioned you: A nation among nations. (Rashi, Deut. 32:6)

Here Rashi emphasizes that the Jewish nation is exceptional among the nations of the world.

Rashi penned these words almost a thousand years ago, at a time when the Jews were a persecuted minority dispersed throughout Europe and the Middle East. At the time there were no Jewish Nobel laureates in physics and medicine, no Jewish Pulitzer Prize winners, no Jewish world chess champions, no Jewish Academy Award directors, and of course no State of Israel. In making his comment, Rashi drew on a glorious Jewish past in which the nation of Israel was led by kings and prophets. His words remain equally resonant in the modern era, in which the Jews have again demonstrated they are a nation unlike any other.

Questions for Discussion

1. Are there any countries you consider "exceptional"? If so, which ones and why?
2. In what ways do you believe the nation of Israel is distinctive from other nations? To what do you attribute these differences?
3. At the start of the twentieth century, the British were a dominant world power, of which it was said, "The sun never set on the British Empire." By midcentury, the United States and the Soviet Union had become the leaders in military might and ideological influence. The twentieth century closed with the collapse of the Soviet Union, and the twenty-first century began with the 9/11 attack on the World Trade Center and the rise of ISIS (Islamic State of Iraq and Syria). Which countries do you foresee being the dominant powers of the twenty-first century? What elements of "exceptionalism" have they demonstrated that lend support to your prediction?

❖ Loyalty

During the forty years that Moses led the Jewish people through the wilderness to the Promised Land, he had forged such a strong bond with the people that on the final day of his life, when he prepared to leave the world, they refused to let him go.

וַיְדַבֵּר יְהֹוָה אֶל מֹשֶׁה בְּעֶצֶם הַיּוֹם הַזֶּה לֵאמֹר: (דברים לב, מח)

That very day the Lord spoke to Moses: (Deut. 32:48)

Rashi explains the significance of the phrase בְּעֶצֶם הַיּוֹם הַזֶּה (on that very day), citing the other instances where it appears in the Torah:

וידבר ה' אל משה בעצם היום הזה: בשלשה מקומות נאמר בעצם היום הזה, נאמר בנח (שם ז, יג) בעצם היום הזה בא נח וגו', במראית אורו של יום, לפי שהיו בני דורו אומרים בכך וכך אם אנו מרגישין בו אין אנו מניחין אותו ליכנס בתיבה, ולא עוד אלא אנו נוטלין כשילין וקרדומות ומבקעין את התיבה. אמר הקב"ה הריני מכניסו בחצי היום, וכל מי שיש בידו כח למחות יבא וימחה. במצרים נאמר (שמות יב, נא) בעצם היום הזה הוציא ה', לפי שהיו מצרים אומרים בכך וכך אם אנו מרגישין בהם אין אנו מניחין אותם לצאת, ולא עוד אלא אנו נוטלין סייפות וכלי זיין והורגין בהם. אמר הקב"ה הריני מוציאן בחצי היום וכל מי שיש בו כח למחות יבא וימחה. אף כאן במיתתו של משה נאמר בעצם היום הזה, לפי שהיו ישראל אומרים בכך וכך אם אנו מרגישין בו אין אנו מניחין אותו, אדם שהוציאנו ממצרים וקרע לנו את הים והוריד לנו את המן והגיז לנו את השליו והעלה לנו את הבאר ונתן לנו את התורה אין אנו מניחין אותו. אמר הקב"ה הריני מכניסו בחצי היום וכו': (רש"י, שם)

That very day the Lord spoke to Moses: In three places the Torah uses the phrase בְּעֶצֶם הַיּוֹם הַזֶּה [on that very day]. Concerning Noah it states (Gen. 7:13), "On that very day Noah entered [the ark]"—when the light of day was in full view. Since Noah's contemporaries said, "We swear by such and such, that if we sense him leaving, we will not let him enter the ark," The Holy One, Blessed is He, said: "I will have Noah enter at midday, and let anyone who has the power to prevent it, come and prevent it!" Concerning Egypt it states (Exod. 12:51), "On that very day, the Lord brought [the Children of Israel] out [of Egypt]." Since the Egyptians said, "We swear by such and such, that if we sense them leaving, we will not let them go," The Holy One, Blessed is He, said: "I will bring them out at midday, and let anyone who has the power to prevent it, come and prevent it!" Here too, concerning Moses's death, it states, "on that very day." Since the Israelites said, "We swear by such and such, if we sense him leaving, we will not let go of him—the man who brought us out of Egypt, split the sea for us, brought down the manna for us, made the quail fly over to us, brought up the wellspring for us, and gave us the Torah—we will not let him!" The Holy One, Blessed is He, said: "I will gather him up at midday." (Rashi, Deut. 32:48)

Rashi explains that the Jewish people felt so indebted to Moses for all he had done for them that they were willing to confront God to keep Moses from being taken from them. Moses is known in Jewish tradition as Moshe Rabbenu (Moses Our Teacher). This episode illustrates the loyalty he instilled in his disciples.

Questions for Discussion

1. Name someone to whom you feel a strong sense of loyalty. How have you demonstrated—or would you like to demonstrate—your loyalty to this person?
2. If you were in a dire predicament and needed extraordinary assistance, who would you call for help and why?
3. How would you describe the difference between love and loyalty? Is it possible to feel one for a person without the other?

❖ Consolation Prizes

The long-running game show *The Price Is Right* likely popularized the notion of a consolation prize. Winning contestants have been awarded valuable prizes, such as a new car, and runners-up have received consolation prizes, such as a year's supply of Rice-A-Roni. A verse in this week's parashah discusses a consolation prize for Moses.

כִּי מִנֶּגֶד תִּרְאֶה אֶת הָאָרֶץ וְשָׁמָּה לֹא תָבוֹא אֶל הָאָרֶץ אֲשֶׁר אֲנִי נֹתֵן לִבְנֵי יִשְׂרָאֵל: (דברים לב, נב)

You may view the land from a distance, but you shall not enter it—the land that I am giving to the Israelite people. (Deut. 32:52)

Rashi explains why Moses was shown the land from afar:

וְשָׁמָּה לֹא תָבוֹא: וִידַעְתִּי כִּי חֲבִיבָה הִיא לָךְ עַל כֵּן אֲנִי אוֹמֵר לָךְ עֲלֵה וּרְאֵה: (רש"י, שם)

but you shall not enter it: But I know that the land is dear to you. That is why I say to you (v. 49), "Go up [the mountain] . . . and see [it]!" (Rashi, Deut. 32:52).

Despite his great love for the Land of Israel, Moses was not allowed to enter the land. However, as Rashi explains, Moses was given a consolation prize, so to speak: the opportunity to view the land from a distance.

There is a modern parallel in Israel to this episode. During the 1948 War of Independence, all the residents of the Jewish community of Kfar Etzion, just south of Jerusalem, were either driven from their homes or killed in a brutal attack that left this area under Arab control. For the next nineteen years—until the Six-Day War—the former residents gathered annually in Jerusalem to gaze from afar at the lone oak tree that marked the site of their former homes. Following the Six-Day War, Jews returned to this area and established the community of Alon Shvut (Oak of Return), whose name is derived from its location adjacent to this iconic oak tree.

Questions for Discussion

1. Describe a time that you did not attain a goal or result that you pursued, but you did achieve a lesser result that could be considered a "consolation prize." How did you feel about it at the time, and how do you feel about it now?
2. In life, things rarely work out as intended. This fact has given rise to the expression: "Life is all about how you handle Plan B." What was the "Plan A" that you once conceived, and how does it compare to the "Plan B" with which you live?
3. Have you ever had a "consolation prize"—or something you didn't even then recognize as a prize—turn out, at

a later time, to be more valuable or important than the prize you thought you wanted? If so, what happened? Alternatively, have you ever won or earned a valuable prize, only to later assess that it wasn't as valuable as you had thought?

VE-ZO'T HA-BERAKHAH

❖ The Last Lecture

In 2007 Randy Pausch, a forty-six-year-old professor of computer science at Carnegie Mellon University, delivered a talk entitled "Really Achieving Your Childhood Dreams." Because he had terminal cancer, this was his last lecture. It formed the basis of his book *The Last Lecture*, which was translated into forty-eight languages and sold more than five million copies. In Parashat Ve-zo't ha-berakhah, Moses delivers his "last lecture," a series of blessings for the tribes of Israel.

וְזֹאת הַבְּרָכָה אֲשֶׁר בֵּרַךְ מֹשֶׁה אִישׁ הָאֱלֹהִים אֶת בְּנֵי יִשְׂרָאֵל לִפְנֵי מוֹתוֹ: (דברים לג, א)

This is the blessing with which Moses, the man of God, bade the Israelites farewell before he died. (Deut. 33:1)

Rashi comments on the seemingly superfluous phrase "before he died":

וזאת הברכה, לפני מותו: סמוך למיתתו שאם לא עכשיו אימתי: (רש"י, שם)

This is the blessing . . . before he died: Close to his death, for if not now, when? (Rashi, Deut. 33:1)

As Rashi explains, Moses was cognizant of his impending death, and therefore decided to bless the Jewish people now, while he still had the chance.

Our lives are replete with deadlines, some more flexible than others. However, just one deadline—death—comes with no possibility of reprieve. Furthermore, we do not even know when it will arrive. Being reminded of the fleeting nature of life can help us focus on living our lives more fully while we still have the chance.

Questions for Discussion

1. What was a childhood dream of yours? Did you bring this dream to fruition? Why or why not?
2. If you were to deliver your own "last lecture," who would be your desired audience and what would you say?
3. If you knew the next year would be your last, how would you live it differently? Is there a compelling reason not to live it that way now?

❖ Forever Young

So powerful is the desire to regain lost youth, a legend arose about a Fountain of Youth that would restore youthful properties to whoever drank from it. Spanish explorer Ponce de León is said to have been searching for this mythical Fountain of Youth when he discovered Florida in 1513. One of the blessings in the parashah addresses this aspiration to hold on to one's youth.

בַּרְזֶל וּנְחֹשֶׁת מִנְעָלֶךָ וּכְיָמֶיךָ דָּבְאֶךָ: (דברים לג, כה)

May your doorbolts be iron and copper, [a]nd your security last all your days. (Deut. 33:25)

Rashi comments on the end of this blessing:

וכימיך דבאך: וכימים שהם טובים לך, שהן ימי תחלתך ימי נעוריך כן יהיו ימי זקנתך, שהם דואבים זבים ומתמוטטים: (רש"י, שם)

[a]nd your security last all your days: Like the days that are beneficial to you—meaning your early, youthful days—so may be the days of your old age, which [generally] flow downward, droop, and decline. (Rashi, Deut. 33:25)

As Rashi explains, this blessing expresses the hope that one's health in old age should be as in youth, despite the decline that generally accompanies aging.

More generally, the Torah imposes an affirmative obligation to safeguard one's health: "guard your life exceedingly" (וּשְׁמֹר נַפְשְׁךָ מְאֹד) and "Be extremely cautious for your lives" (וְנִשְׁמַרְתֶּם מְאֹד לְנַפְשֹׁתֵיכֶם) (Deut. 4:9,15).

Today's medical knowledge enables us to live more healthfully than ever before. It is now universally recognized that regardless of one's genetic makeup, lifestyle choices can strongly influence one's health. By eating healthfully (studies recommend five to seven daily servings of produce, for one), exercising regularly (the American College of Sports Medicine advises 150 minutes of aerobic exercise and two to three strength-training sessions weekly), sleeping at least seven hours per night, and avoiding harmful habits such as smoking, a person can extend his or her life by years and significantly reduce the chances of suffering from heart disease, diabetes, and cancer. In addition, by performing strength-training exercises that work all the major muscle groups in the human body (such as the combination of push-ups, pull-ups, and squats), adults can prevent and even reverse age-related muscle loss that can translate into difficulties opening jars, carrying heavy packages, walking up stairs, and rising from the couch.

Questions for Discussion

1. Do you agree with this statement: "While you can't avoid getting older, you can avoid feeling older"? Why or why not?
2. Discuss a lifestyle choice you have made—or would like to make—to enhance your health. What impact has it had or do you anticipate it will have?
3. What is the appeal of the notion of "eternal youth" and at what stage in life does this become appealing?

❖ Shalom in the Home

The institution of marriage has been in decline in the United States. In 1960, 72 percent of American adults were married; 51 percent were married in 2011. During this same period, the average age of marriage rose from twenty-three to twenty-eight for men, and from twenty to twenty-six for women. While there are a number of reasons for this development, one possible contributing factor is the difficulty couples face in achieving marital harmony. Judaism regards marriage as a sacred institution whose preservation remains a top priority, as Rashi indicates in a comment on this verse from the parashah.

וַיִּבְכּוּ בְנֵי יִשְׂרָאֵל אֶת מֹשֶׁה בְּעַרְבֹת מוֹאָב שְׁלֹשִׁים יוֹם וַיִּתְּמוּ יְמֵי בְכִי אֵבֶל מֹשֶׁה: (דברים לד, ח)

And the Israelites bewailed Moses in the steppes of Moab for thirty days. The period of wailing and mourning for Moses came to an end. (Deut. 34:8)

Rashi contrasts the mourning for Moses with the mourning for his brother, Aaron:

בני ישראל: הזכרים, אבל באהרן מתוך שהיה רודף שלום ונותן שלום בין איש לרעהו ובין אשה לבעלה נאמר (במדבר כ, כט) כל בית ישראל, זכרים ונקבות: (רש"י, שם)

The Israelites: [Only] the males [wept for Moses]. However, concerning [the mourning for] Aaron, since he pursued peace—making peace between neighbors and between women and their husbands—it states (Num. 20:29), "All the house of Israel" [wept for him]—both males and females. (Rashi, Deut. 34:8).

In comparing the verses describing the mourning for Moses and for Aaron, Rashi focuses on word *kol* (כל, all), which appears only in reference to Aaron, indicating that both men and women bemoaned his passing because they were grateful for his involvement in restoring marital and neighborly harmony.

Jewish tradition relates: "There were thousands in Israel who were called by the name of Aaron, for if not for Aaron, they would not have come into the world. Aaron made peace between husband and wife . . . and they would therefore name the child that was born after him" (*Avot d'Rabbi Nathan* 12:4). The fact that Aaron, both the High Priest and a prophet, made it a priority to help couples resolve their marital issues—and that he was remembered specifically for this—demonstrates the importance Judaism attaches to healthy marriages.

Questions for Discussion

1. Why do you think the prevalence of marriage has declined in recent generations, and the age of marriage has increased? Do you regard this as problematic? Why or why not?

2. The current divorce rate in the United States is estimated to be between 40 and 50 percent. What do you believe accounts for the prevalence of divorce? Do you believe reducing the incidence of divorce is in the couple's or society's best interests? Why or why not?

3. Aaron was renowned for making peace between husbands and wives. What do you believe is the relationship between making peace and having a happy marriage? Is it possible to have one without the other? What do you believe are the most important components of marital harmony?

SUBJECT INDEX

Aaron: death of sons of, 83; golden frontlet of, 62–63; inauguration of, 64; mourning death of, 182–83; refraining from consuming Rosh Hodesh offering, 84; turning Nile into blood, 45

Abiram: Korah's influence upon, 127; rejection of Moses's peace overture toward, 129

Abraham: compared to Noah, 6; and covenant of Land of Israel, 10–11; ha-Ivri, 7; hospitality of, 12; as immigrant, 9; marrying off Isaac, 15–16; muzzling camels, 16–17; as nemesis of Nimrod, 7

Adam, sin of, 5

adversity: attitude toward, 15; overcoming, 18

affection, 77

age, obligations related to, 65

Ai, 10

alcohol, 83

Amalek, 51–52

ancestry, 69

anger, management of, 128, 142

appreciation: for any benefit, 168–69; of blessings, 172

Ark of the Covenant, 60, 69–70

assistance: duty of recipient of, 167; obligation to provide timely, 104; to one whose life is threatened, 97

assumptions, mistaken, 71–72

attention to detail, 72–73

attentiveness to others, 28–29

Babel, 6–7, 7–8

Balaam: blessing Jews, 136; interpreting prophecy, 135–36

Balak, Midian consulting, 134

bar and bat mitzvah, 65

beauty, importance of, 16

Beer-sheba: departure of Jacob from, 21; and Jacob's offerings en route to Egypt, 34

Benjamin, 31–32, 33

Bethel, 10

Bethuel, 18

Bezalel: as creator of ark, 69–70; pairing with Oholiab, 69; qualifications of, 65–66

blessings: for children on Sabbath, 37–38; by Jacob for Manasseh and Ephraim, 36–37; by *kohanim*, 100

blood libel, 94

business, integrity in, 25, 99

challah, 124–25

charity: assessing recipient's need for, 161; priorities in, 57

children: blessing, 37–38; educating, 12–13; encouraging decision-making in, 123–24; favoritism toward, 27–28

cities, aesthetics of, 146

clothing, 80

coexistence among Jews, 45–46

commitments, 10–11

communication: effectiveness of, 82; and knowing your audience, 47; and offering choices, 135–36

community: contribution to, 59; laying the groundwork for Jewish, 34–35

compassion: misplacement of, 57–58; as sign of power, 30; and the wilderness sojourn, 144

conflict: and cooling-off period, 127–28; Jewish imperative to resolve, 129

consequences: bearing, 123–24; of misdeeds, 86

contemplation, 78

courage, 42–43

Creation, 3–4, 4–5

criminals, penal system and, 56–57

criticism, sensitivity in offering, 82, 149–50

Dan, and lost objects, 122

Dathan: Korah's influence upon, 127; rejection of Moses's peace overture toward, 129

death: and burial, 36; impending, 19–20; as spur to action, 181

decision-making, 31–32

decorum, 22

dignity: preserving others', 149–50, 163–64; of workers, 105

disappointment, 179–80

dreams, interpretation of, 29

Edom, denial of passage to Jews by, 131

education: and differentiation, 61; information versus insight in, 66; of Jewish youth, 94; and pedagogy, 52; and primacy of Torah study, 34–35, 106

effort, maximum, 160

Egyptians, duty to not hate, 168

Eleazar, 93, 142

empathy, 174

environment: influence of, 6, 80–81; protecting the, 164–65

Ephraim, Jacob's blessing for, 36–37, 37–38

Esau, Jacob's appeasement of, 24

evil eye, 36–37

excellence in service to others, 160

exceptionalism, Jewish, 177

excuses for others' behavior, 98

Exodus and the Song at the Sea, 50

fame, attraction of, 150

family, priority of, 143

favoritism, Jacob's toward Joseph, 27–28

neighbors, impact of, 114–15,
127
nepotism, 93
Nimrod: rebelling against God,
6–7; as unifier of people, 7–8
Noah, righteousness of, 6

offerings: disqualifying thoughts
concerning, 101; musical
accompaniment of, 116
Oholiab, 69
Old French, 64, 85
order, 138

Paddan-aram, 18
Parenting: allowing children
to fail, 123–24; encouraging
versus punishing, 66–67;
teaching children Torah,
94
Passover: and Jewish calendar,
161–62; sanctity of, 49
peace: between husband and
wife, 182–83; hostility toward
Israel by her neighbors as
basis for, 134–35; and Jewish
unity, 53–54; lesson from
the plague of hail, 45–46;
Moses's pursuit of, 129;
Nimrod's achievement of,
7–8; primacy of, 107
perceptions, subjectivity of, 151
persecution of Jews in Spain
and Germany, 14
perseverance, 62, 70, 106, 160
perspective, reframing, 81–82
persuasion, 6–7, 120
priorities, exertion for, 62

proactive measures, 103–4
procrastination, 20
property, avoiding liberties with
others', 16–17

Rabbi Akiva, and loving one's
fellow, 98
Rebekah: and background
of wickedness, 18; and
suitability for marriage to
Isaac, 15–16
recognition, 69–70, 100
reminders, 63, 125–26
Rephidim, 54
respect for parents versus
grandparents, 34
responsibility: for decisions,
5; for others, 104, 165; to
rescue others, 97; for what is
valuable, 172–73
retirement, 120–21
Reuven giving precedence to
flocks, 143
righteousness, impact on city
of, 21

Sabbath: and melakhot, 68;
preparation for, 54–55; resting
on, 4–5
sabbatical year, 103
Sarah, 15
scouts, and consequences of
mission of, 123
Shechem, Jacob's arrival in,
26
Shemini Atzeret, 102
sibling rivalry, 27
silence, significance of, 141

Sinai, 53–54, 118
slaves, Hebrew, 56, 105
Sodom, 13–14
speech: and lashon ha-ra, 88, 90;
and tweets, 90
storytelling, 53
strengths, capitalizing on one's,
131–32
Sukkot, 102

Tabernacle: and attention to
detail, 72–73; contributions
to, 59, 71
technology: enslavement to,
4–5; and impact of Internet,
175; and impersonalization,
41
Ten Plagues, 44–45, 45–46, 48
theft, punishment of, 56
Torah, study of, 35, 106, 115, 175
Tower of Babel, 6–7, 7–8
Tree of Knowledge, 5, 135
tzara'at: causes of, 86;
examination by priest for,
87; of houses, 91, 91–92; and
lashon ha-ra, 88, 90
tzitzit, 63, 94, 125

United Nations charter, 7, 107
unity: among Jews, 53–54;
among nations, 7–8

value, sentimental or symbolic,
25
vision, 87
vitality in performing mitzvoth,
136, 171
vows, endorsement of, 141

war: exemption from, 163,
169; preparation for, 24;
protection of environment
during, 164
wastefulness, 92
wealthy, definition of, 26
words, power of, 6–7

Zelophehad, and daughters'
inheritance, 138

INDEX OF SOURCES

In the JPS Study Bible Series

The JPS Rashi Discussion Torah Commentary
Steven Levy and Sarah Levy

The JPS B'nai Mitzvah Torah Commentary
Rabbi Jeffrey K. Salkin

To order or obtain more information
on these or other Jewish Publication
Society titles, visit jps.org.